MW01611219

The Best Dogs for Apartment Living

The Complete Guide to Training and Care for 32 Breeds

MIA MONTAGLIANI

Copyright

Your Dog Needs You is an online resource for dog owners looking for simple and fun dog training tips. The founder of Your Dog Needs You, Mia Montagliani, is a highly sought after dog trainer and is well known for her uncanny ability to empower dog owners to bring the best out from their dogs.

Copyright © 2013 by Mia Montagliani

All rights reserved. With the exception of quoting brief passages for the purposes of review, no part of this publication may be reproduced without prior written permission of the author.

The information in this book is true and complete to the best of the author's knowledge. All recommendations are made without any guarantee on the part of the author, who also disclaims any liability incurred in connection with the use of this material.

The author recognizes that some words, model names, and designations herein are the property of the trademark holder. The author uses them for identification purposes only.

To contact the author, find out about my other publications, or affiliate information, please visit http://YourDogNeedsYou.com.

ISBN: 978-0-9875130-1-4

Author: Mia Montagliani

Editing, Layout & Cover Design: Viva La Vida Pty Ltd

Health Glossary reviewed by Laura McLain Madsen, DVM

Table of Contents

Acknowledgements

I would like to thank my mom and dad, Georgette and Francesco, for always encouraging me to follow my dreams. It takes wise parents to know the difference between what is best for them and what is best for their children.

Thanks to all the owners and their dogs I have trained for allowing me to refine my craft – because of what I have learned from you, I was able to make this an invaluable resource for others.

I would also like to thank my friends: Ingrid, Julia, Naomi, Merrin, Yvonne and Penny for encouraging me throughout the writing of this book.

I would like to thank all the precious dogs I have had the privilege of owning throughout my life. You all taught me much more than I could ever teach you: unconditional love, loyalty and trust. My gratitude knows no bounds – you are all in my heart.

Introduction

Dear fellow dog owner,

Congratulations on buying *The Best Dogs for Apartment Living: The Complete Guide to Training and Care for 32 Breeds.*

My name is Mia Montagliani and I am the dog trainer at http://yourdogneedsyou.com, the premier online resource for dog owners. I help owners train and care for their canine companions humanely, effectively and without stress.

As a dog trainer I am often asked by people who are thinking of owning a dog as to which dog is most suitable for them. Many of these people live in apartments; they are not sure if any type of dog would be happy in an apartment, but they still dream of finding the perfect dog for their lifestyle.

It's not easy to choose a good apartment dog this is because many breeds are too big or too active for apartment living. That's why I decided to write this guide; through my research I found 32 breeds perfect for apartment living. Not only will you find useful breed profiles in this guide, but also instructions for the training and care of apartment breeds, ranging from health, obedience to dietary tips.

Potty training can be challenging in an apartment setting, so I have also included special instructions to ensure your dog learns to potty where you want.

This guide is designed to equip you – apartment resident and dog owner with the right tools and techniques to give complete care and training to your dog.

Again, I congratulate you on buying this guide and trust you and your precious dog will benefit from it.

Regards,

Mia Montagliani

Does Size Matter?

Most dogs that are suitable for apartments will be small, but that does not mean that all small dogs make suitable apartment pets. In fact, there are larger dogs that would make better apartment pets than some smaller breeds! Take the Great Dane, for example. You may be surprised to find that these dogs would be more suitable for an apartment than a Jack Russell. Why? It all comes down to a breed's activity level. Despite their huge size, Great Danes are quite placid and require only a certain amount of exercise per day. They are not very active and tend to enjoy lounging about. The smaller Jack Russell, on the other hand, can be quite active, boisterous and requires lots of exercise. An apartment will frustrate a Jack Russell, while a Great Dane can be very comfortable in the same apartment.

Therefore, the breeds I have chosen for this guide have two particular qualities:

- They are happy with a certain amount of exercise per day

- They tend to be comfortable indoors or in smaller spaces

It's also important to consider the size of your apartment when choosing a breed. The most important question to ask is: "Will the dog be able to wander around comfortably in my apartment?" Some apartments will simply be too small for a larger breed. You must also consider how much free space your apartment has. It's important to be honest with yourself when it comes to the size breed your apartment can house. In this way, you won't feel guilty about your dog's comfort level.

In short, when choosing an apartment dog, consider three factors:

- The size of the dog

- The size and spaciousness of your apartment

- The dog's activity levels

In the next chapter, I'll discuss how you can help your dog live comfortably and safely in your apartment.

10 Steps to Make Your Apartment Safe and Comfortable for Your Dog

Dog proofing your apartment essentially means keeping your dog safe in your home. If you live in an apartment, dog proofing basically entails:

- Keeping harmful foods and items out of your dog's reach

- Teaching your dog how to behave in your home

- Securing your home so your dog cannot run away

- Protecting your dog from hazards

- Arranging your furniture so your dog can move around the apartment safely and easily

Dog proofing your apartment is important because the danger is not always obvious. The seemingly harmless, yet common household plant or food may be poisonous, and even deadly, to dogs. Furniture and fixtures may seem innocent enough, but may contribute to injury. A curious dog can get herself into any kind of danger in the same way a baby or toddler can. However, a dog can potentially get into even more trouble - a dog's sensitive nose can sniff out intriguing materials in hidden places that a very young child would never find. Puppies are especially vulnerable because of their natural curiosity, lack of training and small size.

The old adage "the best defense is a good offense" also holds true for your dog's safety. Therefore, I recommend you take a proactive approach to your dog's safety; the process of dog proofing your apartment should therefore begin even before you bring your dog home. However, even if your dog is already home, it's not too late to dog proof your home.

Although there is never 100% protection, the ten measures I suggest will significantly increase your dog's safety and bring you peace of mind, especially when your dog is left alone in your apartment.

Here are ten ways to dog proofing your home:

1. Remove Poisonous Plants

Dogs enjoy eating or chewing plants and grass. If you have some plants in and around your apartment, you may have never given any thought to whether they are poisonous. The leaves and stems of some plants contain substances that can be irritating and even toxic to dogs. Common houseplants that are harmful if swallowed include Dieffenbachia (or Dumb Cane), Philodendron, Caladium and Elephant's Ear. Many yard plants such as flowers, shrubs, and trees are also dangerous to dogs. The bulbs of flowers such as Amaryllis, Daffodils, Jonquils, Narcissus, Hyacinth and Irises are poisonous, as are Azaleas, Holly berries, Hydrangea, Ligustrum, Oleander, Privet hedges, English Ivy, Jasmine and Wisteria. Of course, some mushrooms and toadstools are deadly too.

For a list of plants that are toxic to dogs, check out http://www.aspca.org/Pet-care. Scan your apartment, balcony and courtyard and remove any plants listed in ASPCA's site. Don't forget to also remove the bulbs and roots of any poisonous plants. Do not leave them in the trash either in, or around, your apartment, as your dog may sniff them out! Better yet, keep your trash in a latched cabinet.

2. Remove Medicines from Easily Accessible Areas

Common household medicines such as Aspirin, Acetaminophen (Tylenol and similar products), Ibuprofen (Advil and similar products), cold or cough medications and diet pills can make your dog sick, or even kill her. Given these medicines may be necessary to have in your home, it's important they are either locked away or placed in inaccessible shelves.

One way your dog may gain access to medicine is by raiding your purse. So, keep your purse out of your dog's reach.

Also, take medicines when your dog is in another room. In this way, you can pick up any pills you accidentally drop before your dog has a chance to snatch them.

3. Remove or Securely Store Antifreeze

According to the United States Humane Society, antifreeze poisoning kills an estimated 10,000 animals each year. Antifreeze tastes and smells sweet (because of its ethylene glycol content), thus making it a dangerous temptation for dogs. Even small spillages pose a threat, so it is best to ensure that any amount of antifreeze cannot be consumed by your dog. Ice-melting products can also be very dangerous to your dog.

4. Remove or Securely Store Toxic Foods

There are foods that are fine for people, but potentially deadly for dogs. Chocolate is a prime example. Macadamia nuts are another example. For a list of foods that are toxic to dogs, see my list below. Scan your apartment and pantry for these foods and make sure they are unreachable. Do not leave these foods in the trash either in, or around, your apartment, as your dog may raid the trash to get a snack!

Remain vigilant if you eat these foods or offer them to visitors. To avoid any accidental consumption of poisonous foods by your dog, follow these quick tips:

- Ask visitors not to feed your pet.

- Do not give toxic foods to children or visiting children, or if you do so, watch them carefully.

- Do not leave toxic food unattended on dinner tables, coffee tables or counters - some dogs will go so far as to 'counter surf' to get a snack! Times to watch for are when you are eating whilst watching TV or reading. A quick trip to the bathroom gives your dog ample time to steal food.

- Some dogs can master the art of opening fridge and pantry doors. Consider child proof locks, latched cabinets or high shelves.

5. Designate No-Go Areas

Have a room or area that you do not want your dog to enter? One of the best ways to ensure certain areas remain out of bounds is to use a baby gate. Some baby gates enable you to create a safe area for your dog, either as a fully enclosed play area, or as a way of stopping our dog from entering a room altogether. Many gates are not self-latching so exercise caution when using them. A good use for a baby gate is to stop your dog from rushing the front door. Whilst some dogs are great at remaining indoors, some dogs see open doors as an opportunity to escape – a well-placed baby gate can stop this from happening.

6. Mark Glass Areas

Many apartments have glass sliding doors. In order to keep your dog from running into glass doors, place bright stickers or labels at dog height on the glass sliding doors and panels. The stickers can also be used in any other glassed area that you might be concerned about. Make sure that glass areas are well lit at all times, especially at night. Where transparent glass is not essential you can use a patterned, translucent glass.

7. Make the Balcony Safe

Although I have never heard of a dog jumping off a balcony, I have heard of cats doing so. Having said that, it is certainly possible a dog may – through curiosity or accident – fall victim to this hazard.

There are several things to look for when checking the safety of your balcony:

- Are there any gaps wider than two inches on your balcony?

    If the railings on your balcony create any gaps that are wider than two inches, you'll need to make some modifications to stop your puppy or small dog from squeezing through. One option is to cover the railings with plastic garden fencing, sheets of clear plastic or Plexiglas. Some of these materials can be difficult to work with and so the services of a handyman or carpenter may be required.

- Does your balcony have horizontal bars?

    A dog may be able to climb any ladder-like horizontal bars on railings. Therefore, make sure you install plastic garden fencing, sheets of clear plastic or Plexiglas to the exposed part of the railing. In this way, your dog won't be able to use the balcony as a ladder. I don't recommend using shade cloth or other soft material as a barrier as some dogs can simply chew through it.

- Is there furniture next to your balcony's railings?

    Keep furniture and other items away from the balcony's railings – your dog may be able to climb the furniture in order to reach the top of the railing.

    Breeds like the Chinese Crested, Miniature Pinscher and Italian Greyhound can be particularly adept at climbing; so be especially cautious about the balcony railing and balcony furniture if you intend to get any of these breeds.

- Does your balcony have a shaded area?

  Some balconies may be at the mercy of the elements, particularly rain and the hot afternoon sun. Therefore, make sure your dog is able to settle comfortably in a shaded, enclosed area on your balcony. In this way, your dog is protected from the weather when outside. A kennel may do the trick, but ensure - as with other furniture – that it does not allow the dog access to the top of the balcony's railing.

8. Position the Kennel in a Safe, Comfortable Position

Not many people put too much thought into their dog's kennel, let alone its position. Having said that, it is important your dog comes to love her den as this will prevent restlessness. Your dog's kennel can also offer protection against the elements. Your dog's kennel should allow your dog to live within a comfortable temperature range; some dogs are more sensitive to hot or cold weather, so check your dog's breed profiles in this guide for more information. You could also ask your veterinarian to determine the most comfortable outside temperature for your dog.

Here are some matters to consider when positioning your dog's kennel in your courtyard or balcony:

- If you live in a wet climate, place the kennel in a higher area with good drainage. Of course, a kennel should have a floor so your dog doesn't have to sleep on the cold, damp ground.

- Ensure the kennel has a raised floor as this provides extra insulation. Some kennels are designed with raised floors. You might want to surround the elevated area with boards or place hay or other material underneath it so the wind won't whistle under the kennel. For further protection from the wind, the kennel's door should face south or east. As rule of thumb, coldest winds come from the north, west or northeast.

9. Remove Cleaners, Poisons and Other Items from Easily Accessible Areas

Common everyday items in your home can pose a danger to your dog. They are:

- Cleaners like bleach, ammonia and pine cleaners.

- Aluminum foil, batteries, coins, moth balls, liquid potpourri and small items can cause intestinal blockages.

- Snail bait, ant and rodent poisons, insecticides and herbicides can be fatal to dogs. If you have a dog, do not use rat or snail poison in your house.

Just because something is poisonous, don't think your dog will avoid it. Dogs will happily lick or eat many items just to see what they taste like. Like antifreeze, snail bait can smell and taste delicious to a dog. Scan your apartment for these items and ensure they are out of your dog's reach.

10. Watch for Elevators, Stairs and Escalators

Stairs and escalators can be particularly hazardous for dogs. There have been reports of injuries suffered by dogs after having their paws or legs stuck in escalators. Avoid using escalators with your dog or exercise extreme caution when doing so.

Stairs that are not enclosed present an obvious hazard: a dog may fall off the side or fall through the gaps between the steps.

Never leash a dog by or on stairs as this can lead to strangulation.

Never leave your dog unattended near an elevator; you would not want your dog to get her legs stuck in the gap at the foot of the elevator doors or fall victim to closing elevator doors.

Nine Apartment Danger Zones

Even after taking steps to dog proof your apartment, there are still nine danger zones to keep in mind when protecting your dog against injury and poisoning:

1. Trash Bins – Anything you discard could be raided. Discarded sharp objects like razors and broken glass can harm your dog. Ensure anything potentially dangerous to your dog is immediately taken out of the apartment or, as I said before, place the trash can in a latched cabinet.

2. Purse – Dogs have no qualms about raiding a purse! Medicines, gum or sweeteners are just three of the toxic, and potentially deadly, materials your dog might find in your purse.

3. Kitchen Counter – Poisonous foods left unattended present an overwhelming temptation for canine thieves!

4. Front Door – Some dogs may see an open front door as an opportunity to escape.

5. Laundry Basket – Dogs have eaten underwear, socks and pantyhose. These items can represent a choking hazard or cause internal blockages.

6. Baby gates, lids and doors – I have personally seen a dog open an unlocked baby gate. Dogs can be amazingly dextrous – they can open lids, doors and unlocked gates. So, if you are hoping to stop your dog from accessing certain cabinets or areas, ensure their doors and lids are locked or properly closed.

Poisonous Foods –Twenty Things Your Dog Should Never Eat

Here is a list of 20 foods you should never feed your dog. This list is by no means exhaustive, but it covers the most common undesirable 'foods' available:

1. Grapes can cause kidney failure in dogs and can be fatal.

2. Raisins like grapes can cause kidney failure in dogs and can be fatal.

3. Onions contain thiosulphate which is toxic to dogs. They can cause dogs to develop hemolytic anemia (where the red blood cells burst while circulating in the body). Any and all forms of onion can pose a problem, including dehydrated onions, raw onions, cooked onions and table scraps containing cooked onions and/or garlic. Left over pizza, Chinese dishes and commercial baby food containing onion, sometimes fed as a supplement to young pups, can also cause illness.

Initially, dogs affected by onion poisoning show gastroenteritis with vomiting and diarhea. They will be disinterested in food and will be dull and weak. The red pigment from the burst blood cells appears in an affected dog's urine and the dog becomes breathless. The breathlessness occurs because the red blood cells that carry oxygen through the body are reduced in number.

The poisoning occurs a few days after the pet has eaten the onion.

Onion poisoning can occur with a single ingestion of large quantities or with repeated meals containing small amounts of onion. For a ten kilogram (22 pound) dog, a single meal of 21-28 ounces (600-800 grams) of raw onion can be dangerous, whereas a daily dose of 5 ounces (150 grams) of onion for several days is likely to cause anemia. The condition improves once the dog is prevented from eating any further onion.

4. Garlic is toxic to dogs for the same reason as onions, however garlic is less toxic and large amounts would need to be eaten to cause illness.

5. Chocolate contains theobromine, which is naturally found in cocoa beans. Although it is not harmful to humans, this substance is highly toxic to dogs (and other domestic animals, such as horses). Theobromine is a stimulant (similar to caffeine) and so affects the central nervous system and heart.

6. Caffeine Products (coffee, coffee grounds, tea and tea bags): drinks and foods containing caffeine cause many of the same symptoms as chocolate.

7. Macadamia nuts and walnuts: Macadamia nuts can cause weakness, muscle tremor and paralysis. You should limit all other nuts as they are not good for dogs in general; their high phosphorous content may lead to bladder stones. An exception to this rule is peanut butter which can be a wonderful treat, especially if hidden inside a dog's toy that is designed to hold food, such as a Kong. Always use salt and sugar free organic peanut butter.

8. Animal fat and fried foods: excessive fat can cause pancreatitis.

9. Cooked bones can splinter and damage a dog's internal organs. A dog chewing on a raw bone should always be supervised as a piece can always break off and cause problems. Try frozen oxtails or frozen knuckle bones, then take the bone away before the dog can swallow a final small piece whole. Bones are a great, natural way to clean teeth.

10. Tomatoes can cause tremors and heart arrhythmias. Tomato plants are very toxic to dogs, and tomatoes themselves are unsafe.

11. Avocados: The fruit, pit and plant are all toxic to dogs. They can cause difficulty breathing and fluid accumulation in the chest, abdomen and heart.

12. Nutmeg can cause tremors, seizures and death.

13. The seeds or pits of apples, cherries, peaches, mangos and similar fruit contain cyanide, which is poisonous to dogs as well as humans. Unlike humans, dogs do not know to stop eating at the core or pit and easily ingest them. However, these fruits are generally good for your dog, so remove the pit or seeds before feeding them to your dog.

14. Raw eggs may cause salmonella poisoning in dogs. Dogs have a shorter digestive tract than humans and are not as likely to suffer from food poisoning, but it is still possible. Try organic or scrambled eggs (with no salt).

15. Excessive salt intake can cause kidney problems.

16. Some types of mushrooms can be fatal, so never let your pets chew on mushrooms found in your yard. Safe mushrooms are shiitake, maitake and reishi.

17. Xylitol (a sweetener used in breath mints, gum, mouthwashes and toothpastes). Even a small amount can cause liver failure and death. This is why it is important not to use human toothpaste when brushing your dog's teeth.

18. Sugar and corn syrups: honey and molasses are acceptable in small amounts but should never be given to dogs prone to cancer.

19. Human medications: medicating your dog using medicines designed for people may have serious health implications for your pet. Always seek veterinary advice on what medications to give your dog.

20. Raw potato, skins and potato plants: potato poisonings among people and dogs have occurred. Solanum alkaloids can be found in green sprouts and green potato skins, which occur when the tubers are exposed to sunlight during growth or after harvest. The relatively rare occurrence of actual poisoning is due to several factors: solanine is poorly absorbed; it is mostly hydrolyzed into

less toxic solanidinel; and the metabolites are quickly eliminated. Note that cooked, mashed potatoes are fine for dogs, and are actually quite nutritious and digestible.

In the next chapter, I'll discuss how to teach your dog good manners so she does not become disruptive and bossy.

How to Prevent Little Dog Syndrome

Little Dog Syndrome (LDS) describes a cluster of undesirable behaviors by any type of toy or small breed of dog. LDS is a symptom of a power struggle between the dog and owner. Typically, the dog asserts leadership through an array of behaviours which makes the dog seem uncontrollable, disobedient or spoilt. This behaviour is the dog's way of saying "this is my domain, I'm your leader and I'll do what I want!"

LDS manifests through a mix of some - or many - of the following behaviors:

- Disobedience
- Tantrums
- Aggression towards the owner, visitors or strangers
- Growling
- Nipping
- Possessiveness of people, objects or furniture
- Pottying in inappropriate places
- Destruction
- Excessive barking
- Jumping on people

LDS arises when the dog has decided to take the lead role in a household. The dog decides what she can get away with, and compensates for her small size by acting big and tough.

What Causes LDS?

The three primary causes of LDS are coddling, poor training and the owner failure to demonstrate strong leadership.

Coddling

Because small dogs are so cute and cuddly, owners tend to treat little dogs as they would a human child. Owners fawn over their dogs, picking them up and letting them lay in their laps. Some owners will even allow their dogs to break the house rules, and so the dog jumps on people and sits on the furniture – things that would not be tolerated in larger dogs. Because the owner appears to be giving tacit approval for this behavior, the dog assumes the leadership role and makes her own rules. This doesn't mean the dog is bad or spoilt; she is merely doing what thousands of years of canine evolution have taught her to do: if she makes the decisions and is fawned over (as occurs in nature when submissive dogs fawn over their dominant counterparts), then she decides she is the leader.

Poor Training

If a dog is not trained well or the training methods are harsh or inconsistent, the dog loses confidence in her owner. When this occurs, the dog takes control. The dog ensures the pack's survival by making up for her owner's inability to properly direct the family's behavior. The dog then creates havoc fuelled by her own sense of dominance and power.

Lack of Leadership

A dog that is never shown firm disapproval assumes she is the leader of the pack, that is, the 'alpha dog'. Dogs understand that leaders mete out discipline and submissive dogs receive discipline. A dog with LDS may therefore discipline her owner with growls, nips or glares.

The leader of the pack is also responsible for the safety of the pack. That's why the dog with this syndrome will nip and bark at strangers. If the dog is taking care of the pack, then she assumes leadership. She has no reason to listen to her owner. Again, this does not mean the dog is bad or mean, rather she is merely doing what thousands of years of canine evolution have taught her to do; protect and govern her family to ensure its survival.

How Can You Prevent LDS?

Preventing LDS comes down to you becoming the leader. Leadership is not about being harsh or gruff with your dog; instead leadership is easily achieved through various physical and verbal cues that your dog easily understands. As a leader you no longer 'negotiate' with your dog, rather you set the rules and ensure your dog follows them. In this way, your dog understands that challenging you will be a futile exercise.

Here are some easy-to-apply leadership strategies:

- Your body language should reflect confidence; your tone of voice should reflect kind assertiveness. Stand tall. This assures your dog of your leadership ability.

- Train your dog to heel either beside or behind you on a leash. She must not be allowed to walk in front of you. You must decide where your dog is allowed to stop and sniff. In the wild, dominant dogs always walk ahead of the rest of the pack. By having your dog walk behind you, the dog clearly understands your intention to lead the way during outings.

- Walk ahead of your dog when entering a room or going through a doorway or gate.

- Your dog must eat only after you have eaten. In the wild, dominant dogs eat first.

- Only allow your dog to eat after she has obeyed the sit command and you have released her.

- Never, ever give your dog any food from your plate or the dinner table. If you do, your dog may develop begging as a bad habit.

- When returning home or seeing your dog after a long absence, completely ignore your dog for about two minutes no matter her reaction (such as whinging, pokes or tantrums). Only when she is calm and not vocalizing, can you pay her attention.

- The dog must not receive anything from you without first sitting. This should be a command that she must follow before getting a treat, meals, before going for a walk or before being given a toy or attention.

- Do not lay or sit on the floor with your dog, unless it is playtime. For the majority of your interactions with your dog, you must remain at a higher level than your dog.

- If someone comes to your house, you must be the one to greet the visitor first. This means not allowing your dog to rush up to visitors first. By being the first to approach visitors, you are showing your dog you decide if a visitor is friend or foe.

- If the dog is always getting in your way, for example, standing or lying in front of you, never walk around, or over, her. Gently move your dog from your path, say "move" and continue on your way. Alternatively, you can gently move your dog out of the way without saying a word. Your dog will soon learn to move out of your way when she sees you coming.

- Your dog should not be allowed to sleep on your bed; her place is at the foot of your bed or in her own doggy bed.

- Do not respond to your dog's demands for attention – poking, pawing, whining, barking or nudging should be completely ignored. Some dogs may even be brazen enough to climb onto your lap without being invited! If your dog climbs onto your lap uninvited, say "no" firmly and remove the dog from your lap. Your dog may persist – the trick is to do this again and again until your dog gives up.

- Your dog must not be allowed to lie on your lap, be on the sofa with you, or sit on a chair with you, unless invited as a reward for obedience. If you are concerned for your dog's comfort, ensure she has a comfy, enclosed dog bed and blanket on the floor.

- Only show affection when the dog has earned a reward, such as obeying a command. If you want to show affection, play with your dog, or to have your dog sit on your lap, then ask your dog to obey a simple task such as 'sit' first.

- Aggression or growling should never be tolerated. Such behaviour should immediately be met with a timeout. Time-out basically involves quarantining your dog in a room for between 2-10 minutes. During this time the dog is to be ignored. The room in which your dog is isolated should not contain food or toys – the room should be 'boring'. When I give this advice to my clients, I remind them that a parent would never allow their child to have time-out with their toys within easy reach!

- If your dog has any object you do not want her to have, find an object for which the dog is willing to trace. If she does not trade, take command and take the object away. Do not chase her as this will reinforce that she is the leader (submissive dogs chase their leader).

Many of these tips are based on an important, but not often talked about, principle of responsible dog ownership, that is, dogs are better behaved if they understand that *nothing is for free*. This means that if a dog wants attention, food, toys or anything from her owner then she must behave. A dog's good behaviour therefore becomes her currency; she can then trade good behaviour for whatever she craves from her owner, whether this is attention, food or an activity. If a dog is able to get what she wants and give nothing in return then the dog will simply exploit this. When in doubt about whether you encouraging LDS, ask yourself "How can I make my dog work for whatever I am about to give her?" In this way, your dog learns that you are a leader because you have firm expectations; only when those expectations are met will your dog get what she wants from you.

In this chapter, I talked about some tactics you can employ to ensure your dog does not become a furry devil! Some of these tactics simply mean a change in how you interact with your dog, whilst others involve some training. In the next chapter, I'll share how you can teach your dog to be obedient and keen to listen to you.

Training and Leadership for Apartment Dogs

Good quality obedience training is essential for your dog's psychological welfare and also ensures dog ownership is a joy, rather than a burden. Obedience training is not just about getting your dog to do what you want, when you want; it's also an essential part of raising an independent and confident dog. Training does not end with formal obedience training. There are, in fact, many ways you can interact with your dog on a daily basis outside of formal training sessions - that will help your dog feel confident. This is especially important as your dog learns to keep herself occupied and contented, even when you are away from your apartment.

How Trainable is Your Dog?

Have you ever wondered what affects a dog's ability to learn new skills? It is very rare to find a dog that is not trainable to some extent, but the fact is some dogs are easier to train than others. In this guide, I have included a trainability rating in each dog profile which is based on the research of notable dog behaviourist, Stanley Coren. In his book *The Intelligence of Dogs*, Coren published the findings of a survey where dog obedience judges in the United States and Canada ranked 110 dog breeds by intelligence. Whether or not you agree with these rankings, it is important to remember not to rely on these rankings as the sole indicator of your dog's trainability. Rather, I recommend you view the ratings together with these other eight factors when determining how quickly and easily your dog will learn a new command:

1. Age

When it comes to peak learning, dogs are like humans – the best learning occurs in the early years. What dogs learn up until 14weeks old will stay with them for life. That's why early training is best. The good news is that a dog's learning capacity is never fully shut off; older dogs can learn new skills, it's just takes more time and patience. However, very old dogs suffering from dementia or other age-related disabilities may be quite difficult to train.

2. Temperament

Your dog's temperament is determined by her genes; her temperament cannot be changed. Generally speaking, a dog's temperament can be classified into one of the following three categories:

- Dominant

- Middle Pack

- Lower Pack

Dominant dog

This may come as a surprise for most people but it is the female dogs that are more likely to be the dominant dog in a pack.

Confident, dominant dogs stand straight with head level. If approached by other dogs, they stiffen in an upright pose. Generally, dominant dogs will not yield to other dogs – they won't lie on their back. These dogs will test their owners and tend not to be owner orientated. They will jump on you and walk ahead of you (unless they have been trained not to do so). Some owners fall into the trap of thinking that they should 'break' their dominant dog. This is irresponsible and dangerous to the dog's mental well-being. Dominant dogs simply require a firmer, more consistent and persistent training approach.

Middle pack dog

These dogs are generally friendly, easy going and compliant and, unless backed into a corner, will not fight other dogs. They will yield to the leader by lying on their back, cowering, lowering their head or darting. However, they will engage their subordinate counterparts by standing upright, stiff and head level. These dogs are generally great to train as they respond well to a confident and strong leader.

Lower pack dog

These dogs are focused on their owners and will always have an eye on them. They generally keep close by and respond quickly to rewards and corrections. They tend to submit to other dogs easily (by lying on their back, cowering, lowering their head or darting) as they do not want conflict. Thus, these dogs are very trainable, but watch out if they 'shut down', that is, totally withdraw from a training session, if the training is too harsh. Don't try to 'toughen' your dog with harsher training methods – this may stress her.

3. Motivation style

When training any dog, it is important to find out what motivates her. This can be different for each dog. There are many things that can motivate a dog: treats, food, toys, praise and dislike of corrections.With food, treats and toys, it can sometimes be a matter of what type of food, treat or toy your dog prefers. For example, my two terriers are not keen on tennis balls but they love their squeaky toy duck.

It's a good idea to experiment with toys, food and treats, to see which ones really excite your dog. It's also a good idea to rotate treats – dogs love to eat an array of foods. This will keep them guessing and interested. After all, variety is the spice of a dog's life too!

Some dogs thrive on praise and their owner's approval; other dogs really hate being corrected or experiencing their owner's disapproval. Surprisingly, you do not have to use harsh corrections – some dogs dislike the idea of their owner showing any sign of disapproval such as a growl or sharp "no!" You can use this to your advantage when training.

4. Health

A healthy, fit and active dog will most likely be responsive to training. Like humans, dogs have their days when they might be feeling a little 'off'. In such cases, the dog may not be as responsive to her owner's instructions. Luckily, this is temporary in most cases. Other longterm conditions, ailments and injuries might mean a dog is experiencing pain, lethargy or physical disability. This can significantly lower the dog's trainability, as she loses her capacity to follow instructions. Furthermore, the dog's desire to please the owner can be diminished.

On a more subtle level, poor diet and lack of exercise can affect a dog's health, even if only to contribute to a dog's general lethargy and malaise. Some dogs may even experience heightened anxiety or depression as a result of lack of enough fun family activity. It is therefore very important for owners to feed their dog a nutritious diet, exercise the dog regularly, give the dog regular opportunities to be trained and play with her owners.

Surprisingly, dogs with hearing and sight impairments can still be trained. In these cases, the trainer should rely on training methods that focus on the dog's other functioning senses.

5. Training experience

Dogs that are familiar with training and the learning process are far more likely to pick up new tricks and tasks than those dogs with limited experience being trained. This is because a dog which has been trained regularly gets to know and understand the learning process. In this way, the dog immediately goes into 'learning mode' where she experiments with her own behaviour, with guidance from the owner, to work out what actions will get her a reward.

6. Confidence and knowledge

Your energy 'travels down the lead' – this means that your own level of confidence is easily sensed by your dog. A confident owner puts a dog at ease; an unconfident one will affect the likelihood of training success. This is because dogs with dominant personalities will walk all over unconfident owners, while nervous dogs will only continue to be at the mercy of their own insecurities when they sense their owner is also unsure.

Knowing exactly what you are doing is the key to dog training. Plan your training sessions and be clear about what you will ask of your dog. Knowledge of good dog training techniques is essential in getting the best from your dog. This will also alleviate your frustration because you'll be more patient and understanding.

7. Complexity of new task

Some tasks are relatively easy to train while others are naturally harder. Generally speaking, the more steps involved in a task, the higher the complexity. For example, 'sit' is easy to teach as the action of sitting can be completed in one movement. However, teaching a dog to retrieve an item is more complex as it involves teaching the dog four separate movements: walking to the object, picking the object up with her mouth, returning to the owner and then dropping the item at the owner's feet. Some dogs learn to fetch quite quickly, but for dogs that are reluctant to, or unfamiliar with, fetch, it can be quite 'complex' to train them because of the number of steps involved.

As you can see, the trainability of your dog depends on many factors. It is essential to be willing to work through any challenges you may encounter in training your dog in a calm and creative way. Apart from dire health and old age issues, you should be able to work through most challenges in order to train your dog well.

The Ground Rules of Dog Training

These basic ground rules for training your dog will allow you to get her to focus and learn. They will also ensure both you and your dog absolutely love training. As you apply these rules you will see a big difference in your dog's responsiveness to any new skill you introduce.

Here are my ground rules:

1. Ensure your dog is healthy, alert and pain-free. If you notice your dog is unwell or tired, your dog is recuperating from illness or surgery or is in any pain, then don't train her until she is well and alert again. There is *never* a reason for making a dog do something that causes her pain.

2. Train your dog at regular intervals. There shouldn't be a long period of time between sessions, especially when you are introducing your dog to a new skill. Ideally, training sessions should not be more than 24 hours apart. If you have been unable to train your dog for a couple of days, remember your dog may have forgotten what she has learned. In that case, you need to do your last session all over again. You can have many training sessions per day, as long as they're short and fun.

3. Train your dog in short bursts. All dogs, especially puppies, have short concentration spans. Training your dog for 2–3 minutes at a time is sufficient. With puppies, sessions can be as short as 10–20 seconds! This ensures that your dog's mind is fresh during training. By dragging the session for too long, you run the risk of frustrating your dog. Too many repetitions are a sure-fire way to turn your dog off training. Your dog will dread training sessions, weakening her desire to learn.

4. Always end the session with a win so you can spend some time praising, cuddling and playing with your dog. A 'win' is when your dog has done well and you have not had to correct her. In this way, your dog will have fond memories of the last session and will eagerly await the next one.

5. Train in a quiet, distraction-free environment. There should be no other dogs, children, people or noisy things around. You can introduce distractions gradually only when you are confident your dog knows the command well.

6. Make sure your family is on the same page when it comes to training the family pet. There is nothing more frustrating and confusing to a dog than to be subjected to different training methods, training schedules and corrections. It's probably best that one person in the family coordinates the training. This person can ensure all family members are agreed on how to train the dog (having them read this chapter would be a good start). It is also vital that all family members are kept in the loop in regard to the dog's progress in terms of what the dog is currently learning.

7. Have a cue for the start and end of training sessions. Dog's love certainty – they like to know what is expected of them at any given time. These cues give them a clear distinction between training and other activities. By using a phrase to clearly signal the start and end of a session, your dog is given an opportunity to perform at her best; this is because she'll know she has a task to do. Dogs actually love working for their owners and these cues give them that satisfaction. I use "Are you ready?" to start a session and "Finished!" to end a session.

"Are you Ready"

"Finished"

What you choose to say is up to you, as long as the same cues are used each time. It's always best to use the same physical gestures with your instructions; I use arms out and palms up to signal the start and arms crossed over my chest to signal the end of a session.

8. Have the right equipment and training space. In this way, you won't be forced to cut the session short because you have run out of treats or cannot find a certain training tool. Later, I'll discuss what training equipment you'll need.

9. Be flexible. Training is a great opportunity for you to develop rapport with your dog. This bond ensures your dog is loyal and

obedient. You develop rapport by really taking notice of what your dog is 'telling' you. If your dog is having difficulty getting a new command or is not responding to a certain training method, then change the way you teach. This may be as simple as changing the types of reward or correction you are using, the length and timing of sessions or the type of training technique being applied.

10. Set your dog up for success. No one likes to fail often – it's demoralizing. Dogs are no different – if they feel they cannot please you, they will simply give up. When faced with constant failure (and punishment) some dogs will even shut down completely; this phenomenon is known as 'learned helplessness'. When a dog is constantly punished no matter what she does, the dog simply gives up. You set up a dog to win by using a good training technique (these are explained later in relation to each command) and by following these ground rules. One of the most important ways to set your dog up for success is to train 'incrementally'. This means teaching your dog a little at a time. For example, when you first train your dog the recall, ensure your dog is right in front of you. If you start with your dog on the other side of the yard, your dog is bound to fail.

11. Mindset is everything. A positive, upbeat approach to training will have a great effect on your training ability. Patience and confidence are essential. A confident owner will in still a strong sense of security in the dog. Never, ever show frustration or anger to your dog during training. By being angry you are signalling to your dog that you cannot handle the situation and your dog may shut down or play up.

12. Your dog decides her reward. When training your dog, carefully observe which type of reward your dog loves. Rewards are a dog's currency – different types of currency are valued differently by each dog. If your dog is a glutton, then use treats. Some dogs may go crazy for certain games like fetch or tug, while others long for affection. Choose the reward based on what your dog values most, not what you think is best. An advanced training technique used by professionals involves using a

reward that your dog values, but then using an even more valued reward for big improvements in behavior.

13. Rewards should be given only occasionally once the dog has learned the skill. Initially, as you teach your dog a new skill, a reward will be given every time she performs as expected or makes a small improvement towards the desired behavior. As the dog masters the new skill, rewards are phased out gradually. If you drastically cut rewards, your dog will lose motivation. This is also the reason why many dog owners report that their dog refuses to obey unless there is a treat on offer – it is because the phasing out of the treat occurred too quickly.

14. Timing is key. Your rewards and corrections must be instantaneous. You have about two seconds to provide a response to your dog's behavior; after that she is unlikely to make a connection between the behavior and your response.

15. Only say the command once. There is no need to repeat the command in an effort to get your dog to obey. Saying a command repeatedly, without the task being performed, teaches your dog that she can fob you off.

16. Never let your dog get away with disobedience. In the early stages of teaching a new command, it would be redundant to punish your dog for not doing what you ask. After all, your dog has not learned the new command yet! But, after your dog has learned a new skill, then she must obey every time you ask. Later, I'll discuss your options when your dog disobeys.

17. Always have you're your dog on a leash during training. There'll be times when a leash is unnecessary, but this will be indicated in the training instructions. A leash is important as it is a way to keep your dog under control. But, you should not rely on the leash as your only means of control. Your confident handling skills, clear communication and body language all go a long way to making sure you have good control over your dog.

18. Don't expect too much from your dog. This means in each session the dog should only be exposed to one step at a time. If your dog succeeds in learning a new step, then give an extra reward and give your dog an opportunity to reinforce this step by having her do that particular step repeatedly over a few training sessions.

19. When teaching a new command, have the overall goal in mind. Then break it down into steps – these steps will then form the basis of the smaller goals you will need to achieve in order to achieve the overall goal.

20. When training, use clear communication. Use high tones for praise, neutral tones for commands and low, guttural tones to indicate disapproval. Each verbal command should be accompanied by a special hand signal. It doesn't matter what terms or hand signals you use as long as they are used consistently and come natural to you.

21. Always use a release word. A release word is the equivalent of giving your dog permission to be 'at ease'. By using a release, you are teaching your dog that she should stay in a commanded position until she is released or given another command. The release word can be anything, as long as you use that word consistently. I use the word 'free.' Some people use 'okay', but many professional dog trainers say the word 'okay' may cause the dog confusion because this is too commonly used in general conversation. A reward should only be given *after* you have released your dog (and your dog has performed the task as expected).

Reward and Punishment

In rule 19 above, I discussed using clear communication when training your dog. This means being obvious about whether you approve or disapprove of your dog's behavior. Rewarding your dog can be simply be a matter of using treats, toys, play and affection (see rules 12, 13, 14 above for more information about rewards).

Type of punishments to use

Punishment is a way of expressing disapproval and should be applied humanely. This means the punishment should produce either annoyance, a startle, or some amount of discomfort in the dog – but certainly *not* pain. Studies have shown that hitting, kicking, slapping or using other corporal punishment on a dog causes behavioral issues such as aggression or timidity. Humane forms of punishment are:

- Guttural, gruff tones (such as a growl). These may be accompanied by a tug on the leash or a stare-down.

- A clap or similar very unpleasant sound at medium (but not loud) volume.

- Boss grip (where the owner holds the dog's muzzle firmly, and gently, closed). This is suitable for barking or mouthing issues. This method is unsuitable for some small apartment dogs like pugs, as they have such a flat muzzle.

- Isolating the dog (timeout). This can be done by gruffly saying "enough!" and then firmly leading the dog to a secluded environment and then leaving the dog in that space for a short period of time. This can be the laundry or bathroom of your apartment. A two minute timeout is enough.

The level of punishment you apply should be proportionate to how robust your dog is. A timid, fragile dog may not cope with the same level of disapproval as a confident, robust dog. Many apartment dogs are quite small and somewhat fragile, therefore choose your method of punishment accordingly. Also, a soft punishment such as a low growl may have no effect on a sturdy, dominant dog. It's up to you to learn your dog's level of tolerance and adjust your punishment methods accordingly. If your methods are too 'soft' your dog will likely resume whatever behavior you are trying to avoid. Likewise, if you do not consistently punish unwanted behavior, your dog is unlikely to heed your sporadic efforts.

If you ever feel like using corporal punishment on your dog, remove yourself from the situation. I guarantee you'll feel better if you do. Usually, if a dog does not 'get' something, it's because you've missed something in your training technique. In such circumstances, review this chapter and see how you can improve your training methods.

When to use punishment

In the initial stages of teaching your dog a new command, there'll never be a need to punish your dog. This is because your dog is still learning the meaning of the command. Once it is clear that your dog understands what a certain word means, then you can introduce the punishment for non-compliance. You'll know when your dog has learned the association between the word and behavior when your dog has consistently performed the task about ten times (over the span of several training sessions) without you having to coax the behavior. Therefore, especially during the initial stages of training a new behavior, you will be using rewards more often. When you introduce punishments, keep track of how many you have had to apply. If your punishments are more than one in ten, then your dog has not learned the meaning of the word. In this case, you'll need to go back to teaching your dog the command as if she is new to it.

Distraction-Proofing Your Dog

Initially, training sessions should be conducted in a quiet, distraction-free zone. Once you are certain your dog knows a command very well, that is, nine out of ten times in a row over the span of several sessions, you can slowly introduce distractions. Distractions can be simple things like you moving around, tossing a toy or treat and saying other words (that do not resemble the release word). Later, you can take your dog to the park and have your dog perform the tasks on a short, then long, leash. If your dog is having trouble with the distractions, then you have gone too far too quickly for your dog. Keep to a level of distraction that she can handle and proceed slowly. Remember to set up your dog to win!

Your Dog Training Tool Box

Here is a brief checklist of the things you will need:

1. Your dog will need a flat buckle collar and leash. A nice nylon collar and leash will do very well. You may wish to get a collar that is brightly colored in case your dog wanders away from you. Something bright will make her easier to spot. Her leash should be about six-feet long. You'll also need a longer leash (about 20-30 feet long) which you can use when your dog's training becomes advanced and you would like to do some distance work in a public area.

2. Your dog will need a crate for sleeping and house training. Even if you don't plan to have your dog sleep in the crate on a regular basis, all dogs should be crate-trained. It is recommended that dogs ride in crates when in vehicles (or use a harness), and most dogs must ride in a crate if they fly by plane. Choose a crate that is large enough for your dog to stand up and turn around but not so large that she will be tossed around in case of a car accident. Dogs can be injured in crates that are too large.

3. Make sure that you have toys for your dog. Choose a few things from different toy categories such as balls, ropes, squeakies, stuffed animal-type toys, and so on. Your dog will soon let you know what kind of toy she likes best. Toys can also be used as rewards during training.

4. Treats make great rewards for good behavior during training. Treats should be very small and soft. If you are using commercial treats, then break them into smaller pieces. Natural alternatives are chopped vegetables (no onion or garlic – they are poisonous to dogs).

Your Dog's First Training Lessons

There are some basics every dog needs to learn. You can start training your dog as young as six to eight weeks of age.

Potty training

When you bring your new dog home the first thing you will want to start is your dog's potty routine. How to teach your dog to eliminate outside or in a designated area is explained in this guide.

Confidence building

Building confidence in your dog is about allowing her to become accustomed to your lifestyle. This is so she won't be afraid of new things. Humans lead busy, interactive and noisy lives. We are exposed to a lot of things, situations and people that would be quite foreign to a dog. As such, socializing your dog with different people, places, things, noises and activities is a key aspect of confidence building. The window of opportunity for ensuring your dog is well-socialized is between one and five months. During this short period of time it's your job to provide a stimulating and varied environment – you can do this by:

- Ensuring that your dog grows to like people generally. Take your dog out to meet your friends and family. And let visitors pat her.

- Ensuring that your dog grows to like other dogs. Let her meet other friendly dogs on a leash where dogs are welcome (such as parks, pet supply stores) as soon as her vaccinations are complete (you can check what a typical vaccination schedule will involve in this guide). Make sure you ask the other dogs' owners' permission prior to approach.

- Encouraging strangers to pat your dog. Take treats with you and give them to strangers so they can pat your dog and give her treats. (This won't make your dog any less welcoming of suspicious people. A secure dog knows the difference between friend and foe).

- Enrolling in your dog in a preschool, dog party or dog kindergarten. Here your dog will meet other dogs her age.

She will be able to play, meet other friendly owners, and learn some basic good manners in class. These classes are highly recommended. They are usually offered by kennel clubs, animal shelters, pet stores and dog trainers.

- Ensuring your dog becomes accustomed to different types of noises at different volumes. Sound desensitization is the process of helping your dog become used to some of the many loud and strange noises that she will encounter in life. Many dogs are afraid of loud noises such as fireworks, thunderstorms and sounds they haven't heard before. By using sound desensitization you can gently teach her to accept strange noises and to understand that there is nothing frightening about them. In the next section, I'll show you how to desensitize your dog to strange sounds.

The more confidence you can in still in your dog, the more confident she will be as an adult. Confident dogs are less likely to develop separation anxiety and other behavioral problems later in life.

Sounds of a lifetime

When socializing your dog, it is very important that you ensure she is accustomed to many types of noises, such as:

- Lawnmowers and leaf blowers
- Babies and children
- Phones
- Traffic: cars, trams, dirt bikes and trucks
- Thunderstorms
- Music
- Gun shots and artillery
- Door bells
- Vacuum cleaner
- Hair dryer
- Aeroplanes
- Fireworks

As you can see, these are all sounds that your dog may encounter. By using a recording you can control when your dog encounters these sounds and how loud the noise will be. You can be there with her when she hears these noises. You can encourage her to be confident by being cheerful and relaxed when these recordings are played. You may wish to give your dog treats as she listens, so she understands that nothing bad will happen.

One way to use these recordings is like this: play one of the sounds for your dog and if she reacts calmly you can praise her and give her a treat. If she is scared, stay calm and cheerful, and play the sound again at a lower volume. Encourage the dog to play and ignore the sound. When she plays and ignores the sound, praise her and give her a treat. It's that simple. You can use some of the dog's favorite toys while the sound plays to encourage her to play. Make the sounds fun for your dog.

You could gather each of these items together, such as a vacuum cleaner, a hair dryer, fireworks, and so on, and teach your dog about the sounds individually, but it is much easier to teach your dog about the sounds when you use recordings of the noises. Then your dog can identify the sounds – and know that they are okay – when she encounters them in real life. Playing these sounds at the time and place of your choosing, when you can be positive and encouraging for your dog, can do wonders to desensitize your dog to these and other loud or unexpected sounds.

Sound desensitization helps puppies develop into confident dogs that are not afraid of hearing these sounds in real life.

Independence training

Raising an independent dog means your dog will remain calm and secure, even when she doesn't have access to you at all times. A dog that frets or experiences anxiety in your absence can engage in problem behaviors such as excessive barking, shadowing (this is when your dog follows you around constantly), destruction, hyperactivity and pottying inside.

Here are seven keys to raising an independent dog:

1. Do not acknowledge your dog as you return to your apartment. If you make a fuss, your dog will fret in your absence and long for that special attention she expects upon your return. It's best to ignore your dog for about ten minutes after your arrival, later you can calmly acknowledge her.

2. Give your dog something to do as you leave the house. In this way, your dog sees your departure as a positive event.

3. If you have several people in your home, see that each family member shares responsibility for the dog's welfare. This means that activities such as feeding, walking, play and training should be done by different people in the household. In this way, your dog won't come to rely solely on one person for her survival and therefore won't regard one particular person as her 'savior'.

4. Ignore your dog's demands for attention (via poking, pawing or whining).

5. Make your dog 'work' for your attention and affection. This can be as simple as doing a quick training exercise, then rewarding with play afterwards. Your dog will learn that you do not give away 'freebies' and that she must behave to be acknowledged.

6. Your dog should not have constant access to you. This means that even when you are home there will be times when your dog should not be able to reach you. This can be as simple as ensuring that your dog is in an x-pen or in the courtyard while you are home. Or you can even use a baby gate to section off part of the house. For dogs, initial periods of separation should be very short (a matter of minutes). These periods of separation can then be lengthened gradually.

7. Give your dog her own haven. A special, enclosed space such as a crate can be your dog's 'home'. This is where your dog can sleep, play or relax without interference. This space gives your dog a place to feel safe and secure. Never send your dog to her haven as punishment (otherwise it will no longer have a positive

association). Also, never drag your dog out of this space or allow children to poke or annoy the dog while she's in there.

Crate training

You already know that puppies can be naughty at times; destructive and messy in the house; and sleepy, especially after they use up their energy playing. Crate training is a good solution for some of your puppy's less desirable behaviors, such as chewing and house soiling. It will also keep her out of trouble when you can't be home.

A crate also provides your dog with a safe place to sleep and rest.

What type of crate should you choose?

Purchase a crate that will be large enough for your dog when she's an adult. Most manufacturers give good guidance regarding which crate is right for which breed (or mix) so check the labels or tags. When in doubt, get a crate that is a little larger rather than one that's too small. However, don't get an enormous crate that will be too big for your dog when she's fully-grown. Dogs generally like to feel well-insulated and comforted in their crates, like a den. They won't feel safe in a huge space.

If you choose an adult-sized crate for your dog, then fill the extra space with blankets – this way the dog will not soil the crate as they do not like to pee or poop in their living space. If the crate is too big, the dog may use the crate as a potty, which is exactly the behavior you are trying to discourage!

There are several different kinds of crates: hard plastic airline crates, wire crates, and canvas crates. There are even wicker crates and other unusual crates. They are all fine for different purposes. Canvas, wicker and other crates are usually not a good choice for a dog, however, since they are easily torn or chewed. Choose a hard plastic or wire crate for crate training.

Your dog's first reaction to the crate

It's not hard to crate train a dog but your dog may complain about it at first, depending on her early experiences with a crate. Some breeders use a crate as part of their whelping set-up so some dogs are used to them from birth. They have no objection to spending time in a crate or sleeping in one. To them a crate is a cozy, safe place that they associate with their mother and littermates. Other dogs, however, may not have seen a crate before. Initially, at least, they may think of the crate as a jail. Since you may not know whether your dog has any experience with a crate it's always a good idea to introduce the crate slowly.

Three steps to easy crate training

1. Allow your dog to explore the crate.

Once you have the right crate, allow your dog to explore it. Leave the door wide open. Place a comfortable sheepskin mat or some towels in the crate and put some treats and toys inside. Many dogs will go inside to get the treats. Your dog may decide to take a nap there. That's fine - you should let her sleep there with the door open. Let her get used to going in and out of the crate as she likes. You can also begin feeding your dog meals in the crate, with the door open.

2. Introduce short periods of crate time.

After your dog has become used to the crate you can start closing the door for short periods of time while you are home with your dog. Close the door for a couple of minutes and give your dog something good to chew on while she's in the crate. Some dogs may not notice that you have closed the door. They will be focused on the chewy. Other dogs may protest the closed door. It is best to open the door after a couple of minutes and let your dog out when the dog is quiet. Do this a few times each day for several days. You can gradually keep your dog in the crate for longer periods of time, always making sure that you are home with her.

Your dog should begin to get used to spending some time in the crate. Make sure you always give her something safe to occupy her while she's in there. You should not expect her to spend long periods of time in the crate at this stage, especially if she's very young, as she may soil her space or become distressed.

Eventually you can practice going outside for a few minutes while your dog is in the crate. Your dog may howl but you will need to ignore it. Then, once settled, you can go back inside and let her out. The key is not to make a fuss when you let your dog out. In this way she will not become too excited when you return. Your dog will learn that you will always come back and so she will not fret while you are away.

3. Gradually increase crate time.

You can gradually be gone for longer periods. If your dog whines, howls or freaks out, then cut the time she is left in the crate by half and slowly build up the length of your absences as your dog remains calm in her crate. When your dog is still quite young, remember that she will need to be toileted frequently so ensure she is let out often. If she soils her crate this may lead to a bad habit that is hard to break.

Outcome - a happy crate trained dog!

If you follow these suggestions your dog will be crate trained in just a few weeks. Some dogs learn faster than others. Some dogs will calm down and take a nap when you leave while others may bark and object at first. The keys are to ensure: (i) your dog knows that you will return; (ii) the crate is a pleasant place (never scold or punish her while she's in her crate); and (iii) you do not make a big fuss when you leave and return.

Training Your Dog to Be a Good K9 Citizen

The goal of training is not only about moulding your dog into a confident and secure pet, but also giving your dog clear guidelines for what is acceptable and unacceptable behavior. If your dog knows her 'good manners', then she will turn out to be a loyal, fun and easy-going pet.

Teach your dog to "stand"

Stand is a great position to teach your dog; it is particularly useful when you need your dog to stand for a veterinary check-up. You can teach your dog to stand using your hands to guide the dog into position with these five simple steps:

1. Kneel beside your dog, with your dog's head at your left and her rump to your right.

2. Hook two of your left fingers under your dog's collar so they are pointing towards your dog's tail.

3. Prop up your dog with your right hand by placing it under the dog's chest area (by hugging your dog from above). As you perform this step, say "stand".

4. Keep the dog in this position for three to four seconds, release and reward your dog.

5. Slowly increase the length of the stand (with your hands still in place) and eventually you will be able to allow your dog stand without being guided.

Here are some quick fixes to common problems associated with training your dog to stand:

- *"My dog sits as I try to position her correctly."* Make sure you firmly hold the dog's rib cage up with your right hand and do not allow the dog to sit.

- *"My dog seems uncomfortable and cagey."* Make sure your right hand is under the dog's rib cage and *not* under her abdomen. Applying pressure to your dog's abdomen can cause discomfort.

- *"My dog squirms or won't stay still."* Make sure you firmly hold the dog in place. If you 'give in' when the dog struggles against you, she will learn to get her way by wrestling you.

Teach your dog to "sit"

The sit command is one of the first commands taught as part of obedience training. People assume that the sit and stay commands should be taught separately when, in fact, you can teach your dog to 'stay sitting'. In this way, when you teach your dog to sit, she will eventually learn to remain in the sit position until released or commanded to do another task.

This command can be used to maintain control of your dog and ensures that she understands you are the boss. For example, this is also a great command to teach before every mealtime. This way, your dog learns to sit and wait for her meal.

If teaching this command in your apartment, ensure your flooring is not slippery. Tiled and wooden polished floors make it hard for your dog to stay in a sit position, as their front paws will slowly slide forward when they sit, forcing them to stand in order to avoid slipping all the way down. I recommend using a mat or carpeted area when teaching this command.

There are two ways you can teach your dog to sit. I'll explain both ways and you can choose which method is best for you and your dog.

Using a treat as a 'lure'

1. You and your dog should be standing and facing one another. Take a step away from your dog to encourage her to stand if she's sitting.

2. Have a treat ready in your right hand and hold your dog's lead in your left hand.

3. Allow your dog to see that you have a treat in your hand.

4. In a sweeping motion, move the treat from under your dog's chin to just above the dog's nose (between the dog's eyes).

5. Slowly and gently move the treat towards the dog's eyes so that the dog needs to tilt her head backwards. This compels the dog backwards into a sitting position.

6. Just before your dog sits, say "sit" and give her the treat. Your dog may immediately stand again – this is fine as she is learning a new skill.

7. Once your dog routinely sits, introduce your release word so you can turn sit into stay (see Ground Rule 21 above). You won't have to say "stay", rather the goal is to ensure that your dog will sit until you release her. Initially, releases should be given almost immediately. Then gradually increase the time, initially for a few seconds and slowly to longer and longer periods.

8. Once your dog sits for longer periods (between 30 seconds to two minutes), you can start putting some distance between you and your dog. After directing your dog to sit, take a step away from your dog. Then return to your dog and release her. Slowly and gradually increase the amount of steps you take away from your dog. If you take too many steps too quickly, your dog may move before you release her – so take a gradual and patient approach.

Another way to teach "sit"

If the lure is not working for you and your dog, you can try a different approach. This method is very effective as you are using your hands to carefully manoeuvre the dog into a sit position.

1. Kneel with your dog in front of you. Your dog's head should be to your right and your dog's rump to your left.

2. Hook the index and middle fingers of your right hand under your dog's collar at the back of the dog's neck, so that your palm is facing up.

3. Say "sit".

4. Firmly and gently tuck your dog's rump in towards the ground. If your dog resists, slightly rock her rump sideways as this will destabilize her hind legs and compel her to sit.

Do not push down on your dog's spine – this may cause serious injury!

5. As you are tucking your dog's rump in, you can also very lightly tug up on your dog's collar with your right hand.

6. Hold your dog in that position for a few seconds, release and reward your dog with praise or a treat.

7. Eventually, you'll notice that you do not need to maneuver your dog into a sit position.

You can now start putting some distance between you and your dog. After directing your dog to sit, stand up, then release and reward her. Slowly and gradually increase the distance between you and your dog. Always return to release and reward your dog.

Teach your dog to "drop"

Teaching your dog to drop is very important. It is a great way to keep control of your dog and ensure that she remains calm and relaxed if left in a stay position for longer periods.

Here is how you can teach your dog to drop:

1. Kneel beside your sitting dog, with the dog's head to your right. (Your dog should know the sit command before learning this command).

2. Place your left hand on your dog's rump. Do not push your dog's spine; just keep your dog's rump tucked into the ground.

3. Place a treat in front of your dog's nose so that she sees the treat in your right hand. In a slow sweeping motion, lower it to the floor so that the treat is about 6-12 inches (15 - 30 centimetres) from your dog's feet. Hold the treat still. Do not move the treat closer then farther away from your dog's nose, as your dog will find this 'game of tag' tiresome and unrewarding.

4. Just as your dog lies flat on the floor, say "drop" and give her the treat. Timing is key – say "drop" only as your dog reaches the floor. In this way, your dog will learn to associate the word "drop" with the actual action of lying on the floor. Initially, your dog may immediately stand again – this is fine as she is learning a new skill.

5. If your dog does not move towards the treat, use an item your dog really wants, a tastier morsel food or a beloved toy. Sometimes patience is needed, but your dog will eventually understand what she needs to do.

Never try and push your dog down as she will automatically resist.

6. Once your dog is routinely dropping, introduce your release word so you can turn drop into stay (see Ground Rule 21 above). You won't have to say "stay", rather the goal is to ensure that your dog will stay in the drop position until you release her. Initially, releases should be given almost immediately. Gradually increase the time, initially for a few seconds and slowly to longer periods.

Teach your dog to "come"

The recall command, like sit and stay, forms the basis of good obedience training. A dog that comes when called is more easily controlled and less vulnerable to hazards such as roadways.

Here is the recall training in six steps:

1. Make sure your dog is on a lead and is not looking at you.

2. When your dog is looking away from you, say her name. Praise her when she looks at you.

3. Open your arms wide or lift one arm in the air, say "come!" in an excited tone and take a few steps backwards.

4. As your dog approaches you, gently capture her. Release and reward your dog.

5. Using a longer lead, slowly increase distance between you and your dog. Eventually, you can try this training without having the dog on a lead. Make sure you are in a safe, confined space when you do this (in case your intrepid dog tries to run off!)

Some extra tips to get good recalls

Here are some things you can do to make your recall training even more effective:

- Play little games with your dog where you reward her with treats and affection for giving you attention when you say her name.

- Never, ever call your dog over to punish her or to do something unpleasant (such as a bath or trimming nails). If you do, she will be reluctant to come when called as she might not know whether you are calling her for good or bad reasons. Your dog must know that whenever she is called to you, it's only for good reasons.

- You can crouch down during recall to make yourself more appealing to your dog.

- Before recalling your dog, make sure she sees that you have a toy or treat in your hand. This will entice your dog to come more quickly. If your dog has a canine playmate, you can use that dog as a lure by keeping that dog next to you as you recall your dog.

- Play tag where you are always the one being chased. This way, your dog will come to love 'catching' you. This strategy can be used to great advantage during recall training.

Troubleshooting the recall

Here are some quick fixes to common problems associated with recall training:

- "*My dog refuses to come.*" If your dog does not respond to your recall, then you can behave excitedly and make high pitched sounds like "pup, pup, pup!" You can also gently tug the lead.

- "*My dog runs to me before I say come.*" Praise your dog anyway. Never, ever punish her for coming to you. Have a friend hold your dog and release her when you say "come" – this way your dog is forced to wait until you give the command.

- *"My dog won't come unless I have a treat in my hand."* Play tag, crouch or lie down to entice your dog to come.

- *"My dog seems to veer off in another direction as she nears me."* Simply continue jogging backwards and wave a reward such as a toy or food treat in front of you.

- *"My dog ignores me when I say her name."* Train your dog to look at you when you say her name. See the next section on how to do this.

Teach your dog her name

It's important that your dog learns to give you attention when you command her to do so - this means she must look at you when you call her name. Follow these steps to train your dog to learn her name:

1. Wave a small treat in front of your dog's face so that your dog starts to follow the treat with her eyes.

2. Bring the treat up to your nose - your dog's eyes should follow the treat so that she is looking at you in the face.

3. Say the dog's name, praise and give the treat.

You can do this five to six times a day. Your dog will quickly get into the habit of looking at your face when you say her name.

Teach your dog leash manners

Before teaching your dog leash manners, you must ensure that you have correctly fitted a collar. A collar that is too loose is a dangerous hazard as it may come off when your dog is near a busy road. A collar that is too tight may constrict your dog's breathing.

A collar is a proper fit when you are able to slide only one or two fingers comfortably through the collar when your dog is wearing it.

You can measure your dog's neck with a soft measuring tape, and then adjust the collar to match. Even if you do this, it is likely that the collar will need adjustment once it is on her. However, measuring beforehand means that you will need to only have minimal adjustments once the collar is on the dog.

Make sure your dog's collar has a tag with your contact details clearly etched into it.

Getting used to the collar and leash

Your dog may not like the collar at first and may fuss. So to begin with, put the collar on for short stints. Gradually increase the length of time, making sure your dog is distracted with treats and play. It's normal for a dog to whine or fuss so leave the collar on until the dog has settled. If you immediately remove the collar when the dog fusses or whines, then your dog will learn to get her way by whining.

Once your dog is used to a collar, you can begin getting your dog used to a lead.

Allow your dog to sniff and familiarize herself with the lead. However, do not use it as a toy as this will encourage your dog to bite and play with the lead when you take her for walks.

First, hook the collar to the lead and allow the lead to hang freely on the ground. Allow your dog to explore her surroundings with the lead attached (but not held on to).

You can, if you want, drape the lead over the dog's back and play with your dog.

Once your dog is comfortable with the fact that there is a lead attached, you can pick up the lead. Don't lead her around yet – instead let her lead you to wherever she's going. This first session should be short and fun. You can make subsequent sessions incrementally longer and let her explore the yard and the house as she chooses. This allows the dog to associate freedom of movement with the collar and lead.

If and when your dog strains on the lead, stop and encourage your dog to return to you. Making light-hearted sounds like "pup pup pup!" There is never a need to yank or jerk the lead or pull your dog back to you.

Make this whole process as pleasant as possible; this means you should praise and play with your dog and give her treats or meals while the lead is attached.

Teaching your dog to "heel"

After your dog or dog is comfortable with the lead and you have done some initial lead training, you can begin to teach your dog to heel. Until your dog learns to heel, all walks should be treated as a training session – so keep walks short and fun.

Begin the walk with the dog to your left. Start off and say "heel". Walk briskly, but be mindful of your dog's pace. For example, toy breeds and smaller dogs require a slower pace.

If your dog pulls ahead, you can try these two techniques:

- Stop walking. Never ever keep walking when your dog is pulling on the lead, this only rewards her behavior and reinforces the habit. Do not proceed ahead until the dog is at your side again. You might have to coax your dog back to you.

- Simply turn and walk in the opposite direction. In this way, your dog learns that if she pulls, she won't get any further.

You can make walking fun by walking in zigzags and by giving her rewards. This will serve to stimulate your dog and encourage her to follow you. This is important because when you're both out on a walk you're basically competing for your dog's attention with all the other wonderful sights and smells. So make yourself exciting and fun.

At curbs you can have your dog sit beside you, and as you move off again say "heel".

Teach your dog to calmly greet people

Dogs often lick each other on the face or nether regions as part of their greeting rituals. It is therefore natural for dogs to jump up on people upon meeting them, hoping to engage them in a friendly way. However, this is an unacceptable habit, and it is your responsibility as a dog owner to ensure that you teach your dog to greet people calmly, whether these people are visitors to your home or passers-by in public areas.

Here are some effective tips to deter or prevent jumping:

- Do not pick up a dog in response to jumping as this is seen as a reward and will only encourage this unwanted behavior.

- As your dog jumps on you, fold your arms, avoid eye contact and swiftly turn away.

- Do not tolerate hyperactivity and attention-seeking from your dog when you have guests in your home. This means no jumping, barking or whining when people arrive. Have visitors ignore the dog when they come so the dog does not get over-stimulated. If the dog jumps on people, take the dog away until she's calm. Bring the dog back to where the visitors are and allow the dog to remain while calm. Consistently remove the dog from the room whenever she misbehaves. In order to have control over the dog when visitors arrive, have the dog on a lead.

- Always have a mat, crate or other resting place in your living room so the dog can have a place to settle when people are visiting. Visitors should wait until the dog is calm before gently praising and patting the dog.

How to stop your dog from chewing on things

If you've ever come home to find your favorite shoes chewed into pieces or a ruined remote control, then you probably already know that dogs like to chew. You may not know there can actually be a number of reasons for this type of behavior. Here's a look at some reasons why dogs chew and how you can manage this issue:

1. Like human babies, puppies are born without any teeth. This means that for the first few weeks of life they are cutting teeth and learning to use them. During their first few weeks they will have very sharp little teeth. Between four and seven months, dogs get their adult teeth. This means that your dog will look for things to chew on! She may chew on you, soft things, hard things and anything she can find to put in her mouth. Nothing at all is safe during this time. If you leave things lying around your dog will chew on them.

You can help your dog a lot by giving her lots of things of her own to chew on. Make sure you provide a good variety of chewies – give her things with different textures such as soft toys, hard chews, hard rubber Kongs, and other indestructible chew toys. You can even wring out a wet wash cloth and freeze it for your dog. Your dog will probably like the hard cold texture of the cloth to chew on and it's easy to wet it and re-freeze it again later for her. If your dog has things of her own to chew, the less likely she will be to chew on your things.

2. Loneliness and boredom. Dogs that are left alone with nothing to do all day will often act out and get into trouble by chewing on things. They can become very destructive. A bored dog will find things to chew on. You can help keep your dog occupied by providing her with plenty of her own things to chew on. Give her toys to snuggle with, hard things to chew on, balls to chase and some good interactive toys that she has to figure out in order to get treats.If your dog is lonely and bored you may also wish to leave the TV or radio on for her. Have a neighbor or a friend drop by during the day to see your dog. Perhaps have a dog walker take her for a walk during the day. And, it always helps if you can spend more time with your dog yourself. Make the time you have with your dog count. It will also help if you increase your dog's exercise when you're home. Dogs that get plenty of exercise are more likely to spend their daytime hours resting and less likely to spend their time alone being destructive.

3. Separation anxiety. Your dog may chew on your belongings when you're gone. This can be a sign of separation anxiety. A dog with separation anxiety will also have problems when you leave her alone in a room while you're still in the house. She won't want to allow you out of her sight at all. Dogs that suffer separation anxiety will be destructive or misbehaved in the owner's absence. Increasing a dog's independence and confidence is the best defense against this type of anxiety; for relevant tips and techniques see the section on 'independence training' above.

4. Normal chewing. Keep in mind that some chewing is perfectly normal for your dog. Not all chewing is bad. For your dog, chewing can be very soothing and relaxing since it satisfies a natural instinct. It's a good idea to provide your dog with a regular source of safe chew toys so she can satisfy this instinct. Always

remember that the more toys and chewies of her own that your dog has, the less likely she is to chew on your things.

Reduce your dog's mouthing and nipping

For dogs, biting is a natural behavior that may subside by the time they are four months old. However, it is not guaranteed this problem will disappear on its own, so it is recommended that biting is discouraged from the start. Many owners view this behavior as playful, but the dog may also be testing what you will tolerate.

What are the best ways to stop a snappy dog? Just do what other dogs would do! Dogs first learn from their mother or litter mates that biting is inappropriate. When a dog bites, the other dog may respond by giving a short sharp "yelp", withdrawing, growling or biting back. We all know that biting back is not the way to go! But there is plenty of merit in the other strategies. Let's look at what you can do when your dog nips you:

- The short sharp yelp: A short, high pitched "ouch!" or "yelp!" will startle the dog into ceasing the biting. Make sure the yelp is high pitched but not too loud – the aim is to startle, not frighten, the dog. All dogs instinctively recognize this sound as meaning it has caused pain and it will immediately stop.

- The growl or correction: A verbal correction such as "no" or a low guttural growl will give your dog a clear message that biting is not tolerated.

- Withdrawing: Simply stop and withdraw the part of you that has been bitten. A concurrent growl or yelp will help reinforce the message.

There are also some other things you can do to prevent your dog growing into a snappy dog. They are:

- Reinforce safe play - when dog plays nicely, reward her with affection and treats.

- Correct your dog without using your hands - some dogs grow up having had bad experiences with human hands because they were smacked as a dog; they may bite hands as a way of protecting themselves. It is therefore important that when you are raising your dog that you never smack her, otherwise she may grow up to be a 'fear biter'. Use verbal corrections as discussed earlier.

How to Choose a Good Dog Trainer

This guide serves as a way to empower you as a dog owner to train your dog well, however, you might decide to engage the services of a professional dog trainer to help you out. But there are so many dog trainers. How do you know which one to choose? Here are some things to look for in a great dog trainer.

1. Observe. After you have found several possible trainers you should ask if you can observe them working with dogs. See if you can sit in on their classes if they offer group training. How do they interact with other owners and their dogs? Are they brusque? Understanding? Are they rough with dogs? Do they explain things to the owners? Do they repeat things until the dogs are bored or do they keep the dogs interested and happy? It's important to observe a trainer because this gives a good indication of what your training with your dog would be like.

2. Talk to the trainer about their qualifications. Some trainers are certified by professional organizations for dog or animal trainers although not all are. At the very least you should find out about their training specialties. Is most of her or her experience in training dogs for agility or some other sport? This doesn't mean that the trainer can't teach you and your dog the basics of obedience but it does mean they may have less experience working with some kinds of dogs than others. Ask the trainer about their experience with dogs like yours.

3. Talk to the trainer about her or her training methods. There are a number of different approaches to dog training. These include positive reinforcement such as using a clicker and treats;

traditional dog training which uses a slip chain collar; and combination methods. Ask your trainer what methods he or she uses. Some dogs respond better to one method than another or you may have your own preference. It's best to know how the trainer trains before you sign up to work with her.

4. Do ask about price. However, remember that a trainer's rates should not be the sole determination in choosing a trainer. For example, many pet stores offer training classes. They are usually relatively inexpensive for a few weeks of training. However, you can often find a better, more experienced trainer if you are willing to go to another training center and pay a little more. If you are working one-on-one with a trainer or if a trainer is coming to your home to work with you and your dog, you can expect to pay more. However, you and your dog may progress faster because of the focused attention so you may not need as many lessons. If you have a good trainer, you and your dog may learn more, too. So, try to consider the quality of instruction as well as the price when you are choosing a trainer.

5. Chemistry. There are also some intangibles to consider when choosing a dog trainer. Sometimes you just seem to 'click' with someone. Or your dog may really like a particular trainer. Although you may not be able to give a rational reason for these reactions, you should still respect them. These reactions are important.

6. Read their testimonials. Most dog trainers have a website. Make sure you check it out and see what others owners had to say about the dog trainer. A good dog trainer will have many testimonials from different owners. The testimonials will also give you an idea of which dogs the trainer has worked with and what problems the dog trainer is good at solving. Testimonials are particularly useful if you have not been able to observe the trainer with other dogs.

In summary, when choosing a dog trainer for you and your dog, give consideration to the person's qualifications, training methods, rates and your own reaction to them. And remember to make time to observe them at work with other dogs and owners. If you follow these suggestions then you should be able to choose a great trainer for you and your dog.

Leadership and training is good for your dog's well-being and your peace of mind! In the next chapter, I'll discuss how to keep your dog healthy from the inside out with good eating habits and nutritious food.

How to Feed Your Dog a Nutritious and Healthy Diet

Dogs are amazingly hardy animals. The dog's ancestor – the wolf – was a meat eater but over thousands of years, dogs have adapted to a diet consisting of meat, vegetables and yummy human leftovers! Dog's stomachs are very acidic which can digest bones and fats relatively well. I have noted diet-related sensitivities in each breed profile in this guide, although most breeds do not have any specific dietary requirements outside of what is normally required for dogs. A good diet may ensure your dog encounters few health problems, including stomach and intestinal issues.

The Right Diet for Your Dog

The right diet makes a big difference in your dog's vitality and wellbeing. Here are some signs that your dog is enjoying a healthy diet:

- They poop once to twice daily, their poop being firm, small, brown, relatively of low odor and free of worms (or larvae).

- They have a shiny coat and are energetic.

- They have a reasonable concentration span, which is sufficient for training.

- Their teeth are in good to excellent condition. (You can optimise your dog's oral health by supplementing your dog's diet with dental toys or dental treats.)

There's no one ideal diet for dogs, however feeding your dog cheap supermarket brands is not recommended. The key is to ensure that your dog's food intake consists of the correct proportion of protein, calcium and minerals, which will provide steady growth and development.

When choosing the right diet for your dog, bear in mind that:

1. If you got your dog from a reputable breeder, then follow the breeder's recommendations. Your breeder should be able to provide good nutritional information.

2. If you are unable to get guidance from the person from whom you obtained your dog, then purchase high quality dog food. Do not substitute puppy food for dog food. Dog food does not contain the correct ratio of ingredients for proper development of young dogs.

3. Dogs need a high calcium intake as an insufficient amount can cause bone abnormalities. Having said that, excessive calcium and a diet too high in energy can cause excessive growth spurts and extra weight gain which could damage a dog's joints.

4. Dogs need protein. Protein is required for growth and nutrition, without which a dog can develop malformed bones and joints. However, the amount of protein in adult dog food should be 22% or higher than puppy food.

Do not overwhelm your dog's digestive system by regularly experimenting with new foods or treats.

If you want to feed your dog a raw or home-cooked diet, consult a veterinarian for guidance. Find an experienced person who has successfully raised dogs to adulthood on your proposed diet. This is critical as raw diets can easily go wrong with dogs – calcium levels should be watched, as well as bacterial contaminants (which can cause grave illnesses).

Make sure your dog has access to fresh water at all times throughout her life. Some owners limit their puppy's access to water at bedtime to discourage night time potty accidents.

Feeding schedules for your dog

Follow these feeding schedules for dogs:

- Up to 3 months old: three times a day. (Some veterinarians recommend four times a day for toy breeds).

- Between 2 months and 3 months, you can begin to gradually wean your dog down to two meals a day.

- From three to twelve months old: twice daily. If your dog is fed only once a day, your dog might feel hungry – after all, 24 hours between meals is a long wait! Some toy breeds such as the Papillion may need three small meals a day as their stomachs are too small for larger meals.

Amount of food for your dog

As a starting point, go with the amounts recommended by either the packaging on commercial food, or expert (breeder/veterinarian) suggestions. Adjustments may be needed if you find your dog becoming overweight or underweight. Making adjustments can be tricky, as puppies experience growth spurts and gangly stages. If unsure, consult your veterinarian. Experts generally agree that your dog's weight should err on the side of slender, rather than tubby!

Dog treats

Treats should be given only occasionally and are ideally used as rewards during training sessions. Treats should be very small and soft. If you are using commercial treats, then break them down into smaller pieces. Natural alternatives are chopped vegetables (no onion or garlic – they are poisonous to dogs), cooked meat and unsalted popcorn.

Refusing meals

Puppies may refuse a meal if their mouth hurts as a result of teething. If a dog refuses more than two meals, call your veterinarian.

Preventing Food Aggression in Dogs

Food guarding is a highly undesirable habit. Luckily, it's the easiest problem to prevent. Follow these quick and easy steps at feeding time:

1. After you set your dog's food bowl down, start to teach your dog to sit and wait for her food.

2. Once your dog starts eating, place your fingers in the bowl and allow your dog to eat around your fingers.

3. Pat your dog whilst she is eating so she becomes accustomed to being touched while eating. Do not pull your dog away or taunt her as she eats, as this will only serve to annoy her and encourage aggressive behavior.

The Right Diet for an Adult Dog

An adult dog is generally over one year old, although smaller dogs reach maturity at about 18 months. At this point, the dog will no longer be growing in height, though she may still be gaining weight. This is caused by the development of muscle tone and a process known as 'filling out' – a process that takes a lot of energy. The dog will require this much energy from her food and only a high quality, active dog food source will provide the nutrients that she needs.

Dogs need proteins, minerals, amino acids and fats as part of a healthy diet. Dogs could technically survive on a vegetarian diet, although many dog nutritionists do not recommend this.

Generally speaking, dog owners can choose from three broad types of dog food: commercial food (kibble and canned), raw food, or a blend of the two.

Do not feed the young adult dog food for senior (or old) dogs. This food does not provide the dog with the nutrients that she needs to develop those strong and lean muscles that her body needs to be healthy.

As always, fresh water should be available at all times.

How to read commercial dog food labels

Generally, cheap kibble and canned dog food will not provide enough nutrients for your dog. If your dog has a lacklustre coat, is overly flatulent, in average condition, or has skin problems, chances are you can point the finger directly at what your dog is eating.

A diet that consists solely, or mainly, of wet (canned) food means your dog may be slightly more prone to cavities and tooth decay. This can result in a dog losing her teeth due to disuse and decay. However, this food is ideal for hiding medication because most dogs will scoff it so fast that they won't notice any pills mixed inside.

Remember that slogans like 'Premium Grade', 'Veterinarian Approved', 'Good For Your Dog' and 'Finest Ingredients' are not specific enough to allow you to make an informed decision. When choosing your dog food, disregard the writing on the packaging in favor of reading the ingredients (which are listed in order of highest to lowest quantity). As a friend of mine once said: "Don't be slack, read the back!"

When reading dog food labels, make sure you are able to see the following types of ingredients:

- Animal protein to be listed more than once in the top five ingredients.

- Meats that are clearly listed by type, for example: rabbit, chicken, beef, lamb, duck and venison.

- Whole grains such as millet, rice and oats.

- Naturally preserved kibble.

When reading dog food labels, make sure you avoid dog foods that have the following 'ingredients':

- Cheap canned food that contains 'meat chunks' – these may simply be grain gluten processed to resemble meat.

- 'Animal digest' or 'meat meal' – these labels do not guarantee high grade/quality meat.

- Added colors, flavors or artificial preservatives.

- Grain by-products such as gluten and brewer's rice.

- Food that contains soy which causes allergies in many dogs.

- Products where the first listed ingredient is a corn, wheat, meat-meal or meat by-product.

If you're feeding your dog only canned food and kibble, make sure that most of it is kibble. Canned foods are not designed to provide a dog's complete diet. This is partly because canned food does not offer any health benefits to your dog's teeth; kibble results in less teeth tartar. It will also save you a small fortune!

Daily intake of moist food will mean that dogs require, and therefore drink, less water. If you are changing your dog's diet to include more dry food (e.g. from only moist food to moist food plus kibble), make sure that you have more fresh water out for your dog to drink. You may also need to allow your dog a few more toilet breaks whilst she adjusts to her new and healthier diet.

The raw diet

Raw feeding, also known as 'BARF' (Biologically Appropriate Raw Food), promotes a diet of raw meat, bones and organs (with no grains).

The BARF diet consists of:

- 5-10% organ meats

- 10-15% bones

- 75-85% muscle meats

- Small amounts of vegetables (optional)

A warning about vegetables: do not feed your dog onions or garlic. Although most dogs tolerate small amounts of these vegetables, they can result in your dog's death if she eats too much of them. Veterinarians don't know what the lethal dose, though it may depend in the breed's size, age and overall condition of the dog.

If you feed your dog a raw diet, you have to be aware of possible problems arising from ingesting undigested bone, as well as the bacteria and virus inherent in raw meat. Salmonella and Campylobacter bacteria can be an issue with raw chicken meat, and raw pig meat can contain the virus that causes Aujeszky's disease as well as fluke worms. Both can cause serious illness and even death in canines if left untreated. Members of the dog family tend to eat the organs of freshly caught prey and then bury the remains for days or even weeks before eating it. This allows the meat to start to decay in a more hygienic environment than being left in the open air to rot, which results in a degree of digestion of the raw meat. Of course the additional benefit of burying the meat is that it is far less likely to be stolen by other scavengers.

If you feed a raw diet to your dog, make sure that they are very fresh and haven't been on a supermarket shelf for days. The fresher the food, the smaller the chance of contamination with germs and bacteria. Even if you don't ordinarily feed your dog raw food, I would advise you to refrain from giving your dog meat, cooked or otherwise, that has been in the fridge past its 'Use By' or 'Best Before' dates, or even in the freezer past the freezer's maximum recommended storage period.

Raw diet principles have now been adopted by dog food companies that produce pre-ground raw dog food. This is particularly useful for owners worried that raw bones may remain undigested in their dog's gut. Alternatively, dog owners may elect to grind bones (using relatively inexpensive home grinders).

How much should you feed your dog?

Dogs are meant to know when they've eaten enough (but then so are we!), however they are usually guided by what their owners feed them. It is not uncommon for dogs to eat then walk away from the bowl with food left in it. They might go and run round for a while or sleep and then return to the bowl only to drink the water and will ignore the food still there until later in the day. Obviously, I would only recommend that you allow this with kibble and not with moist/wet foods as the influx of flies alone would be off-putting! Be aware that the feeding recommendations on commercial dog food will always give you higher end of the requirement range. So if your dog tends to become overweight, reduce the amount you feed her gradually, in order to allow your dog's stomach to tighten. Remember how you feel when you go on a diet!

Dogs of different breeds and sizes still have the same digestive system, which means if you own more than one dog you can feed them the same things, but in different quantities. If you have multiple dogs, there may be a temptation to save on dog food expenses by purchasing a cheaper brand – but you should avoid this temptation. It can take several times the amount of cheap dog food to provide the same nutritional value offered by higher quality food. Owners often think they are saving money this way when, in fact, it is the other way around. However, you do not always get what you pay for – which is why, again, you must read and understand the ingredients label and the recommended quantities. Some inexpensive dog foods may be nearly as good, if not as good, as some of the more expensive brands.

I would recommend you visit your local supermarket and local pet food shop, and even a farm supplies shop, with a pen and a pad and write down and compare all of the brands. You may find that you can feed your dog just as well with a little less food (fewer poops) and for a little less money. If you change brands, spend a week or two mixing both the old and new brands, slowly reducing the old food and increasing the new.

The total daily quantities recommended below assume you will be feeding your dog high quality, nutritionally rich food.

Dog Size	Raw Diet*	Dry Food	Dry & Wet Food
Toy 2-4.5kgs (5-10lbs) Toy Poodle Pomeranian Shih Tzu Chihuahua	40-90g (1.4-3.15oz)	70-230g (2.5–8oz)	up to 55g (2oz) & ¼ can
Small 4.5-9kgs (10-20lbs) Dachshund Scottish	90–180g (1.4-6.3oz)	230-510 g (8-18oz)	115-285g (4-10oz)

Terrier			& ½ can
Medium 9-23kgs (20-50lbs) Beagle Spaniel Bull Dog Poodle	180–460g (6.3-16oz)	510-850 g (18-30oz)	225-560g (8-20oz) & 1 can

*In a raw diet, a dog should eat approximately 2% of its ideal body weight per day.

Please note: This chart is an approximation only – the quantity needed also depends on a dog's metabolism and activity level. A good test to see whether your dog is eating enough is to feel her ribs – any dog within the ideal weight range will have a small amount of fat and muscle covering the ribs.

Types of treats

There are some great treats that you can use to train your dog or offer as a snack:

- A great tasty treat, high in protein and used by good dog owners to reward their dogs for obedience, is freeze-dried beef liver. You can also try freeze-dried chicken.

- Many dogs absolutely love bully sticks. They're softer than rawhide, and so easy to digest. They will also keep your dog occupied for a long time as they are quite chewy. I recommend giving your dog a bully stick before leaving the dog alone at home, so she has something to occupy herself.

- Although dogs love rawhide and pigs ears, these can shatter or break apart leaving the sharp pieces to wreak havoc on your dog's digestive tract. Make sure the rawhide is compressed. Also, watch for cheap rawhide imitations that are too salty and contain lots of chemicals.

- Brussels sprout stalks are good for your dog. They're also tasty and tough and can be used in fetch games.

- Sugar cane is a great way to reward your dog every once in a while.

- Beef bones from the hip or knuckle of a cow, with the marrow providing a tasty surprise. Brisket bones are good too, and can be eaten quicker than the beef bones. Ensure you don't give your dog too many bones as they can cause constipation. Never give your dog cooked chop or chicken bones as they splinter and can puncture their digestive tracts.

How many treats should be in my dog's diet?

If providing treats or snacks, reduce the volume of your dog's main meals accordingly. Treats should never constitute more than 15% of your dog's overall diet.

Food throughout a Dog's Life

The later years

Dogs are considered 'seniors' when they have lived to about two-thirds of their expected life span. A large breed dog, such as the Great Dane with a life expectancy of around nine years, may be considered senior at six. Meanwhile, a small breed with a life expectancy of 13 years will be a senior at about nine years.

This does not mean that every 'senior' dog behaves like a senior dog and should be fed and handled like a senior. Just as there are many senior people who still lead very active lives, there are senior dogs that are more active than others.

Two particular health issues may arise as your dog ages:

1. Weight gain – older dogs are prone to gaining too much weight, as they often exercise less and eat more. Obesity can then lead to serious health problems such as diabetes, kidney failure, heart disease and dental problems.

2. Arthritis – most dogs will suffer some degree of arthritis from a certain age onwards. The more overweight a dog is, the more pain she will experience from her arthritis.

Most senior or mature dog foods are low in calories. The food will still offer the right balance between fats, calories and carbohydrates, and there is an increase in fiber. Wheat bran can be added to further increase the fiber in the dog's food, helping prevent constipation. Most senior dog foods are high in fillers because the senior dog is not as active as a young adult dog, but is used to eating a specific amount of food and wants to continue eating the same of food.

Supplements may be necessary at this stage of your dog's life for her comfort and health. Supplements that help to support joint health can greatly reduce the pain and inflammation caused by arthritis.

Some dogs have trouble with solid kibble pieces as they begin to age, because of the poor condition of their teeth. If this is the case, then your dog may need to be kept off solid dry dog food and introduced to canned or homemade dog food.

Make the change gradually to prevent gastrointestinal indigestion. You could also add a small amount of wet food to the dog food or add water or broth to the food to soften it.

On top of that, get your veterinarian to check the teeth regularly in case they need cleaning. Older pets benefit from more frequent examinations and regular blood tests. This way any potential problems can be caught in the early stages, and a lot of pain and discomfort can be prevented this way.

Sporting breeds

Sporting dogs are dogs bred for hunting small game. These are naturally very active dogs. These dogs can be of any breed or mix breed and vary in size.

Most people think of the hunting dog when they think of sporting dogs. However, there are many sports that dogs can participate in. The fastest growing sports for dogs include Agility and Fly Ball. Both of these sports are fast paced and require a lot of energy and concentration from your dog. Other sports can include sledding and weight pulling. These are endurance and strength sports that demand even more from the dog's physique.

Food that is geared especially to the sporting dog is higher in protein and fat than the average dog food. The increase in protein helps the dog to keep muscles strong and ligaments supple. This also helps to make the dog feel full for a longer time, helping her perform better during the competitions or throughout a highly energetic day.

A high fat content helps replace calories that the dog burns during her activities. These calories help to give the dog the energy she needs to be active longer.

Sporting dog foods might also contain supplements that will support the high nutritional needs of the active dog. These might include probiotics to assist the dog's digestion. Glucosamine and chondroitin sulfate are joint supplements that are often added into sporting dog foods to assist in the protection and lubrication of the joints.

Fish oil is often added to the food as well to help support the heart and the skin of the dog. Anti-oxidants are added to help eliminate the free-radicals that intense exercise causes. These free radicals can hinder your dog's performance and can even cause serious conditions such as cancer in the long term.

Your sporting dog will also require a lot of water. Water is essential to her bodily functions and will help her to remain active.

Make sure water is always available, especially at the sporting events that she will be attending.

Feeding a pregnant bitch

Just like a pregnant woman, a pregnant bitch needs special food and care. Specific nutrients and calories will allow the pups develop correctly, and will also ensure her health and well-being through pregnancy, birth and lactation.

Pregnancies last around sixty-three days in dogs – that's about 9 weeks in total.

During the first 5 weeks of the pregnancy, all you need to do is make sure that the bitch gets enough water. At this stage, the dogs are not growing much and aren't very taxing for her body. However, she will experience an increase in blood volume during this time as the fluid-filled sacs that hold the dogs are developed.

Around the third week after mating, a lot of bitches go without food for 7-10 days. During this period, they might experience some nausea, just like a woman might. Vomiting during pregnancy is very uncommon in dogs though.

During the first part of the pregnancy, do not give your dog any medications that have not been suggested and approved by your veterinarian. Do not add any supplements to her food, unless instructed to do so by your veterinarian, because the dogs are very vulnerable at this stage of their development.

Bitches do not usually show any discharge from the vagina during pregnancy. If you notice any discharge, especially if it's yellow or green in color or has a strong smell, consult your veterinarian immediately. The dog might have lost the pups and developed an infection.

During the last 4 weeks of the pregnancy, the dogs will begin to grow rapidly. At this stage, you will need to increase the mother dog's food intake by around 25% every week. This means that by the eighth week, you must double the amount of food that you were originally feeding.

In week six or seven, it is a good idea to start splitting the meals into two portions if you are not already doing so, and in the last week into 3 portions. Her belly will feel very big by then and she simply won't have the stomach to take in a whole meal at a time.

Nursing

Once the dogs are born, the bitch will still need a large amount of high quality food. At this time, her dogs will be feeding on her milk. It is called the lactation period. It is a common mistake to reduce the amount of food to the bitch while she is nursing, but producing the milk takes a lot of energy. The mother's food intake will drastically affect the amount of nutrients that the dogs get, and insufficient nutrients can have devastating effects on the health of both the bitch and the dogs.

A nursing bitch requires special food and care. She will need food that has a very high amount of protein and calories. Remember that now she is feeding herself and her dogs.

The milk that she is producing contains a lot of calcium. The calcium in the milk comes directly from the blood stream and the bones of the mother. Sudden depletion of calcium can lead to a serious condition called 'eclampsia' or milk fever.

Symptoms to watch out for are panting, lethargy and sudden disinterest in her dogs. Her muscles might start to twitch and she might develop serious cramps all over her body and have a fever. This is an emergency situation and you must take her straight to the veterinarian. The veterinarian will administer calcium (usually through an intravenous drip) and this usually leads to faster recovery.

If in any doubt about your canine mom's nutritional needs, talk to your veterinarian. He or she will also help you decide if your bitch needs extra calcium or other minerals.

A nursing dog will also need a lot of water because milk production takes a lot of fluid from her body. Water should be available at all times. Elevating the water bowl can prevent the dogs from spilling the water or falling in and drowning.

At the end of the nursing period, your dog should ideally weigh what she did before the pregnancy. If her weight has decreased, take extra care to bring her back up to her usual condition as soon as the pups have been weaned.

A decrease in weight can affect her during her next pregnancy and for some time after the pregnancy and whelping process.

Is Your Dog the Right Weight?

Checking your dog's weight is important to ensure your dog is within the healthy weight range. You don't need to use a scale and weight chart to find out if your dog has a healthy weight. All you need to do is answer these three simple questions:

1. Can you see the ribs? If you can see the ribs easily, your dog is at least a little underweight. But if they are only slightly visible, then your dog is within the healthy range. If you view your dog from above, you should notice your dog's tapered waist line.

2. Can you feel the ribs? If you can feel the ribs easily as you are stroking her across the ribcage, your dog is of the right weight, with a thin fat cover. If you are having difficulty feeling the ribs under moderate or thick fat cover, then your dog is at least a little overweight.

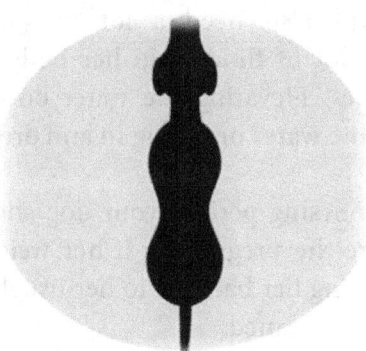

Healthy Weight

Over Weight

Very Heavy Weight

3. Has your dog got an hourglass shape when viewed from above? If your dog's body goes in radically behind the ribcage, this indicates that she is underweight. However, if your dog's waist tapers in slightly, then she is within the normal weight range. If your dog's back is broader at the waist, she is overweight.

Other signs your dog is not within a healthy weight range

If your dog is the right weight, she will be reasonably active and energetic. If your dog is lazy, easily worn-out and hesitant to go for walks, she could be either overweight or underweight.

If you believe your dog is overweight or underweight, consult your veterinarian to confirm or allay your suspicions. If your veterinarian recognizes that your dog needs help with her weight, then you can discuss how to improve your dog's health with diet and exercise.

Your dog is considered obese if she weighs 15% more than the standard accepted weight for the dog's height.

Varying Your Dog's Diet

After reading this guide you may want to change your dog's diet. People often debate whether a dog can get bored with her diet. Although dogs do enjoy variety in their diet, dogs are capable of thriving on the same diet for long periods, as long as the diet is nutritious and balanced. Therefore, you can choose to stick with a certain diet or you can change it to provide your dog with some variety. Dogs can be very sensitive to regular dietary changes, so don't disrupt their diets too often.

How to change your dog's diet

When changing your dog's diet, do so gradually. Initially your dog's meal should mainly consist of the 'old' food, with a small amount of the 'new' diet. Slowly increase the amount of new food whilst simultaneously decreasing the amount of the old diet. Eventually, the new diet will be 100% of your dog's meal.

Alternatively, you can have the same diet and add some supplements to give your dog some variety.

Four Tips for a Fussy Eater

Often dogs can get quite picky about their food. I often see this problem in smaller dogs. Try these tips and consult a veterinarian if your dog skips more than two meals.

1. Apple cider vinegar – a small amount a day mixed in with some moist food will encourage your dog to eat. A teaspoon a day should be enough for 40 pound (18 kilogram) dogs, or a little less for smaller dogs.

2. Crush freeze-dried beef liver and sprinkle over your dog's food. This is also a good source of protein.

3. Leave your dog's bowl out for ten minutes at feeding time. After ten minutes, remove the bowl, even if your dog did not eat. Then do the same at the next scheduled feeding time. Do not allow your dog to have access to any food in between mealtimes. Most dogs will quickly get the message and eat their food within the ten minute time limit lest they miss out! This may seem like a heart-wrenching thing to do for any loving dog owner, but dogs are amazingly adaptable and – if there are no pre-existing health issues – will not suffer from having missed just one meal. (In my experience, that's all it takes!)

4. Instead of feeding your dog from a bowl, use their meal as training treats. All you need to do is separate their meal into smaller portions and give each portion as a reward for obedience. Your dog will come to associate reward with food as well and you are giving her a reason to eat.

Feeding a Pack

When feeding two or more dogs, it is important to make sure every dog gets their own share of food. This can be a little challenging because dogs operate in a hierarchy, which means that dogs higher in the pack may get first dibs at any common food on offer at the expense of lower pack order dogs.

There are a number of things you can do to avoid dogs missing out on their share:

- Each dog should have her own separate bowl and separate feeding area (you might need to ensure each dog cannot get access to another's bowl).

- Supervise feeding time so you can make sure that there is no food stealing.

- Teach all your dogs to sit and wait for their food.

- Ensure you feed each dog the correct amount of high quality, nutritious food.

- Give each dog enough time to eat their food: 10 minutes should be enough.

- Have numerous bowls of fresh water available in different spots. (Buckets are ideal as they are hard to tip over when you have dogs jostling nearby.) Big tubs can get dirty as dogs tend to bathe in them.

Digestive Aids

If your dog has stomach problems, diarrhea or is taking antibiotics, then the good bacteria known as Lactobacillus acidophilus dies out, meaning your dog's digestion will not be as effective as it could be.

Yoghurt is a great source of Lactobacillus acidophilus – try giving your dog a teaspoon at mealtimes to help those bacteria grow and thrive.

Remember, that many dogs who are lactose intolerant will suffer from diarrhea if they eat yoghurt. The good news is that you can ask your veterinarian for Lactobacillus acidophilus supplements.

Why dogs eat grass

Dogs get only a nominal amount of nutritional value from eating grass because their digestive system is not equipped to cope with it. The most likely reason a dog eats grass is because it encourages them to vomit, which can be useful when the dog has undigested fur or bone in her stomach.

Hot Spots

Beware of 'hot spots' on your dog's body. These might be caused by an allergic reaction to dog food. Hot spots refer to a warm spot on the body accompanied by hair loss in the same region. The skin may also take on a different color or texture in that region. This is most often caused by an allergy to the carbohydrate and/or animal proteins in a dog's food. Some dogs cannot tolerate grains and will exhibit this allergy as hot spots. If the dog presents these symptoms, consider changing brands of dog food from one that offers grain to one that does not. These alternative foods use potatoes as their form of starch and carbohydrates. These ingredients are not considered potentially dangerous to your dog and they have not been shown to produce hot spots in dogs. The most common potatoes to use are the sweet potato and the red potato.

When it comes to a healthy dog, providing a nutritious diet is only part of the equation. In the next chapter, I'll discuss 14 ways you can give your dog the best chance of living a full, long life.

Short Dog, Long Life! 14 Ways to Keep Your Dog Healthy

When it comes to your dog's health, prevention is always better – and cheaper – than cure. The best health comes from understanding that most of your interaction with your dog, whether via training, grooming or other activities, will have a real impact on your dog's mental and physical health. Therefore, look at all your interaction with your dog as a way to boost your dog's vitality. Your dog's development and general health should be monitored in collaboration with your veterinarian, as this guide is not meant to be a substitute for veterinary or medical advice.

The 14 ways in which you can boost your dog's vitality are:

1. Understand Your Dog's Changing Needs as She Ages

Newborn puppies are deaf, blind and are unable to regulate their own body temperature (hence they keep warm by sleeping bundled against their littermates). However, they are born with a sense of taste, touch and smell. At this stage, dogs toilet only after being stimulated by their mother. At about three weeks, puppies begin to learn to potty away from their sleeping and eating area.

Puppies are completely dependent on their mother for milk until three weeks, at which time they can start to digest soft food. They are completely weaned by six weeks. They grow quickly: their weight doubles in the first week.

From two to four weeks, puppies start to gain their sight and hearing, and puppy teeth emerge. At about three weeks they start investigating their environment and start learning from their mother and littermates.

By five weeks a puppy's eyesight has developed. They recognize people and become more interested in interacting with their littermates and carers. Their mother will begin to discipline them, which is how they learn to respect hierarchy and rules of interaction. For example, a dog who is not disciplined by her mother or any littermates for biting too hard can grow up to be quite nippy as an adult.

Because dogs learn from their environment at birth, puppies that are handled and talked to are more confident and resilient than their counterparts who are raised in an isolated environment like cages or puppy mills.

Take home age

It is usually between eight and twelve weeks that a puppy is taken home by a new owner. Because a dog learns from her littermates and mother, a dog might lack the complete set of skills necessary to interact properly with other dogs if she is taken away earlier than eight weeks of age.

At this age dogs are still learning a lot about their environment; in fact, how a dog is taught and what she is exposed to at this stage can determine how well a dog will be socialized to deal with sounds, people, things and their environment.

Dogs will engage in behavior that may seem odd or annoying. This is quite normal and it is important that you don't punish your dog for:

- Chewing and biting – redirect your dog to chew toys.

- Humping – this behavior is not sexual. Rather it's a way of experimenting with how to interact with others. Discourage your dog from doing this with people.

- Temper tantrums and growling – this is especially true for dogs with bossy personalities. Be firm, consistent and provide structure, without resorting to punishment.

- Hyperactive episodes – there'll be times when your dog may rocket around the house like a lunatic. This is normal and is usually followed by a nap or resting time.

- Bursts of play and sleeping – your dog will play, wrestle, demand attention and then suddenly will want nothing more than some alone time and some sleep.

- Startles and nervousness – between eight and twelve weeks some dogs may become nervous and startle easily. Too much affection and reassurance during these episodes may result in the dog thinking it's okay to be scared. Assuming the object of the fear is benign, don't acknowledge your dog's fear; instead handle and talk to the object and reward any show of bravery with praise and treats.

Adolescence

A dog's adolescence usually occurs between four and 18 months of age. This period can be difficult; your dog may be defiant and forgetful of her obedience skills. This is normal and requires patience and revision of lessons.

During this period your dog will become an adolescent and reach sexual maturity. A female dog can have her first estrus (or heat) between five and 10 months old. A heat can last about three weeks, during which she might lose drops of blood or serum (a watery form of blood). You can purchase protective bloomers from a pet store. She might behave nervously or depressed, and might try to run away. If she manages to escape, there is the danger that she might find herself a mate and get pregnant. If you wish to breed your female, many veterinarians recommend that she should not be allowed to become pregnant on the first heat.

A male dog's testicles will descend between two and six months. If they have not at six months of age, see your veterinarian as health complications may arise. A male dog's testosterone levels will make him responsive to females on heat, as well as possibly challenging other male dogs. Your male dog will go from squatting to cocking his leg for potty and he will be able to father a litter at age six months.

De-sexing your dog

Spaying refers to the removal of the female reproductive system. This includes the ovaries and the uterus. Neutering is the removal of the testicles of the male dog. Speutering is a term used to cover both.

Most dogs are spayed or neutered when they are between five and eight months old. However, it is possible to spay or neuter a dog at as young as two months old without affecting the dog's growth patterns. The risks and benefits of pediatric speutering should be considered in consultation with your veterinarian. Neutering male dogs early on in life often leads to dogs less aggressive than dogs who have not been neutered (or ones that have been neutered later in life). The removal of the testicles inhibits the dog's desire to mark in inappropriate locations, such as in the house.

Neutered dogs don't get distracted by other dogs (especially female dogs) so much which means they pay more attention to training. They tend to be significantly calmer than dogs who have not been fixed. In addition, without sex drive dogs tend to be much more laid back. The neutering process also prevents future health problems in male dogs, in particular prostrate problems and testicular cancer, both fairly common problems in aging, intact males.

Spaying of a female dog is considered a routine surgery and the risk of complication is low. However, your dog will have to go through the healing process for 7-10 days, and will need to be monitored and kept relatively calm during this period.

The benefits of spaying before the first heat include a decrease in breast infections and a measurable and significant decrease in the chance of getting breast cancer. Once spayed your female dog won't have to go into heat anymore. Spaying also prevents false pregnancies as well as 'pyometra' (infection of the uterus). Pyometra is a very serious condition that often results in expensive emergency surgery as it can be difficult detect in its early stages. Symptoms of an infected uterus include increased drinking, depression and even collapse. Pyometra can be fatal, if left untreated.

Maturity

At this time, all your hard work, training and care will begin to pay off. With the trials of adolescence over, you'll now begin to enjoy a sensible, healthy adult dog. Remember, though, that learning for dogs never stops. Even the best behaved dogs need refreshers on obedience skills. You can even capitalize on your dog's skills and natural abilities by teaching your dog simple tricks like barking on command, rolling over and fetch. Even though your dog will be less work, she will still have needs: keep her mind and body active so she stays alert, happy and healthy.

Senior dog

Small dogs reach their senior years at about 10 years of age, whilst some larger breeds can be considered senior at five.

As your dog ages you'll being to notice these changes:

- Your dog will spend more time napping and be less energetic.

- Tolerance to exercise may drop, so she may not be able to walk as fast or as far as she once could. It's important to adjust her exercise routine, so your dog does not become overly tired, stressed or injured. Having said that, do not stop exercising your dog altogether as your dog may miss these fun times and also put on weight. Instead, opt for shorter sessions as tolerated. Exercise is a great way to keep your dog's muscles as lean as possible, which may assist otherwise sore or arthritic joints.

- Your dog may become prone to weight gain and need smaller meals.

- The muzzle may become greyer and she may get fatty lumps under her skin or warts around her face. Many lumps are harmless, but have a veterinarian check them just in case.

- Your dog's hearing, eyesight and sense of smell may diminish. That's why when training your dog, it's important to use both verbal and hand signals so when her senses start to fail you can communicate with her in different ways.

- An otherwise housebroken dog may potty inside the house; do not punish her as these are accidental. Talk to your veterinarian about treatment options.

- Your dog might display confusion, aggression or forgetfulness. These behaviors may have underlying physical causes, so have a veterinarian check her out.

Apart from certain dietary changes (see my chapter on how to feed your dog a nutritious diet), it's important that you provide your dog with a comfortable place to rest and sleep. Ensure that her bed is soft and caters to arthritic dogs.

Joint pain and arthritis are very common in aging dogs. As a general rule human medications can harm (and can be fatal) to your dog, but supplements made for people such as fish oil and glucosamine can help ease your dog's joint stiffness. Before giving your dog any supplements, talk to your veterinarian about correct doses for your dog's breed and weight.

2. Observe Your Dog and Watch for Healthy and Unhealthy Signs

A healthy dog generally copes with her environment better (that is, experiences less stress and frustration) and has a stronger immune system than her unhealthy counterparts. Checking your dog for signs of health need not be a formal exercise, you can simply observe your dog to see that she consistently exhibits:

- Steady development (before she reaches adulthood)
- Active and alert (between periods of sleep and rest)
- Flexible, smooth, pale pink to brown or black skin color depending on the breed
- Glossy coat, which is smooth to touch
- Healthy weight
- Well-formed, firm and brown poop
- Bright, clear, shiny, healthy pink area around eyeball (conjunctiva)
- Clean and pink skin inside the ear
- Short nails
- Gums are firm, pink, or pigmented with black.
- Clean, sparkling teeth (23 for puppies and 42 for adult dogs)
- No odd lumps in the tissue or indentations of the muscles
- Urine is clear and yellow

Signs Your Dog Is Unhealthy

The following are signs that your dog's health is suffering due to an illness, disease or parasite:

- Lethargy

- Irritability

- Pale eyes or discharge coming from the eyes

- Coat and skin will have dandruff, bald spots, excessive oiliness, skin irritation, fleas, ticks or parasites

- Ticks, redness, swelling, excessive yellow or brownish wax or bad smell from the ear

- Your dog needs to strain to poop, or her poop is runny, watery, black in color, contains blood or whitish bits that look like rice

- The dog's paws seem red or inflamed

- Foul smelling, thick, bubbly, yellow or green nasal discharge

- Pale or red, inflamed gums

- Blood in urine or excessive urination within a short period of time

The above list offers general guidelines on how to spot a problem with your dog's health. If you see any of these signs, consult your veterinarian for an accurate diagnosis and treatment.

3. Know How to Check Your Dog's Vital Signs

Temperature

If you suspect your dog is unwell, but want to make sure, then you can check your dog's internal temperature. There are two ways in which you can take your dog's temperature, via the ear or the rectum:

	Ear	Rectum
Normal Temperature	100.0°F – 103.0°F (37.8°C – 39.4°C)	100.5°F – 102.5°F (38.1°C – 39.4°C)
Equipment	Pet ear thermometer	Digital or mercury oral/rectal thermometer
Instructions	1. Place the thermometer deep into the horizontal ear canal. 2. Insert thermometer for length of time as per manufacturer's recommendations (usually 1-3 seconds). Pet-Temp's ear thermometer will 'beep' to signal that it's okay to remove it from your dog's ear. 3. Remove the thermometer and read	1. Enlist the help of another as some dogs don't like this. 2. If using mercury thermometer, use your wrist to flick it until the mercury is below 94°F (34.4°C). 3. Lubricate the thermometer with petroleum jelly or water-based lubricant. 4. Have the other person hold the dog's head and front torso with a tight

	the temperature.	hug. 5. Lift the tail and insert the thermometer carefully and slowly about 1 inch (2.5 cm) into the rectum. The rectum is located just below the tail's base. 6. Hold the thermometer in place for two minutes for mercury thermometers (or until the digital thermometer beeps).
Action	If your dog has a body temperature less than 99.0°F(37.2°C) or over 104.0°F(40.0°C), contact your veterinarian, pet ambulance or pet hospital immediately. High temperatures could mean an infection or heat-related illness. Low temperatures can denote serious problems such as shock.	

Can you determine your dog's temperature by checking her nose or fold beneath her leg and body?

A cold and moist nose is generally a sign that your dog is healthy and hydrated. However, don't solely rely on this to gauge your dog's health. This is because a warm, dry nose is not necessarily a bad sign. For an accurate assessment of your dog's internal temperature, use a thermometer as described above.

Placing the thermometer in the fold between her leg and torso does not give an accurate reading. The temperature in the fold is typically one to two degrees lower than your dog's actual temperature.

Your dog's heart rate

Dogs have heart rates ranging from 180 to 220 beats per minute. The average heart rate for resting adult dogs is generally lower, between 50 and 130 beats per minute, but this depends on the size of the dog.

Make sure you check your dog's heart rate when her health appears normal and she is resting, so you have a clear indication of your dog's typical heart rate. This will give you a point of comparison if you're checking your dog's rate because you're concerned for her health or when exercising together.

There are two ways in which you can take your dog's heart rate:

	Chest	Femoral Pulse
Instructions	1. Place your hand in your dog's armpit, and lay your other hand flat along her chest. 2. Count her heart beats for 15 seconds, then multiply that number by four	1. The femoral pulse can be felt on the inside of the dog's thigh. 2. Find the femur (long bone of her leg) and gently put your fingers in the groove next to the bone. 3. Count her heart beats for 15 seconds, then multiply that number by four.
Action	You dog's pulse should be steady and regular. A weak or irregular pulse can be a	

sign of illness, disease or parasite. A heart rate that is considerably above the norm may be a sign that your dog is in distress. In either event, contact your veterinarian, pet ambulance or pet hospital immediately.

At rest, a dog's respiratory rate can be as low as 20 to 24 breaths per minute. However, when dogs are excited they can pant quickly. Your dog should be breathing without difficulty. If your dog is coughing, wheezing or is using her belly muscles to breath, then she might be distressed or ill.

Respiratory rate

To measure your dog's respiratory rate all you need to do is count how many times she breathes in 15 seconds and multiply that number by 4.

4. Choose the Right Veterinarian for You and Your Dog

Choosing the right veterinarian is incredibly important and can have a massive impact on your dog's health and longevity, as well as your wallet. Your veterinarian will be your first point of call whenever your dog encounters any health concerns, so it's important to choose someone you can trust. Here are five tips to choosing the right veterinarian for your dog:

- Make sure you find a veterinarian before, or soon after, picking up your new puppy. Call or visit your local veterinarians and have a chat. This way you can make a considered decision.

- When inspecting different veterinary practices, have a look at their kennel area. This will give you an idea of their level of hygiene and care. The kennel area should be clean and warm. The area should also smell relatively clean, however such areas are difficult to keep fresh!

- For practices where there is more than one veterinarian in attendance, ask whether your dog will be assigned to one veterinarian only. Some practices have a 'one-veterinarian, one-pet' policy, whilst others simply make appointments based on which veterinarian is available.

- Your new veterinarian should make you feel welcome and take your concerns seriously. A good veterinarian will answer your questions and freely share information.

- Check their prices, but don't base your decision solely on price. The old 'you get what you pay for' adage applies to veterinarians as much as it does to other professional services. On the other hand, choose a veterinarian within your budget because there is no point choosing a veterinarian that you cannot afford.

When comparing prices you should look at these particular procedures:

- Vaccinations: ask for the price of the yearly booster. First vaccinations and 'top ups' are usually all priced differently, so to get a comparable price you must ask for the booster price. Vaccinations are independent of your dog's weight so should be the same across the all breeds and sizes.

- De-sexing: ask for the price of the standard neutering procedure of a 10kg (22lbs) female dog. This way you'll make sure that there's no confusion, and you'll get to compare some real prices for the exact same procedure. Spaying bitches is a relatively 'big' operation, since it requires opening the abdomen. It is therefore a really good procedure to compare prices, because the price will include a general anesthetic, a surgical procedure and follow-up visits.

- X-rays: ask for the price of a standard abdominal x-ray for a 10kg (22lbs) dog. Make sure this includes the price for sedating your dog.

When it comes to prices, pet insurance can help ease the cost of care (depending on what type of cover you have). So, ask your veterinarian for a recommendation for pet insurance as well as researching alternatives. Later in this chapter, I'll explain how pet insurance works.

5. Help Your Dog Become Familiar with the Veterinarian

A dog which is normally confident and calm at home may become panicky, aggressive, shy or cautious at the veterinarian's surgery. The strange sounds, unusual walking surfaces, new smells and sights might alarm her. Fortunately, there are a few ways you can help your dog familiarize herself with the veterinarian.

The first steps involve preparation. If your dog is normally inside and only taken out to relieve herself or for occasional walks, socialize her with new people and places. Taking her out in public around new people and in new environments will not only help her when you take her to the doctor, but might also make her a calmer dog inside your home. Different places will allow her to see new people of all ages, different clothing styles, and various smells. Try to vary the walking surfaces between tiles, gravel, and dirt or asphalt so that she will not feel as unsure in the veterinarian's office. Try exposing your dog to new sounds, whether it is vehicles passing by, children playing or umbrellas opening. Exercise patience, though, because your dog may act up the first few times you change her environment.

You need to make sure your dog obeys and responds to you. Educate yourself about obedience training, teach her to lie down, stand up, stay, and sit on your command. If your dog trusts you to set boundaries, she will follow your lead. In addition to training, your dog should also be comfortable with the way a veterinarian will handle her. Several times a day, pick your dog up and put her on a countertop so that she will not be afraid of the height of the examination table. Touch all of her body parts as if you are massaging her. Make sure you examine her face, body, legs, and paws, inside her mouth and ears and tail. Squeeze her shoulders and hips gently and lightly touch her spine. Get her acclimatized to having various body parts touched. In addition, your veterinarian will give her a bear hug from the front and behind, as well as a belly rub, the position for x-rays, so try these positions, too. Do not forget to reward her with treats!

Before your veterinarian appointment, drive there, sit in the parking lot a few times and give your dog treats. Ask the receptionist to make a big deal over your dog and reward her with treats. It is usually best to make the appointment when the doctor is least busy and arrive early so you and your dog are not frazzled and whisked away. You can ask the staff to give your dog treats and either ask them for a towel or bring one yourself for your dog to lie on.

Your dog may be more comfortable on the floor, so ask your veterinarian if the examination can be performed there instead of the examination table. Remember to give your dog treats throughout the appointment.

If your dog is still having difficulty going to the veterinarian's office, ask if you can go immediately from the car into the room, bypassing the reception area altogether. You might also consider giving your dog calming herbal remedies or arrange for a home visit from the veterinarian (if this option is available).

6. Arrange Pet Insurance ASAP!

Although pet insurance has been available in the United States since 1982, it's estimated that only 1-2% of pet owners actually have insurance for their pets. Pet insurance is slightly more popular in Canada (an estimated 9% of Canadians have pet insurance) and some 20% of Europeans have pet insurance. Only about 2% of Australian pets are insured.

Why have pet insurance?

Whilst some veterinarian procedures are inexpensive, there are many procedures that can cost thousands of dollars, such as emergency care resulting from tick paralysis or being hit by a car. Surgeries on the knee, leg, heart, spine and brain can each cost thousands of dollars. If you think you cannot afford these expenses and therefore would be faced with choosing between money and your dog's life, then pet insurance is a way to avoid this. Pet insurance is ideal for those wanting to save money on surgeries, procedures and preventative treatments (such as heartworm and ticks) as well as ensuring their dog gets the best possible care.

Pet insurance is most worth considering for the following types of owners:

- People who have a high maintenance pure-breed dog such as a Basset Hound or Pug.
- Dogs that are accident prone or sensitive.
- Owners who frequently leave their pets in kennels or who vacation with their dogs.
- People on a limited budget.

Types of pet insurance

Pet insurance varies a great deal so, if you are considering purchasing pet insurance, consider what kind of insurance you would like to have. Your premium will depend on the kind of insurance you choose. Most pet insurance does not cover well-pet visits, such as vaccinations and a yearly physical. If you do choose this kind of coverage, you can expect to pay a very high monthly premium.

Many plans cover accidents and illnesses up to a cut-off point which will vary, depending on the company. However, existing conditions and hereditary illnesses are almost never covered. Some plans do cover cancer treatments.

Deductibles will also vary a great deal, depending on the plan you choose.

Some plans offer coverage for spaying and neutering, dental procedures and other needs, above and beyond ordinary veterinary visits. You will pay substantially more for these plans in monthly premiums.

Types of plans

There are many options for pet insurers and many of them offer different policy levels, so you will need to read the policies carefully in order to choose which one best fits your dog's needs.

In most cases you can get either a basic plan or a premium plan from an insurer. As you might imagine, the difference is usually what is covered by the plan. Most basic plans will cover accidents and injuries. If you want a plan that covers more, you will have to get a premium plan and pay a premium rate.

In all cases, pet insurance is based on the owner paying the veterinarian up front and submitting a claim to the insurance company for reimbursement. Companies generally pay 70–90% of the claim submitted, minus any deductible or coinsurance amount.

Range of costs and benefits

In the United States, monthly insurance rates for pet insurance range from USD5.75 per month for a basic policy (USD200 deductible, coverage for accidents; no illness coverage), to USD76.79 per month for a deluxe policy with a low deductible

(USD100 deductible; accident and illness coverage to 80%; spaying and neutering covered; essential preventive care; rabies vaccination; free lost pet recovery tag; annual physical exam and dental cleaning; continual coverage for some chronic and long-term conditions that may have arisen in the previous policy year).

You can find all kinds of policies and rates in between these two extremes.

You should be aware that actual premiums may vary depending on your pet's age, breed and where you live.

Keep in mind that most policies allow you to use any veterinarian you like when you have pet insurance. You are usually not limited to using a veterinarian chosen by your pet insurer (though you should check the policy wording).

Pet insurance does help protect you from large, unexpected veterinarian bills that can result from accidents and, in some cases, from illnesses, depending on your policy. However, you must make sure that your policy covers your pet's problem, or potential health problem. Otherwise the policy won't be any use to you. So, if your dog develops cancer and you have a pet insurance policy that doesn't cover cancer, the policy won't pay for anything. This is something to consider before choosing a policy or deciding if you want to get pet insurance.

What to look for in pet insurance cover

These are the costs and features that you look at when considering which cover you'll buy:

- Monthly premium
- Type of cover it provides (accident, illness, comprehensive)
- Annual limit on claims
- Excess costs
- Exclusions (for example if you live in a tick prone area, make sure tick paralysis is part of the policy)
- Extras

- • Age limit on joining. Insurance companies realize that older pets get more problems and so many won't insure pets over the age of 8

Contact information for pet insurers

The best place to compare policies and get contact information for pet insurers online for Canada, United Kingdom and United States is <u>here</u>. They compare policies, provide information about pet insurance, and link you to reviews given by current customers. A similar online <u>service</u> is available in Australia.

7. Vaccinate Your Dog

Vaccines work by stimulating your dog's immune system to attack any unwanted diseases. It works much the same way for humans. As with the humans, the vaccine helps the dog's immune system create antibodies that protect against certain diseases. Vaccinations cannot provide a 100% guarantee. However, vaccinations along with a safe, sanitary environment and good nutrition are the best means of protection for your dog.

A vaccination involves your veterinarian injecting antibodies for certain diseases into your dog's shoulder or into the large thigh muscle. Once a course of 2-3 injections are given to your puppy, she will then be required to receive a booster. The timing of boosters has long been the subject of debate; with experts arguing whether boosters for some diseases are even required on an annual basis.

When puppies ingest their mother's milk, they're basically given antibodies that help fight diseases. This immunity starts to fade after about six weeks of age. At this time, it is vital that the vaccination is given over a course of 2 to 3 injections about 3 to 4 weeks apart. Vaccination schedules can vary, so you should follow the recommended schedule of your veterinarian.

In 2011 the American Animal Hospital Association (AAHA) Canine Vaccination Task Force updated their vaccination guidelines. The gist is that vaccines for distemper, parvovirus, hepatitis and canine cough are now recommended at intervals of 3 years or greater, after the initial revaccination at one year. This is despite AAHA's finding that immunity for parvovirus and distemper vaccinations lasts for 5 years, and 7 years for adenovirus (canine cough and hepatitis).

AAHA still recommends an annual rabies booster.

If you want to keep up to date with their protocols, you can check out their website at http://aahanet.org.

Always discuss the correct level and type of vaccination with your veterinarian. To see if a booster is actually necessary, you could ask for a 'blood titer' which shows the level of immunity in your dog's system.

After vaccination most dogs experience no reaction. But some might feel unwell for a few hours. Serious reactions are quite rare. If you notice unusual symptoms within 24 hours of vaccination, call your veterinarian immediately. After your puppy hasher first set of vaccination, you should still be careful for several weeks. Avoid taking your puppy to pet stores, parks, animal shelters and other public places where dogs congregate until your puppy is fully immunized. Diseases can be passed around animal shelters so you should be very careful about any puppy or dog that you adopt from the shelter. If you have other dogs at home, it's a good idea to try and quarantine your new puppy for the first few days so that any disease won't be passed along to other dogs.

Diseases

When you purchase your dog, you should get relevant papers that indicate which vaccinations your puppy has received and when. Always keep these records up to date and easily accessible. Your veterinarian will update this record every time vaccination is given. You'll need these records for emergency care, training classes, grooming or boarding. If you travel with your dog, keep a copy of these records in the vehicle.

These are some of the diseases for which a veterinarian will generally recommend vaccinations:

1. Distemper

    Often fatal, distemper is a highly contagious and stubborn virus. This virus attacks many organs and can cause permanent damage to the nervous system. Symptoms may include listlessness, fever, coughing, diarrhea and vomiting, with convulsions heralding the disease in its final stages.

2. Canine cough

    Highly contagious, canine cough is a respiratory tract infection created by airborne viruses and bacteria. Dogs often catch this disease in places where lot of dogs live such as a boarding kennels, hence the nickname 'kennel cough'. The most obvious symptom is a dry hacking cough.

3. Parvovirus

    Highly contagious, parvovirus is extremely deadly to puppies and unvaccinated adult dogs. Symptoms include lethargy, bloody diarrhea and vomiting. Parvovirus can be fatal.

4. Hepatitis

A potentially fatal disease, hepatitis can be spread via bodily fluids and secretions such as infected urine, saliva and feces. Hepatitis can cause liver failure, eye damage and breathing problems. Symptoms might include listlessness, fever, coughing, diarrhea and vomiting.

5. Rabies

A preventable viral disease, rabies is often transmitted between animals (including humans) by the bite or saliva of an infected animal. The rabies virus infects the central nervous system, ultimately causing brain damage and death. The early symptoms of rabies in people include fever, headache and general weakness or discomfort. As the disease progresses, the other symptoms are insomnia, anxiety, confusion, some paralysis, agitation, difficulty swallowing and hydrophobia or fear of water. Death usually occurs within days of the onset of these symptoms.

It's important to know that rabid dogs may not show any of these symptoms. So it is best to stay away from strange dogs.

Dogs don't have rabies in such countries as New Zealand, United Kingdom, Ireland, Taiwan, Japan, Hawaii, Mauricio's, Barbados and Guam. Although Australia and the United Kingdom have rabies amongst their dog population, anti-rabies vaccinations are not a requirement in these countries.

Rabies has been eradicated amongst dog population in the United States as a result of the ongoing legally-mandated vaccine used. However, rabies is still carried by urban wild life in North America such as skunks and bats. Thus, dogs in the rural and city areas of North America still need protection.

8. Prevent Intestinal and Heartworm Infection

Worms are essentially parasites. They feed off your dog. Whilst some parasites can cause discomfort, others can have a disastrous effect on our dog's health. Depending on the type of worm and/or intensity of infection, symptoms range from mild discomfort, to diarrhea, nausea, coma and even death.

There are many different ways dogs can become infected with worms or their larvae. Common ways are through eating other dog or cat poop, and coming into contact with other infected dogs, animals, vermin and dirt. This is why it is important to ensure that you give your dog the best level of protection against worms.

In this chapter, I'll discuss two types of worms – intestinal worms and heartworm - and what measures you can take to ensure that your dog is protected against them.

Intestinal Worms

Intestinal worms, in particular, steal much needed nutrients from your dog's digestive system. This, in turn, can leave your dog lacking certain nutrients, which the dog needs for her growth and health. In the dog's digestive system, most nutrients are absorbed in the small intestine, and this is precisely where intestinal worms do their best thieving! Dogs can pick up these worms from ingesting dog and cat poop, and from other infected dogs.

The most common worms are: whipworm, hookworm, roundworm and tapeworm. I'll discuss each of these in turn:

- Whipworm

Whipworms actually look like little whips! They get their nutrition by drinking the blood of the host dog. Whipworms are smaller than other intestinal worms, ranging in size between 1 and 2 inches (3–5 cm) in length. Dogs can get infected by eating infected poop or infected dirt (as whipworm eggs can live in dirt).

How can you tell if your dog has whipworm?

Whipworms can cause recurring diarrhea (which may be bloody), weight loss, anemia and colitis (inflammation of the large intestine). Whipworms are hard to detect as dogs do not generally display symptoms, however when the infestation is serious, visible signs may include bloody poop, weight loss, dehydration and anemia.

The bottom line: Whipworm is not generally life threatening, however it can cause significant discomfort. Having said that, on rare occasions when severe infestation occurs, death can come about as a result of dehydration and anemia.

- Roundworm

Many dogs are born with roundworm as these worms pass from the dam to the dog prior to birth or during whelping. Puppies and adult dogs can also catch roundworm by eating infected poop or vermin (such as rodents).

In adult dogs, roundworm larvae can infest the respiratory system and lay dormant in other organs, only to resurface many years later. In younger dogs, the larvae live in the respiratory system and are regurgitated.

Once regurgitated, the dog reinitiates the cycle by eating its own vomit, thereby allowing roundworm to mature in the intestinal system from which it is passed with the feces.

How can you tell if your dog has Roundworm?

Roundworms can cause diarrhea and vomiting in adult dogs and puppies. Puppies may just look unhealthy or have a pot-belly appearance. They may also pass whole roundworms in their poop. You can see these worms in your dog's poop: they are approximately 2 to 4 inches (5–12.5 cm) long, spaghetti-like and white.

The bottom line: Roundworm is not generally life threatening, however it can cause discomfort.

- Hookworm

Hookworms can enter the body through the skin or by being swallowed. Once inside they settle in the dog's small intestine or lungs. Just like whipworms, hookworms feed on the dog's blood rather than on the nutrients that pass through the system.

How can you tell if your dog has hookworm?

Hookworms can cause itchy feet, a rash on the dog's feet, coughing and wheezing, diarrhea, abdominal cramps, nausea, and bloody or black poop. In advanced cases, hookworms can cause anemia and death. Dogs are particularly vulnerable and can die if infected.

The bottom line: Hookworms are difficult to detect and can be life-threatening. Consult your veterinarian for regular testing, especially if you don't use a preventative.

- Tapeworm

Tapeworms live in a dog's small intestine and absorb the nutrients there. Dogs can get tapeworms from eating an infected flea whilst self-grooming or licking their coat. Tapeworms can grow to about 15 feet (about 4.5 metres) long, however they shed in segments ranging from ¼ to ½ inch (1–1.5 cm) long. The segments can be found in your dog's poop.

How can you tell if your dog has tapeworm?

Symptoms include abdominal discomfort, nervousness, itching around the anus, vomiting and weight loss. The itching may result in your dog 'scooting' her bum along the ground. Segments of tapeworm can be found in your dog's poop. The segments are small, wide and flat and look like grains of uncooked rice or sesame seeds.

The bottom line: Tapeworm is not life threatening, however it can cause discomfort.

The prevention of intestinal worms

There are a number of easy, inexpensive measures you can take to prevent your dog from becoming infected with intestinal worms. They are:

- Ask your veterinarian for a 'broad-spectrum' worming preventative. This will protect your dog against heartworms, roundworms, whipworms, hookworms and, depending on which medication you use, even fleas. No preventative can offer 100% protection, however, properly administering the monthly tablet on time, is the best protection you can give your dog.

- If getting a new dog, ask the breeder or the dog's seller, whether your dog had commenced with a worming preventative at about two weeks of age.

- Keep your dog's area clean and remove poop regularly.

- Keep your dog from eating wild animals and vermin as they can be infected with worms.

- Keep your dog from eating animal carcasses such as birds, rodents and rabbits.

- Dogs should not be allowed to eat offal from any animal.

- Ensure that the areas and parks that your dog visits are clean and well maintained – raise this issue with relevant municipalities, if necessary.

- As part of your dog's annual check-up, have your veterinarian conduct an examination of your dog's poop.

- Ensure your dog's toys, bones and chewy items are relatively free of dirt.

The treatment of intestinal worms

If your dog is infected or has not been given a worming preventative, consult your veterinarian. Treatment is very important, and any treatment of worms in dogs should be repeated over time to effectively kill all live and dormant larvae and eggs. Treatment usually involves de-wormer medication. Even if you find a de-wormer that does not require a prescription, you should still use it under your veterinarian's supervision. This is because doses can vary depending on your dog's size and the severity of the infection. Your veterinarian will be able to tell you what dosage is right for your dog.

- Heartworm

Heartworm is a parasitic disease that is spread by mosquitoes, so all dogs are vulnerable. These long, spaghetti-like worms infest the dog's heart and can grow to anywhere between 6 and 10 inches (17–27 cm) long. This disease can also affect cats, ferrets, foxes, wolves, sea lions and horses.

Heartworm is a serious condition and should be considered in any preventative worming regimen.

How can you tell if your dog has heartworm?

Most dogs do not show any symptoms until several years after the initial infection, by which time the disease has progressed to an advanced stage. Chronic infection can cause loss of appetite, weight loss, lethargy, intolerance to exercise, coughing and breathing difficulties. Acute infection can result in shock, vomiting, diarrhea and fainting.

Cases of heartworm that are advanced and untreated can kill a dog within 3 days of symptoms appearing. If you suspect your dog is infected, take her to a veterinarian immediately.

How can you prevent heartworm in your dog?

In order to ensure your dog does not become infected with heartworm, you have two options: the first is a monthly tablet (or chew) and the second is an annual injection (given by a veterinarian). No preventative can offer

100% protection, however, properly administering the monthly tablet or annual injection on time, is the best protection you can give your dog.

Annual injections do away with the need to remember monthly doses. It is important to enter the annual injection appointments into your diary so that there is no gap in coverage. Some veterinarians will send you a letter before each yearly injection is due, however it is best not to rely on this as your sole reminder.

What if your dog has never received any heartworm prevention?

Before starting a monthly dose or annual injection, ask your veterinarian to perform a simple test to confirm your dog is free of the disease. This is necessary because heartworm preventative works best and will not cause further health issues if the dog is free of heartworm.

Heartworm treatment for an infected dog

The best course of action for the treatment of an infected dog is best discussed with your veterinarian. Treatment options can include injections and, in severe cases, surgical removal of the worms might be necessary. Both options can be risky and even dangerous to dogs that already have other pre-existing conditions such as disease of the liver or kidneys.

The bottom line: This parasite can be fatal, if left unchecked. If you have any concerns about your dog and you suspect heartworm you should see your veterinarian immediately.

3 Things You Must Know Regarding the Monthly Prevention Of Heartworm and intestinal Worms

If you choose to give your dog a monthly tablet as a preventative against heartworm or intestinal worms, and to afford your dog the best protection, make sure you:

1. Give monthly doses on the same date each month. Irregular doses can reduce the effectiveness of the coverage.

There is a margin of error, so if follow these guidelines if you have forgotten to give your dog a monthly dose on schedule:

- If you are up to 15 days late, immediately dose your dog and continue with the original dosing schedule.

- If you are between 15-30 days late, immediately dose your dog and ensure that doses are administered on time for at least the next two months to ensure complete protection.

- If you are more than 60 days late in administering a dose, consult your veterinarian immediately.

2. Ensure that the correct dose is given according to your dog's weight. The required dosage amount per month will depend upon your dog's weight. Therefore, consult your veterinarian or the pamphlet provided with the drugs for the correct dosage guidelines.

3. Set reminders for heartworm and intestinal worm prevention. Apart from adding the dates in advance to your diary, you can take advantage of a free monthly email or text message reminder service offered by many drug companies when you buy their product.

9. Learn How to Give Your Dog a Pill

There are a few ways to give your dog a pill. You can always hide the pill in their food. Some dogs will eat the food along with the pill. While other dogs will be able to separate the food and pill; they then eat all the food and ignore the pill!

If your dog dislikes pills, you can always administer pills to your dog manually in four easy steps:

1. Kneel beside your dog and gently squeeze your dog's mouth open with your thumb and middle finger of your left hand.

2. With your right hand, push the pill as far back into the dog's mouth as possible.

3. Now gently keep your dog's mouth closed with your left hand and rub your dog's throat with your right hand to stimulate the dog's impulse to swallow. Ensure your dog has swallowed at least two-three times before releasing your dog.

4. Watch your dog for a few moments, just to make sure she does not regurgitate the pill.

If giving pills to multiple dogs at the same time, watch them closely, as some dogs see pills as treats and may steal them from their pack mates.

10. Guard Against Fleas

If your dog is constantly scratching herself, then she might have fleas.

Fleas can be a year-long pest, but tend to have less chance of survival in colder climates.

You can check if your dog has fleas by combing through her fur with a fine-toothed comb. Use a white piece of kitchen towel or tissue to collect any debris and dirt that is caught with the comb. Carefully moisten the tissue with water. Any debris that dissolves into a reddish-brown, rust-colored stain is flea poop or the digested blood of your dog.

Even if you find one flea, or only one of your dogs has fleas, chances are there are hundreds about. So, treat all your dogs with spot treatment and wash (or replace) all bedding and blankets.

You can purchase 'spot' preventatives from your veterinarian. These spot treatments are put directly on the skin between the shoulder blades (withers) and disperse throughout the skin, without entering the dog's bloodstream. You may have to shave a small area to apply the spot treatment for dogs with very heavy coats.

If fleas are an ongoing problem, then you may have to consider treating your house for fleas.

Flea treatments for dogs are potentially fatal to cats, so don't use canine flea control on your cats. You must use a cat specific flea control for your felines.

Flea Allergies

The most common allergy in dogs is the flea allergy. The mere presence of fleas and their bites can cause any dog to itch, but with flea allergies the symptoms are much more severe. A dog that has a flea allergy can suffer severe bouts of itching from just one single bite. Often, a dog will be severely itchy despite there being no actual evidence of fleas on the dog. Dogs suffering from flea allergy react to substances in the saliva of the flea. When the flea bites its saliva is transferred into the dog's blood stream and causes the itch. Only your veterinarian can make the final diagnosis, but if your dog experiences severe itching as described above, with redness and dryness of the skin, then a flea allergy should be considered even if your dog has been treated for fleas.

11. Guard Against Ticks

Ticks are a blood sucking parasite that lives off an animal. There are hundreds of species of ticks worldwide. In North America, the most common ticks are deer tick, brown dog tick, lone star tick and American dog tick. Most flea spot treatments also repel ticks, but there is no current vaccine for the tick's toxin. Ticks can potentially transmit diseases, such as Lyme disease, ehrlichiosis, Rocky Mountain spotted fever, anaplasmosis and babesiosis. However, many are without disease. The symptoms of most tick-borne diseases include fever and lethargy, and others cause weakness, lameness, joint swelling and anemia.

Dogs in Australia can be vulnerable to paralysis ticks. Symptoms of tick paralysis include: appetite loss, vomiting or dry retching, excessive salivation, difficulty swallowing, difficulty breathing, coughing, changes to the dog's bark, noisy panting and difficulty swallowing. In the latter stages your dog may experience weakened limbs, incontinence, paralysis and coma.

There are many species of ticks in different parts of the world. If you are worried about whether there is a tick problem in your area or you are considering travelling with your dog, ask your veterinarian about this.

Tick prevention

Here are three ways to prevent a tick attaching itself to your dog:

1. Keep your garden area trimmed and mown.

2. Treat outdoor areas with a pet and environmentally friendly pesticide.

3. Apply a monthly tick prevention product directly onto your dog. Or you can use a tick collar.

What to do if your dog has a tick

Keep your dog as calm as possible. Remove food and water as the dog may choke if she is experiencing difficulty swallowing. Remove the tick, if you can. Take your dog to the veterinarian immediately.

This is how you can remove your tick:

1. Wear latex gloves to protect yourself and use a pair of tweezers. There are also specialty tick removal tools that you may be able to purchase at pet supply stores or online.

2. Use tweezers to grasp the tick at the point where it has attached itself to your dog, as close to the dog's skin as possible.

3. Do not squeeze the body of the tick, as this may cause bacteria and disease to be injected into the dog.

4. Carefully pull the tick straight out from the skin; this must be done steadily, slowly and without twisting or turning the tick. It's normal for some of your dog's skin to come off with the tick.

5. Once removed, the tick should either be flushed down the toilet or placed in a small container so you can show your veterinarian.

6. After tick removal, clean your dog's skin at the bite area with mild soap and water. If your dog is bleeding, apply light pressure. Do *not* apply any type of alcohol (including methylated spirits), lit or hot matches, nail polish, petroleum jelly or chemicals to the area – these may cause more harm to your dog.

12. Monitor Your Dog's Skin

I recommend a brief check of your dog's skin, including belly, leg folds and inner ears on a regular basis. A simple check allows you to quickly detect is anything abnormal arises which you can then address in its early stages. Here are common skin conditions:

Warts

Dog warts are caused by the canine papilloma virus. Warts are not typically considered to be serious. Some people refer to this as the doggie chicken pox because it can look a little like human chicken pox.

Dog warts appear as small lumps and are often found in the dog's mouth. They can look like a little cauliflower or a raspberry. They are not cancerous and will often go unnoticed unless you brush your dog's teeth or your veterinarian notices them up during a check-up.

Dog warts are passed on to your dog from other infected dogs. They may be picked up in kennels, the veterinarian's office, during dog classes or at dog parks. The warts cannot be transmitted from your dog to humans or even other animals.

If you notice warts in your dog's mouth, see a veterinarian to ensure that the warts don't interfere with the dog's eating habits.

Provided there are no problems with the dog eating, no treatment is necessary. The warts will heal in their own time. Once she has had the condition, a full immunity will develop and she will not have this condition again unless her immune system is weakened as a result of another illness or disease.

Extreme cases can be cause for concern. A dog with an abundance of warts might have a weak immune system. If the warts hinder the dog's ability to eat, drink or breathe, they might have to be surgically removed.

Other skin disorders

Skin problems are common in dogs and can be attributed to one or more causes including allergies, mites and autoimmune disease. They can also result from serious underlying issues such as glandular diseases, cancer, a malfunctioning thyroid and Cushing's syndrome (a hormone disorder caused by high levels of cortisol in the blood).

With skin problems, a visit to the veterinarian for a biopsy examination of the dog's skin culture may get you the proper diagnosis. However, a visit to a dermatologist may be required if the veterinarian's efforts to diagnose and treat a skin problem are unsuccessful. Unfortunately, some skin problems can be quite tricky to diagnose and treat. When discussing your dog's condition, discuss the possibility of fish (or other) supplements, dietary changes, medicated shampoos and steroid injections.

Fungal problems

Fungal skin problems are often found in dogs with allergies (for more information about allergies, see the next section). Some fungus is highly contagious (like ringworm), whilst others – such as yeast – are not transmitted as easily. Fungal skin infections can manifest as either crusty red lumps or red and black swollen skin. They can have a similar appearance to mange, and the dog will also have a distinctive, strong odor.

Mange

Mange is a contagious skin disease caused by parasiticnites. This condition presents as flaky skin, bald patches and itching. Several types of mites can be passed to humans (a human infection is known as scabies). Diagnosis of mange can be difficult, particularly with one type of mite (sarcoptic) as their already relatively low numbers may be removed by the dog's chewing.

There are three ways in which mange might be diagnosed:

- The simplest and most common method is via the *Pedal-Pinnareflex* which is when the dog engages one of its hind legs in a scratching motion as the veterinarian gently scratches and manipulates her ear.

- Examination of a skin culture under a microscope.

- A serologic test, which is available in some countries.

Bacterial infections

A dog's skin may become infected after it has been compromised and damaged by an underlying health issue or via the actions of the dog when dealing with itching (such as incessant scratching and chewing). In these cases, your veterinarian may recommend antibiotics.

13. Take Measures to Relieve and Manage Any Allergies

There are four types of canine allergies – food, fleas, inhalants (such as dust, mould, different grasses or pollen) and contact allergies to chemical. Inhalant allergies are more common than food allergies, with only 10% of allergic reactions being attributed to food. Contact allergies to chemicals are quite rare, but should be considered if diagnosis proves difficult. Flea allergies were discussed above.

Often food allergies are caused by the carbohydrates and starch used in the food, for example wheat, grain and rice. Other dogs react to proteins, displaying beef and chicken allergies for instance. Soy allergies are very common. Fish allergies are rare, as are allergies to rarer animal protein such as bison or deer.

Some breeds are more prone to allergies, including bulldogs, poodles and some terriers. A predisposition to allergies is often genetic, so dogs with allergy prone parents might be affected too.

Symptoms for canine allergies may include:

- Intense itching – this is the most common symptom. Dogs may use their paws or an object to rub their face or torso, or they may scoot their hind along the ground.

- Raw skin – this is a result of the dog chewing the affected area. Flea allergies may result in the dog chewing her hindquarters raw.

- Hot spots – these are localized rashes that can feel very warm to the touch. They commonly appear on the shoulder or on the hind quarter of the dog.

- Visible rash – inhalant and food allergies may also result in itch, reddened feet.

- Watery, red eyes.

- Frequent ear and bladder infections and increased susceptibility to illness – this is because the dog's skin is damaged and bacteria are allowed to thrive.

- Vomiting and diarrhea – food allergies may lead to the symptoms listed above, but they may also manifest in this way.

When talking to your veterinarian about possible allergy treatments, remember the following points:

- There is no real cure for an allergy – just prevention and relief.

- The source of any allergy is often difficult to identify. The possibility of a flea allergy should be considered even if your dog has been treated for fleas. Using flea preventatives will help reduce the likelihood of flea allergy.In severe cases, steroids can be used to lessen symptoms of flea allergies, but in the long term steroids can suppress the immune system.

- Food allergies are identified through elimination diets, undertaken under the supervision of your veterinarian.

- Your discussion with your veterinarian should be centered on managing the symptoms.

- Your veterinarian may be able to procure a culture from the affected skin, to see what type of medication can be prescribed.

- Antihistamine may be a good idea to reduce symptoms. Your veterinarian can talk to you about whether this is appropriate and in what dosages.

- You could be referred to a canine dermatologist who may be able to isolate the cause and prescribe injections that will alleviate the symptoms. This option is more expensive, however.

- Vaccinations that are given too often may make an allergic response worse, so consider discussing the frequency of vaccinations and the use of blood titers.

When it comes to managing allergies there are many things you can do at home to reduce the symptoms:

- Itchy skin can be soothed by using medicated or oatmeal shampoo and supplements like fish oil capsules.

- Keep your dog's ears clean to prevent a build-up of yeast.

- Cranberries or cranberry supplements can help prevent bladder infections (that may arise from food allergies).

- Use an air purifier in the home.

- Wash your dog's bedding regularly.

- Keep the house vacuumed and use natural, non-toxic cleaners.

14. Care for Your Dog's Bones

Dogs have about 320 bones in their bodies, compared to 206 for humans. The actual number of bones depends on whether the dog has dew claws (located on the inside leg above the paw) and the length of the dog's tail. To help your puppy's growing bones develop properly, make sure the dog avoids stressing her bones or joints with activities such as jumping or strenuous exercise until she's fully grown.

Signs of joint pain

If you notice your puppy or adult dog showing the following signs, then your dog may be suffering from joint pain:

- Stiffness
- Lameness
- Abnormal, hesitant or labored gait
- Favoring a limb
- Difficulty sitting or standing
- Hesitant to get up
- Difficulty with climbing stairs
- Yelping when moving or stopping
- 'Bunny-hopping' type movements

The most common ailments that can cause joint pain are:

- Arthritis
- Elbow and hip dysplasia
- Slipping knee joints (luxating patellas)

Arthritis is an inflammation of any joint or spine; it can cause pain and swelling. Arthritis is most common in older dogs, but hip or elbow dysplasia can also lead to early onset arthritis.

In each breed profile I have indicated whether a particular breed is prone to dysplasia. Dysplasia can be first noticed in dogs under one year old. Hip and elbow dysplasia are common in dogs, more so in larger breeds. Mixed breeds, purebreds and dogs of both genders can be affected by dysplasia, with more males affected by elbow dysplasia. Dysplasia is hereditary, but you might be able to avoid it by staying clear of breeds that are commonly affected. Choosing a responsible, certified breeder can help avoid this issue – ask if the parents of the relevant litter have been certified to be free from dysplasia. As dysplasia is genetic, it is unlikely that your dog will be affected if both her parents are free from the disease.

Slipping knee joints can affect any dog, but toy breeds tend to be more susceptible. A slipping knee cap is a common problem that affects dogs of all ages and sizes. In affected dogs, the knee cap is not held securely against the joint but rather floats along the leg.

If you suspect your dog to be suffering from joint pain, have her examined by a veterinarian who will be able to make an accurate diagnosis via gentle movement of all joints (to check for range of movement as well as pain) and x-rays. Just be aware that elbow dysplasia can be more difficult to diagnose.

Treatments for the causes of joint pain

Treatment options should be discussed with your veterinarian because they will depend on the veterinarian's preferences as well as your dog's age, health, your budget and the type of condition your dog suffers from.

Treatment options range from simply modifying the dog's exercise and activities to supplements, medication for easing pain, and surgery.Here are some things to note when you are discussing these options with your veterinarian :

- Mild cases of dysplasia, slipping knee joints or arthritis may not require surgery. However, severe cases may require surgical intervention. If your veterinarian recommends surgery, get a second opinion from an orthopedist, who will have up-to-date information on available medications and procedures.

- A total hip replacement is the most common surgery for dealing with hip dysplasia. This surgery includes removing the entire joint and then replacing it with a synthetic hip. Hip replacements can only be undertaken once the dog has finished growing, and there is usually a two to three month wait between replacing the two hips. Femoral head and neck excision is a procedure in which the head and neck of the thigh bone are removed. This is a relatively easy and cheap procedure and can work well in dogs under 20kgs (44lbs). The range of movement and the stability of the hip that can be achieved with this procedure is not as good as it is with other procedures, but can be satisfactory. The veterinarian will suggest that the dog is given limited exercise and a low calorie diet after the surgery, but once the dog has healed, she will be allowed to exercise as before. Limiting her weight will help to reduce any complications that she may otherwise experience.

- Any surgical procedure requires follow up attention with the dog's veterinarian, along with physiotherapy in many cases. Pet physiotherapists can be very helpful with building the muscles and pain management.

- Your veterinarian may also recommend pain medications. Drugs won't correct the condition, but they can significantly reduce pain, inflammation and stiffness. In the long term, pain killers (also known as anti-inflammatory drugs) can have significant side effects, such as stomach ulcers and kidney failure. So, monitor the length of the dog's drug usage in consultation with your veterinarian. Unless they are time release capsules, you can make giving your dog pills easier by dissolving them in water or grinding them up and mixing them with the dog's food. You could also use a pill-gun or pet-piller which works by 'injecting' the pill into your dog's mouth.

- At no time should you consider giving your dog pain medications meant for humans. Aspirin, for example, is not suitable for dogs, and dosages for pain medications that are considered appropriate for people can prove quite deadly for dogs.

- Many supplements are available from veterinarians and over the counter that can help to reduce the effects of inflammation seen with arthritis. Glucosamine extracted from green lip mussels, for example, can be very effective without the long-term side effects of pain killers. Supplements do not reverse arthritis, but they can slow down the process. Supplements such as glucosamine and chondroitin are commonly prescribed to dogs with hip dysplasia. These supplements help to repair cartilage in the joint and support the lubrication of the joint. Better lubrication means less pain and less destruction of the joint. The supplements are easy to obtain and are often sold over the counter at your local pet supply store, but their effectiveness varies widely.

- Most joint support supplements made for humans are fine for dogs too, as they contain the same active ingredients.

- Alternative forms of treatment for arthritis may include gold implants and acupuncture. Some veterinarians are certified acupuncturists.

- An exercise regimen that encourages a slow and steady pace suits dogs with joint pain best, whereas abrupt stopping and starting motions should be discouraged. This includes mounting and descending stairs (if it can be avoided), jumping out of the boot of the car and throwing sticks or balls (as this means your dog will start, stop and turn abruptly). Consider exercises such as swimming as the weightlessness helps build up the muscles without placing stress on the joint and tendons. Pet physiotherapists may be able to provide access to special dog pools, some with underwater treadmills. Frequent, gentle exercise also serves to increase muscle mass which also helps to reduce the stress that joints experience.

- If your dog is carrying too much weight, losing the excess weight should be your first priority. This is because too much weight places extra stress on your dog's joints. Weight loss can have a massive impact on reducing pain.

- Perna mussels are edible shellfish, known for assisting with joint health. This shell fish has a high level of glycosaminoglycans (GAG's) which are known to assist in the formation and repair of connective materials within the joints. This makes it an ideal fish for dogs (and people) that have arthritis and hip dysplasia problems. Unsaponifiables are components in avocados and soybeans which are thought to help rebuild cartilage and prevent arthritis pain and degradation.

- Polysulfated glycosaminoglycan can also be injected directly into the joints on a weekly or monthly basis. This treatment is thought to help rebuild the cartilage within the hips. It is injected directly into the muscles surrounding the joints. The treatment has a good track record, often providing promising results.

Keeping your dog healthy is not your only job as a dog owner. In the next chapter, I'll discuss how you can enrich your dog's life so that she does not miss you when you're away from home.

4 Ways to Keep Your Dog Occupied When You're Not Home

Dogs were bred to accompany humans and other dogs, however today's lifestyles do not allow people to have their dogs with them all day. Because of that, many dogs are left alone for long periods of time while their owners work or go about their day's activities. Dogs are naturally endowed with heaps of energy and they burn this energy with mental and physical stimulation. Some dogs may sleep or rest in your absence because they are diurnal sleepers; they will then become more active when you return home. Some dogs will burn their energy with or without their owners help! Unoccupied dogs left alone in a confined space such as an apartment, may pace, chew or bark, and become anxious in the process. Dogs are clever and curious, and so require different activities to stave off boredom. The key to alleviating boredom when a dog is home alone is to ensure the dog remains occupied with activities for long periods of time.

There are four ways you can keep your dog occupied:

1. Toys

To keep your dog occupied and entertained during your absence, you can provide her with a range of toys (indestructible toys are better).Don't leave the same toys out for your dog everyday as your dog will get bored with them. Instead, change which toys your dog has access to on a daily basis. Use different toys for different activities: when you are away, when you are home, at the park or playing fetch. In this way, your dog will remain interested in all her toys.Also, the toys themselves will remain intact for longer periods.

In the wild, dogs were accustomed to spending a significant amount of time looking for food. This instinct can be satisfied with the following interactive and food dispensing toys

Kong

The Kong is the toughest of toys, as it is virtually indestructible. The Kong can be stuffed with various treats which will occupy the dog as she will spend hours chewing and working to get the treats out. The irregular shape and rubber also makes it a fun bouncing toy that the dog can bat around and chase.

If you want to lengthen your dog's attention to it, then simply freeze it. This will make the Kong's hidden treats last longer - as it defrosts, your dog will be able to pick out the treats!

Some dogs will eventually work out how to get to a Kong's stuffing inside, so you may want to make their job more challenging. You can do this by packing the stuffing tighter or mixing cheese pieces or spread with food nuggets and then microwaving the Kong (inside a cup) until the cheese or spread melts. Let it cool to a safe temperature before serving it to your dog.

If you want to vary what you put inside your dog's Kong, try these recipes concocted by dog trainers and veterinarians. When trying these different recipes, always remain sensitive to your dog's stomach and don't introduce dietary changes too quickly.

BANANARAMA	
Ingredients	Instructions
1 fresh banana	Mash up banana in a bowl. Add wheat germ and yogurt. Mash all ingredients together and use spoon to add to Kong. Freeze for 4 hours.
2 tbs wheat germ	
1 tbs plain yogurt	Serving
	Makes 1 serving for Medium Kong. Double for every level of larger Kong size.

CHEESY DENTAL KONG DELIGHT

Ingredients	Instructions
3 slices of your pet's favorite cheese Dental Kong Toy	Place the 3 slices of cheese directly onto the grooves of your pet's Dental Kong (if model has rope, make sure cheese does not get onto it). Melt in microwave for 20 to 30 seconds. Give to pet after it cools.

PHILLY STEAK

Ingredients	Instructions
Steak scraps 1 ounce cream cheese	Place small scraps of the steak inside Kong toy. Spread cream cheese in large hole to hold scraps.

FRUIT SALAD

Ingredients	Instructions
Apple and carrot chunks 1/4th of a banana	Place apples and carrots in Kong Toy. Mush the banana in large hole to hold fruit in place. You can include other fruits and veggies like orange slices, peach and/or nectarine chunks, celery sticks, broccoli and/or cauliflower, tomato and black olive mixture.

VEGGIE KONG OMELET

Ingredients	Instructions
1 egg Your choice of shredded cheese Any vegetables that	Scramble egg and fold in vegetables. Put into Kong toy. Sprinkle some cheese over the top and microwave for about 20 seconds. Cool thoroughly before giving to dog.

your pet may like	

MAC 'N CHEESE

Ingredients	Instructions
Leftover macaroni and cheese Small cube of Velveeta, Cheddar or Mozzarella	Melt Velveeta in microwave until gooey. Add mac 'n cheese to Kong Toy. Pour heated Velveeta into Kong. Make sure it has cooled before giving to your pet.

Kong Biscuit Ball

This toy is a round, ball-like variation of the original Kong; the Kong Biscuit Ball can be filled up with biscuits, treats and other dry foods that occasionally pop out as a reward for the dog as she plays with the ball.

Bob-A-Lot

This toy wobbles, spins and rolls when pushed by the dog. As the dog plays with the bobbing toy, food treats are dispensed randomly. Adjustable openings at the top and bottom allow you to control the level of difficulty in removing treats. You may also consider substituting the food bowl with this toy, making mealtime more enjoyable.

Tricky Treat Ball

Tricky treat ball works just like a Kong biscuit ball.

Tug-A-Jug

Tug-A-Jug does not only entertain your dog but it also helps prevent them from eating all their food at once. A treat comes out of the jug as the dog plays with it.

Waggle

Stuff kibble into the sides of the barbell-shaped Waggle; the kibble randomly drops out as the dog holds it in her mouth and shakes it. There are rubber teeth in the holes on the sides that can be trimmed to reduce the level of difficulty.

Buster Cube

As the dog rolls the cube around, the dog is rewarded with kibble as they drop out of the toy randomly. The dog is compelled to think about how to move the toy in order to retrieve the treats inside – this type of mental stimulation is great for dogs. The settings can be adjusted so treats are either easier or more difficult to retrieve.

Puppy Pull

Puppy pull works like a rubber-yoyo-like toy which hangs and bounces while hanging from the knob of a door. It keeps your dog busy, as well as entertained and well-exercised.

2. Chews

Many dogs have a natural tendency to chew and enjoy gnawing on something tasty. A raw egg (still in the shell) once weekly can initially offer a puzzle for your dog; once left in its dish your dog will eventually figure out how to get to the gooey contents! Don't worry about the shell – dogs stomachs are equipped to handle it.

Other chewy treats are:

- Freeze-dried beef liver - A great tasty treat, and high in protein, this treat can be used as a reward for obedience. You can also try freeze-dried chicken.

- Bully sticks - Many dogs absolutely love bully sticks as they're softer than rawhide, and so easy to digest. They will also keep your dog occupied for a long time as they are quite chewy. I recommend giving your dog a bully stick before leaving the dog alone at home, so she has something to occupy herself.

- Compressed rawhide - Although dogs love rawhide and pigs ears, these can shatter or break apart leaving the sharp pieces to wreak havoc on your dog's digestive tract. Make sure the rawhide is compressed. Also, watch for cheap rawhide imitations that are too salty and contain lots of chemicals.

- Brussels sprout stalks – tasty, tough and good for your dog. They can be used in fetch games.

- Sugar cane - a great treat to reward your dog every once in a while.

- Beef bones - from the hip or knuckle of a cow, the marrow of beef bones provide a tasty surprise. Brisket bones are good too, and can be eaten quicker than the beef bones. Ensure you don't give your dog too many bones as they can cause constipation. Never give your dog cooked chop or chicken bones as they splinter and can puncture their digestive tracts.

Quado Bone

This toy is entirely edible and long-lasting; this toy offers a great outlet for dogs who love to chew and also helps freshen the dog's breath. There is no added salt, sugar, sweeteners or artificial preservatives.

3. Hire a Dog Walker

A dog walker or pet minder is a relatively inexpensive way to have your canine friend occupied while you are away. These professionals can spend time with your dog at your apartment or nearby parks and walking routes. If you are employing a dog walker or pet minder, tell them what activities your dog enjoys, so the dog will get the greatest benefit from the pet minding or dog walking service. Encourage the professional to engage your dog's mind with games and activities that are stimulating for your dog. For a directory of dog walkers in:

- the United Kingdom visit http://www.ukdogwalkers.co.uk/

- the United States visit http://www.petsitusa.com/

- Australia visit http://www.dogcaredirectory.com.au/

4. Leave the Radio or TV On

Some dog owners report that leaving the radio and TV turned on offers their dog some comfort, however this is not a cure for separation anxiety. Before using these methods for an extended period of time (that is, going out for the day), test them for short periods, and see how your dog reacts. Then increase the amount of time you spend out of the house on each subsequent occasion. If your dog finds the radio or TV over-stimulating you may want to discontinue using this method.

In this chapter, I discussed how to ensure your dog stays occupied in our absence. What about when you are home with your dog? In the next chapter, I'll discuss fun games you can play with your dog so you can deepen your bond and stimulate her curiosity and playfulness.

Fun Dog Games and Activities for Apartments

Dogs that are not occupied on a daily basis often find their own outlets. These outlets (such as digging or excessive barking/howling) can be quite destructive and frustrating for you as an owner! A key strategy for staving off boredom and problem behavior is keeping your dog occupied. There are many ways you can do this and we will look at each of these options in turn. In this chapter, I'll explain:

- How to organize your dog's daily routine and environment so your dog is confident, happy and occupied.

- How to cater to your dog's particular exercise needs, depending on her breed.

- Fun games and toys that will stimulate your dog and allow you to bond with your dog.

Organize Your Dog's Day

Dogs are creatures of habit. They derive security and balance from knowing they can rely on certain things to happen on a regular basis. I have noticed that dogs with haphazard or unpredictable schedules tend to be a little more restless and insecure than their confident counterparts.

Consider scheduling the following activities as part of your dog's day:

- Ensure your dog eats at the same time every day.
- Play with your dog. The best times to play with your dog is when you have been home for at least an hour. Do not play with your dog as soon as you arrive, or just before you leave, home. If you do, you may accidentally encourage your dog to develop separation anxiety. This is because your dog will fret

in your absence, waiting for the moment you return so play can begin!

- Train your dog once a day. The best time to train your dog is just prior to a play session. In this way, you can use play as a reward. Remember, though, that training should be as fun as play. Training is great for both your dog's mind and her physical health. It's been said that training uses three times more energy than exercising, so training is a great way to tire out your dog! Training in short bursts and ranging in length from just one to fifteen minutes a day can help alleviate boredom.

- Walk your dog every day. By taking your dog for a walk in the morning, your dog will be more contented during the day and less likely to engage in destructive activities such as digging and barking.

Although I advocate a daily schedule for dogs, it is important to ensure your dog experiences nice surprises and variety too. Impromptu visits to dog parks, beaches and friends' homes can contribute to your dog's overall mental wellbeing. Surprise treats and playtime are also recommended. That, along with certainty around when to expect food, exercise and training will give your dog confidence.

Your Dog's Exercise Needs

Regular exercise is an essential part of dog ownership. Different dogs have different exercise requirements. Even though all the breeds profiled in this guide are small, there can still be enormous differences between what type of exercise each dog prefers and can tolerate. Different dogs should have different kinds of exercise; forcing a Pekingese to jog or swim could be inappropriate, whilst these types of exercise may be perfect for a Cavalier King Charles Spaniel.

Here are some exercise suggestions for some of the different groups of dogs recognized by the American Kennel Club. Groups are arranged according to a breed's original purpose so many of the dogs in these groups should be able to do at least some of the kinds of exercise suggested.

Exercise for sporting breeds

Members of the Sporting group include the Cocker Spaniel. Naturally athletic, these dogs were all originally bred to find birds and other game. Some can point, set, retrieve or flush out birds and therefore make great hunting companions. You can provide good exercise for these dogs by taking them jogging or biking with you. They are ideal dogs for people and families with an active lifestyle. Most of these dogs are also very good at agility and other dog sports such as flyball and frisbee or disk throwing. Many kennel or dog clubs provide hunt tests for sporting dogs which are a lot of fun for these dogs since they are able to exercise their natural instincts and get plenty of exercise in the field.

Exercise for herding breeds

Members of the Herding group include the Puli and Welsh Corgi. The members of this group are acknowledged to be some of the most intelligent of all dogs. They were originally used to herd flocks of sheep, goats and other animals, or to drive cattle. They have strong herding instincts and may herd kids and other pets unless taught not to do so. They usually greatly enjoy training and work.

Herding dogs usually need plenty of exercise. They are extremely intelligent dogs and if they don't have enough exercise they can become very bored and unhappy in the home. They are brilliant at agility, flyball and other dog sports. Some of these dogs are very versatile because of their intelligence and can be trained to do many things such as working as guide dogs, bomb detection dogs or doing other jobs. When possible, many of these breeds also enjoy herding work. You can even teach some of these dogs to play soccer and other games with balls that involve pushing or 'herding' a ball into a goal. In an apartment, soccer can be played safely with a soft, small ball and using a doorframe as a makeshift goal.

Exercise for hounds

The Hound group is divided into two groups: sight hounds and scent hounds. Sight hounds include the Greyhounds – even though the Italian Greyhound is classified as a Toy breed, she comes from such stock. These dogs are all extremely fast and they love to run. Scent hounds work by scenting their prey. They have great noses. These dogs include the Basset Hound, Beagle and Dachshund. They may work more slowly than the sight hounds but they excel at tracking their prey.

You can provide wonderful exercise for sight hounds by making sure that they get a good run several times per week. Dogs such as Greyhounds are usually couch potatoes at home and are very laid back, but they do need plenty of exercise. Take them someplace where they can safely run off-leash. Be sure it is a safe, enclosed area because once a sight hound starts running she probably won't return to you until she's tired, especially if she's chasing something. These dogs have a very strong prey drive. Sight hounds also love lure coursing which is a sport which allows them to chase a plastic lure on a wire. Open field coursing is another option for sight hounds, in which they are actually able to hunt hares in an open field.

With scent hounds you can enjoy the sport of tracking. Tracking allows the dog to search for items or, for advanced dogs, a person, using her nose to find them. It requires a great deal of training and practice, but scent hounds are terrific at this sport. Other scent hounds take part in hunting such as coon hunting or rabbit hunting. Dachshunds often take part in Earth dog events, going to ground after rabbits or squirrels.

Exercise for terriers

Terriers are often very active dogs so they appreciate exercise. These breeds include the Miniature Schnauzer, Norfolk Terrier and West Highland White Terrier. They were bred to hunt vermin such as rats and fox, going to ground after them if necessary. They are usually very brave dogs. Terriers often excel at agility since they are small and fast. They can be hard to train but, with persistence, they can do well at obedience. Terriers may also enjoy participating in Earth dog events where they can dig and go to ground after small animals.

Exercise for toy dogs

Toy dogs don't usually require much exercise but they do need some daily exercise in order to stay healthy and sane. Toy breeds include: Affenpinscher, Bolognese, Cavalier King Charles Spaniel, Chihuahua, Chinese Crested, Havanese, Italian Greyhound, Japanese Chin, Maltese, Miniature Pinscher, Papillon, Pekingese, Pomeranian, Toy Poodle, Pug, Shih Tzu and Yorkshire Terrier. Exercise provides a good mental outlet for small dogs and improves their socialization. Many Toy breeds began with roles other than companion dogs. The Pomeranian can't pull a sled anymore and the Yorkshire Terrier no longer hunts vermin, but these little dogs do appreciate having some real exercise.

You can provide good exercise for your Toy dog by taking her for a good daily walk. Do not force a Toy dog to exercise and don't allow them to become overheated. In most cases a good walk will provide sufficient exercise. Some Toy dogs may enjoy obedience or agility work, depending on the particular breed and dog's own preferences.

Exercise for non-sporting breeds

The Non-Sporting group is a catch-all group of dogs that originally had different purposes. These dogs are different sizes and they don't really have much in common. Dogs in this group include the Bichon Frise, Bulldog, Boston Terrier, Chow Chow, Coton de Tulear and Lhasa Apso. Exercise needs for these different dogs can vary greatly. For example, care needs to be taken not to allow the Bulldog to be over-exerted. With her brachycephalic head and other physical traits she cannot tolerate too much exercise.

If you have a Non-Sporting dog you should find out what kind of exercise is usual for your dog's breed and see if your dog is able to do that kind of exercise – the breed profiles in this guide outlines the exercise preferences for these breeds. Always start with a minimum of exercise and work up to more.

Stimulating and Fun Games

Dogs love play. It's an important part of their everyday life; playing is a way of exercising, honing their fighting skills (with mock fighting) and bonding with others in their pack, whether dog or human. Many owners forget how important play actually is; owners often make the mistake of not providing playful outlets for their dogs. Regular play with you or a family member is important to your dog's wellbeing as it can help strengthen the dog-human bonds. Play with or without human company provides your dog with mental and physical stimulation (which helps to stave off stress or depression).

I recommend you not allow your dog to always instigate play. If your dog thinks she can demand attention from you at any time, then you run the risk of raising a needy, attention-seeking brat. Some games are great for general backyard shenanigans, while others are suitable during walks or as part of your dog's daily exercise.

It is easy to know when your dog is responsive to play. Dogs invite play by running around in big circles or adopting the classic play bow stance. Some dogs invite play by positioning themselves next to their owners and nuzzling or poking them. Some dogs will invite you to play with a particular toy or object by adopting a play bow stance with the toy in their mouths. Sometimes a playful challenge is set when a dog either lies next to, or stands over, a toy or other prized object.

Here are some great ways you can play with your dog and have fun together:

1. Fetch

Fetch is a great game you can play with your dog, especially as you can use it to exercise your dog with limited action on your part! Some dogs are born retrievers, whilst others have no inkling of what to do, so you may need to teach your dog the necessary skills. Before teaching your dog to fetch, it's important your dog knows the 'sit' and 'come' commands very well. If your dog does not perform these commands to a satisfactory standard, the job of teaching your dog fetch will be much more challenging.

The following is a step-by-step explanation of how to teach your dog fetch. I have included all the steps as I am assuming your dog may have little or no inclination to retrieve an item; these steps will ensure you have all bases covered. As you proceed through the steps, make sure your dog is consistently performing each step before moving to the next step. If your dog 'fails', then you have proceeded too quickly. All you need to do is return to, and repeat, the previous step until your dog is performing that step consistently.

Start out by choosing a suitable item; it might be one that your dog loves such as a ball, squeaky toy or rope. Either way, make sure the item fits comfortably in your dog's mouth – if it's too big, the discomfort would override any joy your dog might derive from this game. The idea is to make your dog as excited as possible about the item; some trainers refer to her process as making the item 'hot'. You make an item 'hot' by playing with the item, tossing it up in the air, speaking in a high, excited voice, using your dog's name and saying: "Where's the ball? Who's a good girl? Where's the ball?" You can toss your dog a few treats, too, so she learns to associate the item with fun and excitement.

Next you should toss the item a little way. Don't expect your dog to bring it back to you at first, but do encourage your dog to go after it. If she goes to the item and touches it you should praise her and give her some treats. If you keep associating the item with treats your dog should pick up the item and you should give her a few more treats. You can start encouraging her to bring the item back to you once she starts picking it up. Don't chase her if she doesn't bring the item back to you. Once she starts carrying the item around you should hold off on the treats until she actually brings it back to you.

Once you are certain your dog is about to bring the item back to you, say "fetch" in an excited tone. If you say "fetch" when your dog is still in the process of figuring out what to do with the item, then you run the risk of the dog not learning to associate the command "fetch" with the actual act of bringing the item back to you.

When your dog returns to you with the item, praise her and take the object from her mouth. Or show the dog a treat, and when she drops the toy as a trade for the treat, say "give".

When teaching your dog to fetch, you might encounter the following challenges:

- "*My dog does not let go of the object*" or "*My dog drops the object too far from me.*"Your dog should drop whatever she has in her mouth on your command. To ensure this happens, make sure she is on a lead and follow these steps in order to train your dog to "drop it":
  - o Play with the item until the dog has taken it from you.
  - o Coax the dog towards you by jogging backwards. (Do not chase your dog, as this will only encourage the dog to run away with the item).
  - o When you produce a treat, the dog is likely drop the item for the treat – as the dog drops the item, say "give".
  - o If your dog refuses to give the item up, put your hand over her muzzle and squeeze near her back teeth. Take the item, say "give" and reward your dog with play and a treat.

- *"My dog does not pick up the object."* If your dog does not hold the item in her mouth at all, then train your dog the "take it" and "hold" commands. The steps are:
  - Put the item in the dog's mouth and say "take it".
  - Ensure the item is in the dog's mouth and gently squeeze your dog's muzzle shut with your thumb over the bridge of your dog's muzzle and palm under the dog's chin. As the dog holds the item, say "hold".

- There is another way you can teach your dog to pick up an item but it may take longer, so this method requires patience:
  - Make the item 'hot' (that is, irresistible to your dog) by playing with the item or teasing your dog with it.
  - Place the item on the ground and wait.
  - Whenever your dog looks at the item, say "good" and give your dog a treat. (Just remember, that your dog may initially choose to look at you or the treats you have in your hand. That's okay, be patient and your dog will eventually look at the item again).
  - If you do this regularly your dog will quickly realize that she is being rewarded for giving attention to the item.
  - Your dog will eventually look at the item consistently and deliberately in order to get a reward. When this happens, hold off on the reward – this will encourage her to approach the item.
  - Reward your dog for getting closer and closer to the item.
  - Eventually your dog will choose to pick up the item. When she does so say "hold" and

reward her. Repeat this last step to
reinforce the "hold" command.

If your dog drops the ball far away from your feet, then there are
some strategies you can adopt to encourage her to drop it closer.
Coax your dog to run towards you, by slowly jogging backwards.
Hopefully, this will also encourage her to drop the ball closer to
you. Reward your dog if she drops the ball even a little closer than
before. Keep rewarding closer drops and ignoring ball drops that
are not closer than the previous effort. You can also stop the game
if your dog drops the ball far away – your dog will learn that the
fun stops when she doesn't play on your terms.

You can also play a little game called "drop it", where you have
your dog sit (on a leash). Encourage your dog to pick up a ball or
toy. Offer your dog a treat. As your dog drops the ball or toy, say
"drop it" and give her the treat. Timing is important here – do not
say "drop it" until the moment the dog allows the ball to leave her
mouth. Once your dog has mastered this, you can gradually take
small steps away and encourage your dog to come to you, before
dropping the ball in front of you. You can then incorporate this
game into fetch.

2. Hide 'n Seek

Dogs love to play hide and seek. This is an easy game to play. It
helps if your dog knows a couple of basic obedience commands
such as sit and stay. Put your dog in the sit and stay position and
then go hide. That's it! You can give your dog the release
command from afar and let her come looking for you. Or you can
ask someone to hold your dog while you hide. If your dog is really
clever, you can let her hide while you go searching for her. Dogs in
training as tracking dogs have to play hide and seek with their
handlers in order to develop search skills. This game is still
suitable even if you live in a small apartment; small, quick games
where the dog finds you easily can still be fun!

3. Tug of War

Dog trainers generally dismiss tug of war as a game that encourages your dog to challenge your leadership; however what the experts don't tell you is that you can enjoy this whilst maintaining your status as leader of the pack.

The fact is that dogs enjoy playing this particular game with their owners and others in the pack. Dogs that play this do not necessarily use it as a way to challenge other pack members or their owner, and they certainly will not become competitive solely on the basis of playing it. It's fun and entertaining as it gives your dog a chance to bond with you and exercise their strength. It's also a good way to teach your dog several basic commands. You can use a simple toy such as a small rope to play.

Some dogs are more interested in playing tug of war than others but you can get most dogs to play if you wiggle the toy in front of them. You should praise your dog for taking hold of the toy to let them know it's okay with you.

You can teach your dog to "drop it" when playing tug of war. When your dog lets go of the toy you can praise her, offer her the toy again, or give her a treat as a reward. "Drop it" is a good command for your dog to know in case she picks up something she shouldn't eat or something dangerous.

If your dog gets overexcited and pulls too hard, or won't stop playing when you tell her to do so, you can simply stop playing. You can teach your dog to "drop it" when playing tug of war.

When your dog lets go of the toy, praise her and offer her the toy again, or give her a treat as a reward. "Drop it" is a good command for your dog to know in case she picks up something she shouldn't eat or something that is dangerous.

How to Play Tug of War the Right Way

Dogs love games of resistance - that's why many pull on a lead! Games of resistance such as tug of war should be played in such a way that your dog understands the rules and that you are always leader of the pack.

Rule #1: Always be the winner. This game can be enjoyable for your dog even when you win every time.

Rule #2: Ensure your dog understands you are the toy's owner. Even if you occasionally let your dog win, make sure that they understand that the tug toy is yours. In other words, do not allow your dog to become possessive of the toy itself. The best way to retain possession of a toy is to put it away in a place that only you can access.

Rule #3: If your dog gets hyper-excited and yanks on the tug toy too hard, or won't stop playing when you command them to do so, you can simply stop playing. After all, it takes two to play and if you stop pulling the game is over.

Children & Tug of War Don't Mix

Never let children play tug-of-war or chasing games with your dog as they see children as 'puppies' and will try to dominate them, which could lead to problems.

This game can be plenty of fun for you and your dog as long as there are a few boundaries - so enjoy!

4. Tag

Other playful activities such as frolicking and playing tag mean that your dog gets plenty of exercise. Dogs love chasing each other – this is a common and fun game amongst pack members. When playing tag, always make sure your dog chases *you*. If you chase your dog, then your dog may become accustomed to this. She may then run away from you whenever you move towards her, and this can be a frustrating experience if you are moving towards your dog in order to put a leash on her in a public area.

5. Find the Treat

This game can be really fun and rewarding for puppies. Grab three identical, lightweight and opaque containers. Place all three containers upside down on the ground and place a treat underneath one of them. Bring your puppy into the room and with your lead gently coax her towards the containers. As your dog explores the containers say "Where's the treat?" When your puppy gets excited about the container with the treat, overturn the container so she can claim her reward! You can repeat this process, but make sure your puppy does not see in which container you have placed the treat. This game can be varied with more containers, spreading the containers out and using different kinds of treats.

Here are some more advanced games you can teach your dog:

Agility Training

Dog agility training is a sport in which a handler directs a dog through an obstacle course in a race for both time and accuracy. Dogs run off-leash with no food or toys as incentives, and the handler can touch neither dog nor obstacles. Consequently the handler's controls are limited to voice, movement, and various body signals, requiring exceptional training and coordination. Dogs can begin training for agility at any age; however, care is taken when training dogs under a year old so as to not harm their developing joints.

Dog agility is an international dog sport with many different sanctioning organizations and competitions worldwide. For most agility events there are two organizations involved – a club that actually organizes the event and a sanctioning organization. The sanctioning organization sets the rules, maintains competition records and issues titles or certificates when certain goals are met.

Flyball

This is a race where dogs spring over a series of hurdles, run to a box, snatch up an object (like a ball) and race back to the starting point. The object of this sport is for the dog to finish this task in a minimum amount of time. The turn at the box can mean the difference between a win and a loss, so a lot of effort goes into teaching the dog to do this well. This event is just pure fun for many dogs, and it is open to all dogs, mixed breed and purebred alike.

Canicross

This game involves cross-country running while hitched to a dog. The equipment needed is a running harness, waist belt and a flexible line.   In   competitions   there   are   more   detailed requirements as to the length of the line. This is becoming a popular recreational activity for people who simply want to walk, jog, hike or stroll hands-free with their dog or multiple dogs without holding a leash. Joggers can run without compromising their stride while holding leashes.

Dog Soccer

For this game, a soccer ball or similar sports ball and a chair for the goal will do. For the goal, you can drape a towel around the legs of the chair, leaving one side open. The two likeliest ways for the dog to 'kick' the ball are by using his paws or his nose. While some dogs are particularly skilled at using their paws to propel a ball with accuracy, the easiest way to train most dogs is to teach them to use their noses.

Dog Dancing

This is a modern dog sport that mixes obedience training, tricks and dance for creative interaction between dog and owner. The first step is to teach the dog how to work on both sides of the handler's body, not just the left side as in heeling. The trainer breaks the dance routine into phases with only two or three moves linked together. As they progress, these phases are linked together.

Earth Dog Trials

This activity tests the working ability and instinct of terriers. These breeds are natural hunters of vermin and other quarry that live underground. Earth dog trials involve man-made underground tunnels that the dogs must negotiate, while scenting a rat as the quarry. The dog must follow the scent to the quarry and then "work" the quarry, which involves vocalizing and scratching near the quarry's location. The sport is humane as the quarry is protected from any harm as the dog never gains any access to it.

Visit these websites for more information about dog events and activities:

- http://www.docna.com/
- http://www.k9cpe.com/
- http://www.nadac.com/
- http://www.usdaa.com/
- http://www.ukcdogs.com/agility.htm
- http://www.dogagility.org/
- http://www.akc.org

6. Interactive Toys and Puzzles

There are plenty of toys and puzzles that will allow you to stimulate your dog's mind. These games also allow the owner and dog to strengthen their bond and enrich their relationship. Most of these games, with the exception of the 'Go Go Dog Pals' game, are ideal for inside the apartment as they are small, compact and clean.

Dog Domino

This puzzle compels the dog to learn to look for treats by trying to push the discs into the correct position. This puzzle allows the owner to teach the dog to understand words like: "wait", "go", "back" and "find".

Go Go Dog Pals

This interactive toy is ideal for exercising your dog in a park or open area. Basically, this fast and durable squirrel toy is remotely controlled by the owner so that it chases, or is chased by, the dog.

Dog It Mind Games

Three problem-solving games keep the dog allows the owner to choose the game – the dog will need to rely on her natural curiosity to solve this puzzle, and is rewarded with treats.

Chuckit! Indoor Ball Dog Toy

This plush bouncy ball is ideal for indoor play; this dog toy is designed to allow the dog to chase this soft and resilient ball along the floor.

Chuckit! Indoor Roller Dog Toy

This plush roller that is ideal for indoor play; this dog toy is designed to allow the dog to chase this soft and resilient roller along the floor.

Chuckit! Indoor Launcher Dog Toy

This toy allows the owner to play hands-free fetch indoors and is the perfect accessory for the 'Chuckit! Indoor Roller Dog Toy' and 'Chuckit! Indoor Ball Dog Toy'. Perfect for owners who do not enjoy bending down to pick up a roller or ball, or who hate holding toys that are covered in slimy dog saliva.

In the next chapter, I'll discuss how to keep your dog safe and comfortable on vacations and short trips.

Safe Trips and Vacations with Your Dog

Most pet owners will travel with their pets at times, whether it is to go on vacation, short trips or to simply the occasional trip to the vet. If you anticipate car travel with your dog, then plan ahead and make sure your dog will be safe while she's in your vehicle.

In this chapter, I'll explain:

- Ways to ensure car rides are comfortable and safe for you and your dog
- How to manage car sickness
- How to manage domestic and international air travel for your dog

Safe Car Travel

Before you embark on a car journey with your dog, make sure you have the following items with you:

- Lead & collar
- Water
- No-spill water bowl
- Crate/Harness/Carrier
- Treats
- Wipes or cloths
- Recent picture of your dog

Your priority is your dog's safety, therefore consider how you will secure your dog in your vehicle. Ideally, your dog should always ride in the back seat or back area of your car. If you have no choice but to put your dog in the front passenger side (in a truck, for instance) be aware that dogs, like children, can get hurt if the air bag is deployed. Below are three options for keeping your dog secured in your car:

1.   Crates and Carriers

One way to keep your dog secure in your car is by using a crate. A crate can work very well for any size breed as long as the crate fits safely in your vehicle. Airline-approved crates, made of hard plastic, are usually safer than wire crates. They will provide some protection for your dog in case you are involved in an accident. Keeping your dog in a crate will prevent her from being tossed around in the car or propelled through the windshield. Also, in the case of an accident, a crate will prevent your dog (who may be disorientated or panicked) from exiting the vehicle and being struck by surrounding traffic.

Choose a crate that is large enough for your dog to be comfortable. She should be able to stand up and turn around. However, do not choose a crate that is too large as your dog can be tossed around inside it and injured in the case of an accident. Remember, crates can also be used for potty training – if you are looking for a crate that suits both your dog's travel and potty requirements, make sure you choose a hard plastic crate. The crate itself should be secured with a seat belt in your car. For small and toy breeds, you may wish to use a soft-sided carrier. You can then use a harness or seat belt to secure the carrier in place so she won't be tossed around in case of an accident.

2.   Harness

Another option when you are traveling with your dog in the car is to use a harness. This not only prevents the dog becoming a missile in an accident but will also stop her losing her footing on vinyl or leather seats. You might want to protect your car upholstery from dirty paw prints, puke and potty accidents by using a blanket, quilt or car seat covers. (Earlier I mentioned bringing wipes or cloths, these will come handy in such an accident too!)

Most harnesses work like a seatbelt for dogs, strapping over your dog's chest and holding her securely against the car seat, preferably in the backseat. Harnesses generally work best for medium and large dogs. Reward your dog every time you place her in a harness. In this way your dog won't fuss and will also come to love riding in the car and wearing her special seatbelt.

3.   Dog Barriers

A mesh or metal divider in your SUV or station wagon is a great way to confine your dog to the back of the vehicle. Many dividers are sturdy enough to withstand some impact in an accident.

Should your dog be allowed to hang her head out of the car window? I don't recommend this. While it might be a fun activity for your dog, there is always the danger of injury from the dog jumping out or airborne debris hitting your dog's face. Local traffic laws may also make this illegal.

Exiting the vehicle

Always ensure your dog is on a lead before she exits the car so she does not have a chance to bolt. You can train your dog to jump out of the car on command too. To do this, follow these steps:

1. Ensure your dog is in the car on a lead with the car door or hatchback open.

2. Have a friend gently hold your dog inside the car, or use the lead to keep your dog in place.

3. Use excited body language, and coax your dog out of the car.

4. Just as your dog leaps out of the car, calmly say "out!" (or another word of your choice).

5. Reward your dog.

6. Repeat the process until your dog learns to associate your command with the action of jumping out of the car.

7. Make sure the sessions are short and taught over a few weeks.

Do not train your dog to jump out of the car if the car is too high for your dog's size. If your dog is forced to jump down a long distance, she may suffer an injury.

Keeping your dog cool and comfortable in the car

Always ensure the particular spot in the car where your dog (and crate) will be is well ventilated and shady. If unsure, try riding in that area of the car yourself. If you think the spot could do with more ventilation or shade, you can always have a small internal fan or window visor installed.

Take regular toilet breaks to avoid potty accidents in the car.

Car rides can be boring for all concerned! So make sure your dog has access to her toys and that other passengers, especially children, do not tease or annoy the dog.

Safe Motorcycle Travel

It is generally not a good idea to ride with dogs on a motorcycle.

Dogs are not always aware of the danger of jumping from moving vehicles and so having them unsecured on a motorcycle is exposing them to the risk of death or serious injury. There are soft-sided pet carriers for small and toy dogs to ride with their owners on motorcycles. They are similar to the airline-approved pet carriers which allow you to take small pets on planes. You can find soft-sided pet carriers for sale online and in some pet supply stores or motorcycle shops.

Leaving Your Dog Unattended in a Vehicle

When traveling with your dog, never leave her unattended in your vehicle. It can be dangerous to leave your dog unattended in both hot and cold weather. Temperatures inside the vehicle can become much hotter or colder than the weather outside and your pet may be at risk of either hypothermia or heart stroke.

Managing Motion Sickness

The reason why some dogs get car sick is because they only go in the car when it's time to go to the vet. The vet can be a stressful place for a dog, so she soon associates car trips with an unpleasant outcome and her anxiety causes nausea. Motion sickness can also be caused by stimulation inside your dog's inner ear. Many dogs suffer from some degree of motion sickness when they are small but, fortunately, they do outgrow it. However, others will still suffer from motion sickness into adulthood.

If you have a puppy it's best to train her to like vehicles from the start so she doesn't develop, or continue to suffer, motion sickness. You can do this by spending some playtime inside the vehicle with your dog without going anywhere, allowing your dog to get used to the vehicle when it's stationary. There may be odors or other things associated with the vehicle that are triggering your dog's nausea or anxiety; spending fun time together in the vehicle can help overcome the problem.

Then you can slowly introduce your dog to some short trips in the vehicle and give her treats. Make your trips together fun. If you have a litter of puppies then take more than one puppy at a time so your puppy won't be scared or nervous in the car. Speak soothingly to your puppy in the car. Play music. Roll a window down part way if necessary to allow some fresh air into the vehicle. Secure your puppy properly in the car so she can't roam all over the vehicle.

If your dog is sick in the car, make sure that you clean it up thoroughly. Your dog's sense of smell is very acute and if she smells this odor again it could make her become sick again.

If your dog isn't able to overcome her motion sickness by getting used to riding in your vehicle then you can try some simple home remedies for dogs with nausea. Try giving your dog a few ginger cookies about half an hour before riding in the vehicle, or try some RESCUE® Pet (a natural, alcohol free remedy that help relieve stress).

If none of these suggestions help your dog then you should talk to your veterinarian about available medications to give her for motion sickness. There are several over-the-counter medications you can give to your dog but you should not use them without first discussing them with your vet. Dimenhydrinate (Dramamine®), meclizine (Bonine®), and diphenhydramine (Benadryl®) can all be used for pets to help with nausea. However, be sure to talk to your vet so you will know what dose to give. In severe cases your pet may need a sedative prescribed by a veterinarian. Acepromazine and phenobarbital are commonly used sedatives for this purpose, but are available only by prescription.

Safe Travel Tips for Interstate and Overseas Flights

Flying with your dog can be a daunting experience for even the most experienced of travelers. Just as there are plenty of regulations and security measures for passengers, there are also lots of things to be aware of when you are flying with your dog. It's very important to attend to all of the regulations involved in flying your dog; to speak with knowledgeable representatives; and to confirm flight information. With good planning and attention to detail you and your dog will have a pleasant trip.

Domestic Air Travel

If you are flying domestically there are several ways that your dog can fly. If your dog is small enough and you are also flying yourself, you may be able to take your dog with you in-cabin in a small pet carrier. These carriers must be small enough to fit under the seat in front of you. Their dimensions should be about 8-10 inches (20-25 cm) tall, 17-19 inches (43-48 cm) in length, and about 15 inches (38 cm) wide. It's best to have a soft-sided carrier so it can be 'scrunched' under the seat with your pet inside while maintaining good ventilation on the sides and/or ends. Most of these carriers are shoulder-style bags so they are easy to carry. Airlines vary in how many pets they will allow to fly in-cabin but it's usually between two and ten. You should inform the airline that you will have a pet with you when you make your reservation. There is a charge for having a pet fly with you in-cabin. It can range from about $75US to $200. Your in-cabin pet carrier will count as a piece of carry-on luggage.

If your pet is too large to fly in an in-cabin carrier then you will need to fly your pet as excess baggage. To do this, your pet will require a hard-sided, airline-approved crate. These crates are usually made of hard plastic and have ventilation in the upper sides. They also have a metal grill door. The crates will also have a rim or lip along the middle of the crate. This is to prevent other crates and baggage from sliding into them and blocking the ventilation for your dog.

You will need to choose a crate that is amply big enough for your dog but not so big that your dog will be tossed around inside it in case of air turbulence. Your dog should be able to stand up easily in the crate without her head touching the ceiling. She should be able to lie down comfortably.

Check with the airline when you make your reservation to make sure that they can accommodate the size of crate that your dog requires. Some planes at smaller airports cannot accommodate crates that are size 500 or larger. If your dog requires a size 700 crate you can probably only fly on the largest jets with her. Most planes will be able to accept crates up to size 400 without a problem but make sure you talk to the airline representative or even someone in cargo to make certain that there won't be a problem accepting your dog's crate if it is very large.

If you have a large dog you won't be able to push her into a smaller crate in order to get her aboard the plane. Airline representatives are trained to check carefully to make sure that dogs are in appropriate crates. They will refuse to accept your dog and crate if they aren't satisfied that your dog is properly crated.

When you put your dog in the crate for travel you should also place some absorbent material in the bottom of the crate, such as a blanket or some newspapers. The crate should come with small plastic food and water bowls that snap onto the metal door. You should see to it that these are in place and have food and water ready to place in them at the airport. Complete most of your paperwork for the trip ahead of time. This usually includes a health certificate from your veterinarian stating that the dog is healthy and up-to-date on vaccinations (especially rabies). If your dog is flying during cold weather, you may need a statement of acclimation from your veterinarian stating your pet is able to fly at colder temperatures.

You should start preparing your dog for travel a few days or weeks before the trip. Whether your pet will be traveling in a pet carrier or in a crate, you can help her get ready for the trip by letting her spend some time in the carrier or crate and making it a pleasant experience for her. Place treats in the carrier or crate. Let her go in and out as she likes. Leave the carrier or crate down in the floor for her so it's not a fearful object. By the time she's ready to travel the carrier or crate shouldn't be something scary. She should be able to spend a few hours inside without becoming anxious.

Be sure to take your dog to the vet a few days before your trip to get her health certificate. Most states require a health certificate with rabies verification when passing from one state to another, although this isn't usually enforced when driving between states. However, the health certificate can be asked for when you fly with your pet. If you are flying during cold weather, your vet should sign a statement saying that it's safe for your pet to travel at lower temperatures.

Most airlines will not accept brachycephalic breeds (short-nosed) for flights in the summer time, even with statements from a veterinarian.

Be sure to have your dog's identification handy. Some people like to attach ID to their dog's collar in case the dog gets out of the crate. Other people are afraid that the dog may get the collar caught in the crate, so they don't put the collar on the dog in the crate. They tape the collar to the outside of the crate with the ID attached to it. Make sure that you are carrying your dog's paperwork with you, such as a copy of her registration papers, sales receipts, photos and other identifying papers in case she should get lost and you have to prove she is your dog. If your dog is micro-chipped, make sure that you have her microchip contact information with you and that it's up-to-date.

You will need to offer your dog a very light meal about four hours before you plan to fly. This is technically required by the United States Department of Agriculture (UDA) and Federal Aviation Administration (FAA). But please don't force your dog to eat or feed her a large meal. This could make her become ill when she flies.

Be sure to get to the airport early but not too early. Walk your dog before putting her in the crate at the airport. This can help your dog avoid having any accidents in the crate, especially if it's a long flight. If your dog is flying as checked baggage then it's good to get to the airport about two hours before your flight. You will take your dog to the check-in counter where she will be picked up and taken to a waiting area to get on the plane. Once you are on the plane you can ask the flight attendant to double check that your dog has been loaded correctly.

Be very careful about giving any kind of medication to pets who are flying, especially if they are flying as checked baggage or cargo. In these cases there is no one around to check on your dog if she should experience any side effects from the medication. In most cases dogs that fly will sleep throughout a flight and will be better off without any medication.

Overseas Travel

If you are flying overseas with your dog then many of the same things that have already been stated will apply. You will need the same type of crate for your dog and you will need an international health certificate from your veterinarian. If flying into the USA, your health certificate will also need to be endorsed by an APHIS-accredited veterinarian in order to satisfy the USDA. Some quarantine regulations will depend on the country you and your dog are visiting.

Whether you are visiting a foreign country or moving there permanently, it's a good idea to check with that country's consulate or embassy about regulations for bringing a pet into the country. Check http://www.state.gov/s/cpr/rls/fco/ for foreign embassies.

The following countries state that they have quarantine regulations regarding dogs:

- United Kingdom – 183 days; exemptions: dogs from Ireland, PETS qualifiers

- Hawaii – 30 days; exemptions: guide dogs

- Australia – 30 days; exemptions: dogs from Cocos Island, NZ, Norfolk Island

- Guam – 120 days; exemptions: dogs from Hawaii & UK

- Hong Kong 30 days; exemptions: dogs from UK, Ireland, Australia, NZ

- New Zealand – 30 days; exemptions: dogs from Australia, Norfolk Island

- Norway – 120 days plus 60 in home

- Iceland – 56 days; exemptions: 42 days for dogs from UK, Norway, Sweden

- Japan – 14 days; exemptions: military allowed in-home quarantine

- Ireland – 30 days plus in-home 5 months; exemptions: UK

- United States – 30 day maximum following exam and vaccination; exemptions: immune animals 30 days min. from vaccination date

If you are flying to any of these places with your dog then it's best to speak directly to someone in authority who can advise you about how imported pets are handled. For example, although the United States says that it has quarantine for animals coming from abroad, in fact, if a dog has been immunized in its country and shows no signs of illness, it may be brought into the country.

Hundreds of thousands of puppies and dogs are imported into the USA each year under these rules.

The United Kingdom still maintains a quarantine period. However, for dogs that qualify under the PETS qualifiers scheme, they may obtain a pet passport and enter the country as visitors. Each year many dogs from other countries visit the UK and some even compete at the famous Crufts dog show. PETS allows dogs, cats and ferrets entering from fellow EU countries into the UK and other EU countries. Dogs from the United States are also eligible for a PETS passport. You can contact PETS directly for more information about obtaining a PETS passport:

'Pet Travel Scheme' helpline

Telephone: +44 (0)870 241 1710 – Monday to Friday – 8am to 6pm UK time (closed bank holidays).

Email: quarantine@animalhealth.gsi.gov.uk. Please enclose your postal address and a daytime telephone number.

Fax: +44 (0) 1245 458749. There is also a minicom/textphone number for the deaf and hard of hearing: 0845 300 1998

If you are entering the UK from a non-qualifying country then your pet must spend six months in quarantine.

For more information about quarantine regulations for these pets in the UK you can contact the British government directly:

Quarantine section

Telephone: +44 (0) 1245 454860

Email: quarantine@animalhealth.gsi.gov.uk – Please enclose your postal address and a daytime telephone number.

If you are coming from a country that is required to take part in the quarantine, you can choose from different participating kennels around the country. It can be very costly to kennel your dog for several months so you may not wish to do this with your dog.

If you are planning to visit another country with your dog then you will need to check the specific situation in that country and find out their quarantine procedures. For example, if you are sending a dog to Australia from the United States, quarantine times can vary. Blood sampling is done for rabies and pets spend time in one of three government animal http://www.daff.gov.au/aqis/cat-dogs in Sydney, Melbourne or Perth.

For more information about different countries and their requirements you can visit PetFriendlyTravel.com.

In the next chapter, I'll discuss how to care for your dog's eyes, ears, teeth and coat.

Grooming and Care for Your Apartment Dog

Grooming is an essential part of canine care. You should follow a regular and gentle grooming regime from puppyhood. This is because your dog will learn to love the care and attention you provide without resistance or fuss. Plus your dog will reap the benefits of living without the pain or stress associated with bad hygiene.

In this chapter, I'll explain:

- How to prevent ear infections by keeping your dog's ears clean and dry.
- When and how to clip your dog's nails safely, without the need to wrestle your dog.
- Simple ways to keep your dog's teeth clean and her breath fresh.
- How to keep your dog's eyes clean and what to do about common eye, lash and lid complaints.
- How to care for different types of coats and which brushes and combs are suitable.
- The safe and hassle-free way to bathe your dog.

Ear Care

Your role as a dog owner is to ensure your dog's ears are kept clean and dry. This will prevent infections, which are not only very painful but can also lead to other complications such as scarring and deafness. Dogs are particularly susceptible to ear infections if their ears are long; these dogs profiled in this guide are particularly susceptible:

- Basset Hound
- Beagle
- Bichon Frise
- Cavalier King Charles Spaniel
- Cocker Spaniel
- Dachshund

This is because the hair limits air flow which then allows bacteria to build up around any trapped moisture and debris (like grass seeds, for example). These dogs' ears should be checked on a regular basis, at least once a week.

Dogs with short, open ears tend to have less ear issues, so a monthly checkup is fine.

Regardless of your dog's ear type, here is a list of things you can do to look after your dog's ears:

- If you notice a strong, pungent odor or discharge; reddened ears; or reluctance by your dog to having her ears handled, then take her to the veterinarian. You might also notice your dog shaking her head or scratching her ears more often.
- A small amount of brown wax or dirt in the folds of the outer ear is typical and can be cleaned by wrapping cotton, gauze or a soft cloth around your finger and gently wiping the area.
- Trim the hair from the underside of your dog's ear. You can do this yourself or you can ask your groomer to do so. This increases air flow and prevents the hair from trapping debris which can then make its way to the ear canal.

How to effectively clean your dog's ears

Here are seven steps to cleaning your dog's ears:

1. Take your dog outside to do this as this procedure can be quite messy if your dog shakes her head!
2. Have on hand a veterinary ear wash or 50/50 mixture of tepid water and white vinegar. (Do not use apple cider vinegar.) Double check that the water's temperature is actually tepid (between 20 and 30°C which is between 68 and 86°F).
3. Lay your dog to one side and pull your dog's ear up and out.
4. Gently douche the ear cleaner into the dog's ear. Do not poke or squirt anything into her ears as this can perforate her ear drums.
5. Massage the base of the ear until you hear a squishy sound. Allow your dog to get up and shake – you may find that gunk will be released from her ears (which is why this should be done outside).
6. Clean any gunk off the outer ear by gently wiping it with gauze, cotton or cloth.
7. Repeat the process on the other ear.

Nail Care

Most dogs are reluctant for their paws to be handled and so nail clipping can be quite a tiring activity for many owners. There are four things you can do to ensure that nail clipping does not become an upsetting and frustrating experience for you and your dog:

1. As soon as you bring your puppy home, start the daily ritual of handling all four of her paws. Pat and lightly squeeze her paws and give her treats and praise; your puppy will learn that having her paws handled by you is nothing to worry about. I'd also recommend using a pair of 'dummy clippers' (clippers with the blades removed) and pretend to clip your puppy's nails often. Whilst dummy clipping, treat and praise your puppy. This way, your puppy won't know the difference

between the dummy and the real thing! (Just make sure your dummy and real clippers look similar.)

2. Ensure your dog has the opportunity to play and exercise on hard surfaces often. A concrete balcony floor or other hard outdoors surfaces may help in this regard. This has the effect of naturally wearing your dog's nails, thus reducing the frequency of clipping required.

3. Take the time to learn how to properly cut your dog's nails. By doing so, you lessen the risk of injuring your dog. The main injury caused by nail clipping is when owners and groomers unintentionally cut the quick of the dog's nail (this causes bleeding and is quite painful). Later, I explain how to cut your dog's nails in the best possible way.

4. If you are too scared to do it yourself, then take your dog to a reputable groomer or veterinarian. This option is obviously more expensive than DIY, but is worth your peace of mind. Having said that, I have been to a groomer who cut my dog's nails and caused bleeding, so make sure your groomer is experienced and properly trained.

When is it time to cut your dog's nails?

No part of the dog's nail should touch and scrape the ground as she walks. If you hear your dog's nails clicking on the floor, then it's time for a trim.

If you don't cut your dog's nails, you run the risk of your dog developing split nails. Split nails are common in dogs and can be quite a nuisance. The split nails will frequently catch on the carpet, blankets and bedding and this can cause some pain. Splitting nails are not usually an indicator of malnutrition or disease but a product of the nails being overly long and not properly trimmed. Regular walks and regular trimming of nails is the best prevention against split nails. Nail files like the 'Peticure' are excellent ways to prevent nail splitting.

Equipment

There are three main types of clippers:

1. Scissor-type clippers. These are ideal for big dog nails. Make sure they're sharp and properly aligned so they don't mash the end of your dog's nails.
2. Guillotine clippers. These are the easiest to use.
3. Battery operated grinders. These take longer but reduce the risk of cutting the quick (although it's not failsafe).

Avoiding the quick

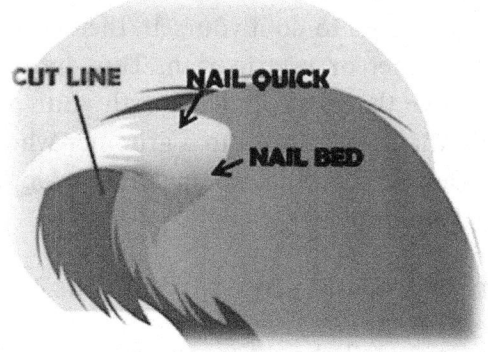

The dog's nail quick contains the blood supply and is the bony base of the nail. The aim of trimming your dog's nail is to cut as close as possible to the quick, without cutting into the quick itself. Dogs with white or light-colored claws have quicks that are visible – the quick is pinkish in color.

It's virtually impossible to see the quick on black nails. Therefore make small nips and start at the tips of the nail. When a small grey area shows in the center of the nail, then you are approaching the quick – it's best to stop at this point.

How to trim your dog's nails

Here are some steps to successfully trimming your dog's nails:

1. Ensure you are relaxed and not in any rush. Have someone assist you.
2. Ensure that you have read the instructions for the clippers and that they are in perfect working order.
3. Choose an enclosed space, so your puppy does not run away if she breaks free.
4. Hold your dog in a hug with your less dominant arm, with the inner forearm resting against your dog's chest. You can then use that hand to hold your dog's paw. Use your other free (dominant) hand to hold the clippers. It's best that your dog is resting in a down position or, for larger dogs, on their side.
5. If your dog fusses or wiggles, don't stop. If you let go, your dog will quickly learn to fuss whenever she does not want you to do something.
6. Align the clipper on the claw, and notice the quick.
7. Cut below the quick to avoid injury (see 'Avoiding the Quick' above) and at an angle so the trimmed nail is about parallel to the floor.
8. If you strike the quick, it is going to hurt and your dog will bleed. Use light pressure towards the nail to prevent the blood flow. However, this may be challenging as your dog may then squirm, squeal and struggle. The bleeding should not last more than five minutes and you can use styptic powder to stop the flow more quickly.

9. Trim the nails straight across, being sure that you haven't left any jagged ends that may catch on carpeting or fabric as the animal makes her or her way throughout the house. Don't forget to reward your pet after you are finished and praise her for staying so good.

Dental Care

Dental care is essential for all dogs. Larger dogs tend to be less susceptible to dental problems than smaller ones. In fact, many of the breeds discussed in this guide fit the profile of the typical small or toy breed that is susceptible to dental problems. These dogs are at risk of dental issues:

- Chinese Crested
- Chihuahua
- Dachshund
- Maltese
- Papillon
- Pomeranian

When a dog enjoys good dental hygiene, her teeth are white and gums are pink, with no redness or swelling along the gum line. Signs of bad dental hygiene include yellowish discoloration, brown residue at the base of the teeth, redness, swelling, bleeding or bad breath. Bad breath can also be a sign of some other underlying medical condition. If you notice discoloration on one side of the mouth and not the other, then your dog may be chewing on one side to avoid pain. This may be the result of a cracked tooth or other dental issues.

Dogs need good dental hygiene routine as much as people do. They don't usually get cavities but they are prone to plaque and tartar (which is the ugly brown buildup you see on some dogs' teeth). Plaque and tartar can lead to bad breath and more serious dental problems. You can keep your dog's teeth pearly white and remove plaque by regularly brushing her teeth.

Brushing is essential to keeping your dog's teeth clean and removing the slight yellowing caused by tartar. Brushing is recommended daily or at least several times a week. There are brushes made for dogs that are angled to fit into your dog's mouth. Some people prefer to use small dental pads or rubber "fingers" that fit over their finger. They can then slip this little rubber piece into their dog's mouth to do the brushing.

There are also toothpastes that are specially made for dogs. These toothpastes come in flavors that are designed to appeal to a dog's taste buds such as peanut butter, beef and so on. Most dogs consider these pastes to be treats so after you introduce them to your dog it's easy to get your dog to open up and let you brush her teeth.

Be warned: human toothpaste is fatal to dogs. Never use human toothpaste when brushing your dog's teeth.

Brushing your dog's teeth is very much like brushing your own teeth. The only real difference is that you will need to make sure you brush far in the back of your dog's mouth since dogs have such long, deep jaws. Make sure you concentrate on the outside of the dog's teeth since many dogs get tartar buildup in this area.

Even with good brushing your dog will probably need to have her teeth professionally cleaned by your veterinarian occasionally. Vets can also talk to you about appropriate mouth washes and toothpaste with special enzymes that help dissolve tarter.

In addition to brushing, there are various other foods or treats that will help keep your dog's teeth and gums clean and suit your dog's size and weight:

- Raw meaty bones
- Marrow bones
- Frozen poultry
- Small Kong toys
- Nylon bones (some are flavored but you can also soak them overnight in meat broth to add flavor)
- Greenies
- Bully sticks
- Dentastix
- High quality grain-free kibble

Fresh Breath

Some people think that it's normal for all dogs to have bad breath, but this is not the case. If your dog's breath smells, then your dog might be experiencing gum disease and bad teeth. The odor is caused by bacteria and infection which, if left untreated, can cause serious dental problems and can be quite painful for your dog.

Your dog may not show signs of discomfort or soreness as dogs often adapt to their lot in life. So, if you notice bad breath but no other symptoms, don't be shy about approaching your veterinarian. Some dogs may refuse their food (as chewing causes further pain).

If your dog's breath is stinky and your veterinarian has given your dog's teeth the all clear, then your dog may be eating some smelly items. Perhaps she found something foul or is eating her poop. You can try to get her to stop paying attention to these things but, in the meantime, it will also help if you give her some better-tasting things on which to chew. Try some good oral chews recommended by the Veterinary Oral Health Council, such as Canine Greenies or a good mint-flavored chew to freshen her breath.

You can also give your dog treats for good breath. There are a number of dog treats that may improve a dog's breath. Some of them are mint-flavored or have other flavors that are more appealing to dogs, such as beef. Try some and see if your dog likes them.

Eye Care

If your puppy's eyes are healthy, then all you need to do is simply wipe some gunk from your dog's eyes with a damp cloth occasionally. There are also various brands of eyewash that can be used to flush out debris, dust or other irritants from your dog's eyes. One such product is called Eye Clens. You can also use eye washes with herbal formulas that have anti-bacterial properties; these include chamomile, calendula and goldenseal.

Tear stains

The most common eye issue is tear stains. Tear stains are especially common among breeds with light or white-colored fur such as the Chihuahua, Lhasa Apso, Maltese, Cocker Spaniel, Toy Poodle, Shih Tzu and West Highland White Terrier. The rusty-colored discharge can be rather unsightly and can emit a strong odor.

Causes of Tear Stains

There are many causes of tear stains, ranging from allergies, diet, poor health, infection and genetic predisposition. Infected tear ducts are a common cause of excess moisture, which will result in staining.

Tear stains can be a sign of a foreign body in the eye, injury, allergies or conjunctivitis. Conjunctivitis usually results in a greenish stain. Genetics, affecting eye structure, may result in excess tears.

Apart from staining, other symptoms of poor health that manifest in dogs' eyes can be cloudiness, inflammation or bleeding. If these symptoms appear, seek immediate veterinary attention.

Staining can also be caused by your dog consuming water with excess minerals.

Cleaning Stains

If your dog is otherwise healthy, then staining can be managed by cleaning the area under your dog's eyes. A very important part of puppy and dog care is cleaning stains regularly, as the dampness can be a breeding ground for bacteria and yeast. Cleaning should be done with care since dogs' eyes are just as sensitive as those of humans.

Here are some options for cleaning stains:

1. Mix equal parts corn starch and peroxide to clean stains and apply the solution to your dog's fur. If you're not comfortable using peroxide on your dog's face, you can try a mixture of boric acid powder and cornstarch instead. Let the mixture dry for at least a couple hours and then rinse your dog's fur thoroughly with lukewarm water. Ensure these solutions do not make contact with your dog's eyes.

2. Mix milk and peroxide in equal amounts. Make a paste by adding in cornstarch and allow the mixture to set for four hours. You can use this preparation to wash and condition the fur of your dog.

3. One product that has been used by breeders and exhibitors to remove tear stains is Diamond Eye Tear Stain Remover. This clears up the staining and also keeps the skin under the eye healthy.

Preventing Tear Stains

The first, and most obvious method, is to gently wipe any sleet or debris from your dog's eyes with a damp cloth. You can use eye wipes especially made for dogs.

Antacids that contain calcium can also be fed to the dog. Such a product is Tums, which can change the dog's pH balance and reduce yeast.

One home remedy that you can use to inhibit the growth of bacteria and yeast is to mix a teaspoon of apple cider vinegar with your dog's drinking water.

If your dog's staining is a result of a genetic 'fault', then eye duct surgical procedures to increase tear capacity may be required; ask your veterinarian.

How Diet Can Help With Staining Issues

Your dog's diet goes a long way in preventing tear stains. Boost your dog's immune system by feeding her healthy, natural food. If your dog has a healthy immune system she will likely not encounter these infections. Feed your dog high-quality food that is devoid of artificial flavors, colors or preservatives.

Cataracts

Cataracts are often associated with older people rather than with dogs. However, dogs can develop cataracts and frequently do. Dogs profiled in this guide that may be prone to cataracts are:

- Bichon Frise
- Boston Terrier
- Chow Chow
- Dachshund
- Italian Greyhound
- Toy Poodle

A cataract is the clouding and loss of transparency of the lens. Cataracts can lead to blindness and are fairly common in old dogs. Cataracts are usually accompanied by other signs of aging such as arthritis of the joints and a general slowing down of the metabolism.

Cataracts most commonly develop with age, but sometimes they can occur after trauma, as a consequence of glaucoma (high pressure in the eye) or diabetes, and due to inherited conditions. So, if your dog develops cataracts, have her tested for diabetes.

Cataracts occur when the levels between water and protein in the dog's lens are disrupted. In a healthy eye, the lens consists of 66% water and 33% protein. If the eye's flushing system begins to fail, the eye will not be able to remove any of the excess proteins. This excess protein makes the lens appear cloudy.

How do you know if your dog has cataracts?

Many dog owners notice that their dog's eyes start to look increasingly white and cloudy. Your dog may start to walk into objects and be reluctant to go out in the dark, as the first thing that deteriorates with cataracts is night vision. In many cases, it is the veterinarian who notices the development of cataracts at a regular check-over.

Can you prevent cataracts?

Keeping your dog at a healthy weight and feeding her a good diet are the only ways to help prevent cataracts. Obesity can bring on cataracts through diabetes mellitus which is a common cause of cataracts.

Free radicals are also thought to accelerate the development of cataracts. Anti-oxidants (found mainly in vitamins) can help prevent damage from these radicals that circulate in our bodies.

What can be done about cataracts?

Cataracts usually develop gradually with old age and can lead to blindness in one or both eyes. Many dogs cope well with the condition. Since dogs don't rely solely on their vision to get around and have their smell to guide them too, blindness does not have to be disabling for a dog. If you make sure that you don't change the furniture around and take some extra care when you walk your dog, you will be amazed how well dogs can cope with blindness. Children should exercise caution when dealing with a dog with cataract as they can startle the dog.

Cataract surgery is an option, especially in severe cases, but it can be expensive.

Conjunctivitis

Conjunctivitis is the inflammation or infection of the conjunctiva in the dog's eye. The conjunctiva is the thin membrane that covers the inside of the eyelid. The condition makes the dog's eye appear red. Conjunctivitis is often called pink eye, especially if the entire eye is red. Discharge can accompany conjunctivitis and this can be clear, brown or yellow-greenish in color. Common causes of conjunctivitis are allergies, as well as bacterial and viral infections.

How do you know your dog has conjunctivitis?

You might notice that your dog's eyes appear red and show some discharge. Conjunctivitis can be very agitating and painful to your dog. Many dogs will paw at their eyes and/or rub their face on a variety of surfaces to eliminate their discomfort.

If the conjunctivitis is due to an infection, the eyes may close up and stick shut, excreting a yellowish or green discharge. Allergic conjunctivitis will often have a thin and clear discharge that is very similar to the dog's natural tears.

What can be done about conjunctivitis?

When your dog shows signs of conjunctivitis, take her to the veterinarian. Conjunctivitis is very irritating and because the eyes are sensitive, it should be treated immediately to avoid further damage. If left untreated, conjunctivitis can also affect other parts of the eye and this can become quite serious and difficult to treat.

Your veterinarian will give the eyes a thorough examination. In serious cases, she might take a swab and send it to a lab to find out what causes the inflammation. If necessary, the veterinarian will prescribe an ointment that might contain antibiotics and/or steroids to help reduce the inflammation fast. Many eye ointments have to be applied often, sometimes 3–5 times daily, to achieve the desired effect.

Dry eye

Dry eye is fairly common in dogs. It occurs when the eyes don't produce enough tears to keep the eye lubricated. In most cases, dry eye is *immune mediated*. This means that the body attacks its own cells, in this case the cells that produce tear fluid. Dry eyes are often very itchy, irritated and painful. The dog may feel the need to keep her eyes closed and feel very depressed with her condition.

How do you know that your dog has dry eye?

Your dog may develop a thick, sticky, yellow discharge. She might appear uncomfortable and rub her eyes on furniture or on the floor. To diagnose dry eye, your veterinarian will perform a simple 'eye strip' test. A thin test strip is applied to the eyes. The strip measures the amount of tears the dog produces within a specified period of time; insufficient tears are a sign of dry eye. Tears have an antiseptic quality and so poorly lubricated eyes are also prone to infection.

What can be done about dry eye?

To treat the condition, you will have to administer eye drops regularly (5–10 times daily) to lubricate your dog's eyes. If an infection is present, your dog might also need antibiotic eye drops for a period of time in addition to the lubricant. In addition, cortico steroid eye drops and eye drops containing cyclosporines (an immuno-suppressant) can help ease the condition. Surgery can be a permanent solution to the problem.

Can you prevent dry eye?

In one word, no. There's nothing you can do to prevent this condition other than avoiding dog breeds that are commonly susceptible to this condition, especially Yorkshire Terriers.

Eye lash and lid problems

There are many different lash and lid problems from which dogs can suffer. These problems can range from the edges of the eyelids being rolled inwards (entropion) or outwards (ectropion), to ingrown lashes. Eye problems need to be evaluated by a veterinarian, and should not be ignored.

Dogs susceptible to entropian are:

- Chow Chow
- Cocker Spaniel (also prone to ectropion)
- Maltese

How do you know your dog has an eye lash or lid problem?

Lash and lid problems generally cause great discomfort and irritation – infections, redness and inflammation may be present. Your dog's eye may be pink in color and discharge may also be present. Most dogs will rub or scratch their eyes, show frequent blinking or winking, and rub their eyes on objects such as blankets and furniture. They may also try to bury their heads in your hands and make pleasurable moans when you rub their eyes gently.

What can be done about eyelash or lid problems?

It is important to remember that your dog is going to be extremely uncomfortable if anything is bothering her eyes. So, if you suspect your dog has some type of lid or lash problem you should take her to the veterinarian immediately. In many cases, surgery can correct the issue permanently.

Coat Care

No matter what kind of dog you have, some grooming will be required. However, different dogs will have different grooming requirements, depending on their coat type and length. Short, smooth coats generally require the least amount of time and attention. Medium-long coats require more care, such as brushing and bathing. And dogs with long coats usually require the most brushing, combing and care. Always brush the dog in the same direction of hair growth to remove all tangles, debris or knots. For dogs that have double coats, continue the grooming process by using your hand to push the coat against the direction of growth, and brush the undercoat to detangle all knots. Finish brushing with a slicker or pin brush for a sleeker appearance.

Smooth coated dogs

If you have a dog with a short, smooth coat you will most likely need a good brush, such as a boar bristle brush, curry brush or a hound glove. A hound glove or curry brush removes dead hair and gives your dog's coat a good glossy shine. As for a bristle brush it is excellent for most types of dogs and is useful to smooth out a dog's coat.

You may also need to use a pair of scissors to trim hair between the toes, around the ears or along the bottom of the tail, just to tidy your dog's appearance. For bathing you can use a good dog shampoo and a dollop of conditioner. No blow drying is necessary - just towel dry your dog.

Short-haired dogs

Short-haired dogs are considered 'wash and wear' dogs because you can simply bathe and towel-dry them. A slicker brush is all that is needed to remove any dead hair.

Medium coated dogs

For a dog with a medium coat more grooming will be necessary. You will need to brush your dog several times per week to keep the hair from tangling or matting. You will require a good brush, such as a boar bristle brush; a good comb, such as a Greyhound comb; and a Pin Brush to separate the dog's long coat and brush it carefully.

With a medium or long coat it is always best to dampen the hair before you brush it with the Pin Brush.

You can use a detangler or mix a small amount of conditioner in a spray bottle and lightly spray it over the long hair before brushing. This will keep the hair from breaking off when you brush it.

For bathing you should look for a shampoo that has conditioners in it. Make sure that you rinse thoroughly. You should then apply a small amount of conditioner and let it sit for a couple of minutes before rinsing thoroughly. You may wish to blow-dry a dog with medium hair to encourage the hair to lie properly and look good. You can brush the hair while you blow dry.

Long-haired dogs

If you have a dog with long hair, such as a Maltese or Yorkshire Terrier, then you will be spending more time grooming your dog. A dog with long hair needs to be brushed daily to keep the hair from matting and to keep it looking good. You will need a good brush, such as a boar bristle brush; a good comb, such as a Greyhound comb; and a Pin Brush. Always make sure that you dampen, but not soak, your longhaired dog's coat before brushing to prevent the hair from breaking. You can use a detangler or put some conditioner in a spray bottle and mix with water then lightly spray over your dog's coat before brushing. For dogs with long hair it is best to brush your dog in sections and brush down to the skin to make sure that no mats are missed. You may want to invest in a grooming table since your dog will be spending a lot of time being groomed. You can teach your dog to lie down on her side to make grooming more comfortable for both of you.

A good brush for long haired or curly haired breed is the slicker brush. The slicker brush is made up of tiny wire bristles very close together. While this type of brush can be very harsh, it is essential for some dog's coats. When used properly, the slicker brush readily removes dead hair and matting.

Choose a shampoo that will condition your dog's coat and rinse thoroughly. Use a good conditioner and let it sit on your dog's coat for several minutes, especially the ends of the coat where the coat may come in contact with the floor. Rinse thoroughly. You should plan on bathing your dog at least once a month. You will probably need to use a blow dryer to help speed the drying process. Again, it will be more comfortable for you and your dog if you teach your dog to lie on her side while you blow dry her hair. Be sure to dry your dog everywhere to avoid leaving damp spots that could become itchy or turn into hotspots for your dog.

Wirehaired coats

Some breeds have wirehaired coats. These coats can be harder for pet owners to groom; you may need to take your dog to a professional groomer. If you wish to groom your wirehaired dog yourself you will need a terrier palm glove to remove loose dead hair, a comb, a good pair of scissors, and clippers or stripping knives, depending on how you intend to groom your dog. You can learn to clip your wirehaired dog's coat yourself and talking to people who groom their dogs. You can also learn to hand strip your wirehaired dog's coat. This is the process of plucking out dead hairs as they become straggly to keep your dog looking neat and tidy. Terrier coats are not conditioned the same way as other breeds. They are not intended to be soft. Instead, they should be harsh and crisp in order to be weather-proof.

Hand Stripping

Although many breeds, including spaniels and terriers would benefit from hand stripping, the breeds that are usually hand stripped are those with wiry coats, such as the:

- Affenpinscher
- Dachshund (Wirehaired)
- Miniature Schnauzer
- Norfolk Terrier

Hand-stripping a dog's coat is an essential part of grooming, especially during summer. Hand-stripping is the process of plucking the outer hairs from the coat after it is dried after a wash. The top coat is pulled out using fingers or a stripping knife. The knife is not used to cut but only to pull the hair out, which is held between the thumb and forefinger. Sometimes chalk, rosin powder or ear powder is used on the coat to help the groomer maintain a firmer grip. Hand Stripping is preferred by most dog groomers over clippers, as hand stripping maintains the proper coarseness of the wire coat. Clipping often makes the wiry coat soft. Without the outer wire coat, the coat color will change and fade, for example a black Schnauzer's coat may fade to gray with continual clipping instead of stripping. Apart from maintaining the proper texture and color of the coat, hand stripping can alleviate certain skin conditions caused by blocked pores, like 'Schnauzer bumps'. Even though some dogs may not like being hand stripped, it is not a painful process when done properly as wiry hair is not attached to the dog's body like other types of coats.

Choosing the right cut for your dog

You may choose to keep your dog's coat in a particular style and cut. The shorter cuts are perfect for busy owners of long-haired dogs as minimal upkeep is required. These short cuts also reduce the coat's heaviness, giving the dog the opportunity to stay cooler in the summer months.

1. Puppy cut or kennel cut

The dog's hair is cut the same length (up to 2 inches or 6 centimeters) all over. This makes brushing and coat maintenance much easier. Always be clear with the groomer exactly how short you would like the coat to be. This cut suits breeds like the Bichon Frise, Maltese, Havanese, Yorkshire Terrier, Cocker Spaniel and Poodle (a pompom at the end of the tail is optional).

2.　Teddy bear cut

This is the same as a puppy cut, but the legs and face are left full and round, giving your dog a cuddly, teddy bear look. A maintenance cut will be required every six to eight weeks.

3.　Lamb cut

This cut is similar to the teddy bear trim, but the hair on the legs and face is cut a bit shorter. A maintenance cut will be required every six to eight weeks.

4.　Schnauzer cut

This cut is great for Schnauzers and Yorkshire Terriers as well as other dog breeds with similar hair. The Schnauzer cut leaves longer hair on the dog's legs, whilst the dog's back and sides are clipped very short. The lower side of the dog's body sports a fringe. The dog also sports a mustache.

5.　Poodle cut

The dog has a trimmed belly and face, leaving the legs, ears and tail thick and fluffy. This cut is not only for Poodles, but also other dog breeds with curly or thick hair.

6.　English saddle cut (Toy Poodle)

This for owners wishing to give their Toy Poodle that classic French look. The face, throat, feet forelegs, and base of tail are shaved, leaving puffs on the forelegs and a pompom on the tip of the tail. The rest of the coat is left full and is shaped according to the owner's preference.

7. Continental cut (Toy Poodle)

The face, throat, feet, rear legs and base of the tail are shaved. Pompoms are on the hips and the end of the tail. The legs are shaved leaving bracelets on the hind legs and puffs on the forelegs.

Shedding

Almost all kinds of animals with fur shed hair, especially dogs. Dogs shed hair in order for them to grow healthier ones or to adapt from the weather. For example, dogs shed their winter coat, so they can feel cooler. Some dogs shed more because of their breed. Dogs that grow longer hair usually shed more hair than the short-coated ones. As a general rule, all dogs shed. However, it's been said that Pulik and Yorkshire Terriers do not shed at all. In reality, they shed very little. Shedding rates for other dogs are as follows:

No Shedding	Minimal	Moderate	Heavy
Puli	Bichon Frise	Affenpinscher	Chow Chow
Yorkshire Terrier	Bolognese	Bassett Hound	Pug
	Boston Terrier	Beagle	
	Chinese Crested	English Bulldog	
	Coton de Tulear	Cavalier King Charles Spaniel	
	Havanese	Chihuahua	
	Italian Greyhound	Cocker Spaniel	
	Lhasa Apso	Pembroke Welsh Corgi	
	Maltese	Dachshund	

Miniature Schnauzer	Japanese Chin	
	Miniature Pinscher	
Norfolk Terrier		
Shih Tzu	Papillon	
Toy Poodle	Pekingese	
West Highland Terrier	Pomeranian	

Shedding is very normal in healthy dogs; however, you can ensure your dog does not shed excessively with:

- Regular grooming. Clean your dog regularly to get rid of parasites that live under their fur. It can also help your dog feel fresh and clean, thus lessens their irritation.
- Visiting your veterinarian regularly. Veterinarians are the best source of information about your pet. A regular visit may help them determine sickness at an early stage or give you assurance that you are taking care of a healthy dog.
- Cleaning your pet's surroundings. This can help reduce your dog's source of irritation and parasites.
- Using the right grooming equipment for your dog.

Excessive shedding

Excessive shedding occurs when dogs are stressed, sick or in poor nutrition. Some dogs might have skin allergies or sensitive skin. Other causes include: fleas, parasites, skin infection and allergies. If you are not sure about the cause of excessive shedding, visit your veterinarian and take not if there are any other symptoms such as: sores, wounds, rashes, bumps, bald spots, loose hair and excessive scratching.

Hypoallergenic Dogs

Some dogs are deemed to be 'hypoallergenic' because they are deemed to cause little or no reaction in people who suffer allergies. However, all dogs produce the same allergen and so the 'hypoallergenic' dog is just a myth. Studies show there is no connection between a dog's shedding rate and capacity to cause allergic reactions. Instead, allergens found in dogs are from their saliva and dander.

Despite this research, people have said that the following breeds are considered to be 'hypoallergenic':

- Bichon Frise
- Bolognese
- Chinese Crested
- Coton de Tulear
- Havanese
- Maltese
- Miniature Schnauzer
- Puli
- Shih Tzu
- Toy Poodle
- West Highland Terrier
- Yorkshire Terrier

Grooming Equipment

Bristle Brush

This brush is typically used on short-haired, smooth-coated dogs that shed frequently. The tightly-packed natural bristles remove loose hair and stimulate the skin. Bristle brushes can be used on breeds such as Pugs, Italian Greyhounds and Boston Terriers.

Slicker Brush

This brush is typically used after brushing with a bristle or a wire pin brush. They are used to smooth the coat and to take out any remaining mats and tangles. Fine wire pins secured to a flat base are bent at an angle approximately halfway down the pin. The slicker brush is typically used on dogs with long coats and those with curly coats. For heavier and thicker coats, a brush with stiffer pins is recommended. This type of brush comes in a wide range of sizes and degrees of pin stiffness.

Hound Glove

This is a glove with a slicker brush on one side and rubber studs on the other, which is great for smooth-coated dogs such as Basset Hound, Boston Terrier, Dachshund, Italian Greyhound, English Bulldog and Pug.

Pin Brush

This wire or wooden brush is often used for dogs with medium to long hair or wiry, wavy, curly coats. The pin brush is able to separate and untangle such coats. Pin brushes with polished or coated pins are better as they do not scratch or harm the dog's skin.

Furminator

Medium Dogs quickly and easily removes the loose, dead, undercoat hair that is the underlying source of every pet owner's major complaint – shedding; and the allergies and cleanliness problems associated with it. The grooming brush's uniquely designed stainless steel edge grabs loose undercoat hair and harmlessly removes it without damaging the topcoat. The fur ejector button cleans and removes loose hair from the tool with ease by simply pushing the button to release the hair.

Combs

Dog combs come in three versions: fine, medium and wide-toothed. Combs are useful to detangle hair and to help remove fleas and their debris. You can always use a spray on detangler to assist with removing tangles. Dogs with silky soft hair, fine hair or medium texture need a fine or medium comb. For coats that are dense and very thick, you should use a wide-toothed dog comb. To combat matting on curly and long-coated breeds, you can use a coat rake, mat comb or mat splitter.

Wide Toothed Comb

This comb is made to carefully untangle and smooth knots in long hair without pulling or breakage. On long haired dogs, start with the shoulder on one side of the dog. Comb in short, slow motions. Avoid pressing the teeth of the comb into the dog's skin. Use this procedure for the other parts of the dog.

Whitening Shampoo

White dogs can become stained due to playing in dirt, licking their fur, use of inappropriate shampoos and conditioners, or accidentally soiling their own fur. This shampoo restores your dog's coat to a brilliant white shine without using harsh chemicals or bleach.

Bathing Your Dog

Washing your dog is not always an easy task; therefore it is very important you make this as easy as possible for yourself and your dog. Some dogs love water, others loathe it and some will just tolerate it.

Bath essentials

Firstly, make sure you have the right equipment ready for the bath: dog shampoo, a plastic water jug (you can use a plastic milk carton), face wash cloth and a towel. Also, have some treats ready. You may also like to have a bathing brush handy. A gentle bath brush can give your dog a nice massage during bath time, as well as stimulate your dog's skin and hair follicles.

Before going any further, let's talk about shampoos. There are many types on the market: there are shampoos specifically formulated to combat fleas and ticks, 'no tears' shampoos as well as tear stain removers, shampoos that are hypo-allergenic, scented shampoos that help combat pet odor, shampoos that give extra body (especially good for double-coated breeds), natural organic shampoos with oatmeal (great for soothing irritated skin), shampoos that brighten white coats, shampoos that enhance the color of darker coats and shampoos for senior pets who may have sensitive skin.

There are many dog shampoos and conditioners on the market so it may be a little daunting to choose a quality shampoo and conditioner for your pet. When looking for a shampoo, go to a reputable pet store and ask the clerk what they recommend. They usually have the dogs' best interests at heart. However, it's best to be armed with good information. Here are six quick tips to ensure you are picking a quality shampoo and conditioner for your dog:

1. Never use human shampoo or conditioner on a dog.
2. Look for a shampoo with a pH that matches your dog's breed. Some shampoos and conditioners for dogs have formulations similar to human products. Although this might seem okay, in fact your dog's skin pH is higher than a person's, so her hair and skin needs are different. A dog's pH varies from 6.2 to 8.6 depending on the breed. If you use a product with a high pH you run the risk of drying out your dog's skin.
3. Look for formulations that have oatmeal and aloe vera as well as omega 3's because they moisturize your dog's skin.
4. Homeopathic ingredients such as spearmint, peppermint, emu oil, jojoba oil, oat, geranium and lavender are also great ingredients in pet hair products.
5. Products with zinc (zinc pca for puppies) are great as they help kill germs and bacteria on the dog's skin (which can cause itchiness and odor).
6. Dogs can also benefit from tea tree oil as this is a soothing agent.

Next, if you are bathing your dog in a sink or bathtub, make sure you use a rubber bath mat to prevent the dog from slipping and getting injured. These can be purchased from any hardware store.

Bath procedure

Before placing your dog in the bath or sink, make sure the water is tepid. Tepid water is between 20 and 30°C (between 68 and 86°F).

In order to place your dog safely in the bath, cradle the dog from underneath, making sure you have a firm hold on her upper and lower torso.

Use the plastic water jug to pour water over the dog. Then, thoroughly and gently massage shampoo into your dog – starting from the top and working your way down to the legs and tail.

When bathing your dog, avoid pouring water on her face and ears. Dogs loathe having water splashed and poured over their face. I am only speculating, but I believe the action of pouring water over your dog's face can trigger panic as a result of an instinctual fear of drowning.

Also, you want to avoid getting water inside your dog's ear canal – after the bath it's always a good idea to check inside your dog's ears. If your dog is not prone to ear infections, then this won't be a big deal: just monitor your dog over a couple of days for signs of ear irritation. If your dog is prone to ear infections and you notice you have accidentally splashed water into her ears, then clean them.

If your dog frets or attempts to leave the bath, hold your dog firmly and give treats so the dog becomes occupied with eating. You can also bring a toy into the bath, if that helps.

Thoroughly rinse your dog. Thorough rinsing to remove all shampoo and conditioner is very important, otherwise your dog may have to endure uncomfortable itchiness. Also, if you do not rinse thoroughly, you'll notice the shampoo leaves a fine powdery residue - it will look as though the dog has dandruff!

For the face and ears, use a small wash cloth. Wet the wash cloth and place the tiniest amount of shampoo on it. Then gently wipe your dog's face. Rinse the wash cloth thoroughly and wipe down your dog's face and ears again.

After you are done, gently lift the dog out of the bath in the same way you lifted her into the bath. Use the towel to dry her. If your dog has long hair, you may want another towel as a backup since it will get drenched quickly.

It's natural for dogs to shake off excess water – so expect to get wet!

A bath once a month is enough. If you wash your dog too often, you will strip the natural oils from your dog's skin which could lead to skin irritation and possibly other skin problems.

If your dog is stinky between washes, you can always use talcum powder or a waterless shampoo (available at pet stores) to deodorize your dog. Lightly shake some powder over your dog's back and legs then brush it through. Make sure you cover your dog's eyes when you apply the talcum powder.

In the next chapter, I'll discuss how to potty train your apartment dog, especially those that are a little stubborn when it comes to this task!

Potty Training Stubborn Small Dogs!

Potty training is the first thing you teach your new dog. A new owner's biggest frustration is the fact that puppies have no clue where to do their business! This chapter gives you clear, easy to follow steps and tips which will make the process easier. If issues around toilet training persist for a long time, consider seeking veterinary advice to make sure your puppy has no bladder or other health problems.

In this chapter, I'll explain:

- The three basic rules of quick and easy potty training.
- The potty schedule which will help you know when your dog is likely to potty.
- How to train your dog to use a crate.
- Tell-tale signs your dog is about to potty.
- How to handle accidents.
- Ways you can reinforce good behavior, so your dog learns to potty in the designated areas faster.

Choosing a Designated Area

As an apartment dweller, your choices for an acceptable place for your dog to potty (that is, a designated area) might be limited. You might choose the balcony or courtyard. If you do not have a balcony or courtyard you might have to consider using an indoor potty or pee pads. The great thing about pee pads and indoor potties is that they can also be used on a balcony and courtyard.

Pee Pads

Pee pads also have two important benefits: Firstly, the pee pads can be used as a place for potty in an apartment when there is no outside area available; and secondly, some dogs profiled in this guide are particularly sensitive to weather extremes and so pee pads are a great substitute for going outside in cold or hot weather.

Indoor Potty

The indoor potty is basically a mat made of a synthetic surface that looks like grass. There is a tray underneath that allows the potty to be cleaned and reduces odor. This potty is ideal for balcony, courtyard or inside apartments.

Three Basic Rules of Potty Training

Your goal as a dog owner is to ensure that your dog learns to potty in the designated area as quickly as possible. This means that your dog should have as few opportunities as possible to potty outside of the designated areas. Three basic rules apply when you are teaching your dog to potty in the right areas are:

- Set your dog up for success
- Recognizing when your dog needs to toilet
- Reward and punish your dog the correct way

Set Your Dog Up for Success

The more success and the more rewarded your dog feels, the more likely your dog will develop confidence and learn to potty in the designated areas quickly. Puppies – especially toy breeds – do not have full control over their bladders until they are between five to seven months old. I have devised this simple timetable to help you know when to take your dog to the designated area to potty:

Timing of Potty

Throughout the night	Take puppy to the designated area if you hear she is awake
6am	Take puppy to the designated area
Throughout the day	Take the puppy to the designated area shortly after the puppy: • Wakes up • Drinks • You have played with, or trained, the puppy
Eating	Take puppy to the designated area to poop 30 minutes later. Eating schedule for puppies is: - 7 weeks through 4 months is 4 times a day - 4 to 7 months is 3 times a day - 7 months onwards is 2 times a day
6pm	Stop food after this time to limit poop
11.30pm (or late as possible)	Last potty before bedtime

Crate training

In between these times, you can confine your dog to a crate for short periods. Puppies have been taught by their mother (dam) not to soil their sleeping area. This effectively means that puppies have been toilet trained since about three weeks old. When you first bring your dog home, it's your job to continue with this training. This means that their sleeping area should be small enough so they do not want to soil it. Having said that, if you keep a dog in a crate for too long then the dog may be forced to potty in it and once this happens your dog may start to develop the undesirable habit of peeing inside her crate.

Being crated can provide your dog with a safe place to sleep and rest. Purchase a crate that will be large enough for a puppy when she's an adult. Most manufacturers give good guidance regarding which crate is right for each breed (or mix) so check the labels or tags. When in doubt, get a crate that is a little larger rather than one that's too small. However, don't get an enormous crate that will be too big for your dog when she's full-grown. Dogs generally like to feel well-insulated and comforted in their crates, like a den. They won't feel safe in a huge space.

If you choose an adult sized crate for your puppy, then fill the extra space with blankets - this way the dog will not soil the crate as they do not like to pee or poop in their living space. If the crate is too big, the puppy may use the crate as a potty, which is exactly the behavior you are trying to discourage!

There are several different kinds of crates: hard plastic airline crates, wire crates, and canvas crates. There are even wicker crates and other unusual crates. They are all fine for different purposes, although canvas, wicker and other crates are usually not a good choice for a puppy since they are easily torn or chewed. I recommend you choose a hard plastic or wire crate for crate training.

It's not hard to crate train a dog but your dog may complain about it at first, depending on her early experiences with a crate. Some breeders use a crate as part of their whelping set-up so some puppies are used to them from birth. They have no objection to spending time in a crate or sleeping in one. To them a crate is a cozy, safe place that they associate with their mother and littermates.

Other puppies, however, may not have seen a crate before. Initially, at least, they may think of being in the crate as jail time. Since you may not know whether your dog has any experience with a crate it's always a good idea to introduce the crate slowly.

Three steps to easy crate training:

a. Allow your puppy to explore the crate

Once you have the right crate you should place it in a spot in your home where your dog can explore it. Leave the door wide open. Place a comfortable sheepskin mat or some towels in the crate and put some treats and toys inside. Many dogs will go inside to get the treats. Your dog may decide to take a nap there. That's fine - you should let her sleep there with the door open. Let her get used to going in and out of the crate as she likes. You can also begin feeding your dog dinner in the crate, with the door open.

b. Introduce short periods of crate time

After your dog has become used to the crate you can start closing the door for short periods of time while you are home with her. Close the door for a couple of minutes and give your dog something good to chew on while she's in the crate. Some dogs may not notice that you have closed the door. They will be focused on the chewie. Other dogs may protest about the closed door. It is best to open the door after a couple of minutes and let your dog out when the dog is quiet. Do this a few times each day for several days. You can gradually keep your dog in the crate for longer periods of time, always making sure that you are home with her.

Your dog should begin to get used to spending some time in the crate. Make sure you always give her something safe to occupy her whilst she's in the crate. You should not expect her to spend long periods of time in the crate at this stage, especially if she's very young as she may soil her space or become distressed.

Eventually you can practice going outside for a few minutes while your dog is in the crate. Your dog may howl but you will need to ignore it. Then, once settled, you can go back inside and let her out. The key is not to make a fuss when you let your dog out. In this way she will not become too excited when you return; your dog will therefore learn that you will always come back and she will not fret whilst you are away.

c. Gradually increase crate time

You can gradually leave your dog for longer periods in the crate while you are absent. If your dog whinges, howls or freaks out, then cut the time she is left in the crate by half and slowly build up the absences as your dog remains calmly in her crate. When your dog is still quite young, remember that she will need to be toileted frequently so ensure she is let out often. If she soils her crate this may lead to a bad habit that is hard to break.

If you follow these suggestions your dog will be crate trained in just a few weeks. Some dogs learn faster than others. Some dogs will calm down and take a nap when you leave while others may bark and object at first. The keys are to ensure: (i) your dog knows that you will return; (ii) the crate is a pleasant place (never scold or punish her whilst she's in her crate); and (iii) you do not make a big fuss when you leave and return.

Controlling your dog's environment

Giving your dog the run of the house means you will have less chance of being able to potty train your dog effectively. Limiting the space to which your dog has access means your dog won't be able to sneak into an unsupervised room and potty. A great way to ensure your dog is safe, comfortable and under your supervision is to use an exercise-pen (also known as an x-pen). Exercise pens are an easy way to confine your dog to a certain place when she is playing, this way you can be sure she is safe. Exercise pens not only provide a safe play area for your dog, but also keep the dog confined between stints of potty training. By making sure it is near where you and your family hang out in the house, your dog will feel involved and occupied too. Make sure there are toys and a water bowl in the pen when your dog is inside it.

Recognizing when your dog needs to toilet

Knowing your dog's schedule for potty is important, however your dog may need to go at other times. Dogs usually signal their need to potty by circling and sniffing the ground. However, some dogs may exhibit different signals, so observe your dog and watch for patterns.

When you think your dog is about to potty, pick her up promptly but gently and take her to the area you'd like her to potty. Be careful not to press your hands against your dog's abdomen as you do this. Doing this calmly and swiftly means you won't startle your dog into eliminating whilst she is being carried.

Once you have taken your dog to a 'designated area' where you encourage the dog to go. Initially, your dog may tend to wander away from the 'designated area'. I recommend you place her gently back in the designated area until she potties; she may fuss and resist. So this will test your patience! You must persevere and continue to place her in the designated area until she potties. If your dog does not potty within ten minutes of taking her to the designated area, then bring her back in, crate her and try again in 15 minutes.

Reward and punish your dog the correct way

Handling accidents

Despite your best efforts, accidents will happen. This is okay and is just part of the process – even seasoned dog trainers experience this with their own dogs! I am often asked by dog owners what they should do if they catch their dog peeing inside.

My advice is not to punish your dog. This is because your dog may think that the act of potty itself is what is angering you, so she will then hide the evidence by eliminating behind furniture or beneath curtains. The best reaction is to simply say "whoops" or "d'oh!" then quickly and quietly take your dog to the designated area. Remember: there's no point punishing your dog after the fact, because she just won't know why she is being punished.

Make sure you clean up any accidents as quickly as possible. You can use an ammonia-free cleaner (dogs are particularly attracted to peeing on ammonia) or a mixture of water and vinegar. Some household cleaners are not strong enough to actually remove the odor (they merely disguise it), so I suggest asking your vet to recommend an enzyme-based cleaner to get rid of the smell completely.

The general rule is that dogs can only hold their bladder for one hour for each month of age. Therefore, an eight-week-old (two-month-old) puppy can only hold her bladder for two hours. This means there may be accidents at night, unless you are prepared to get up in the middle of the night and toilet her. If you do not intend to toilet your dog at night, it's best to provide her with 'pee pads' (these are floor napkins available at pet stores) or a litter tray; in this way your dog does not soil her bedding. It's relatively difficult to wean a dog off soiling her bed once it starts, so make sure you discourage this.

Reinforcing Good Potty Habits

When you have taken your dog to the 'designated area', do not play with her or give treats to her until she has toileted.

You can use treats and play as a reward. Make sure your dog really knows how pleased you are that she has toileted in the right area – this will increase the chances that she will seek to potty in the right area next time.

As your dog toilets say a special word, so your dog learns to potty on command. People tend to use either "potty", "wee", "busy", "go do wee wee" or "toilees". You must say the word just as she begins to potty and only say it once. Timing is the key to teaching a new command, so there is no point saying the word after your dog has finished eliminating. You can choose your own word – just be mindful of choosing a word that you do not mind saying in earshot of others at a park or other public place!

If your dog is quite stubborn about toileting after being taken to the designated area, here is a trick that might help. Leave your dog at the designated area. Watch your dog from afar and when she toilets, go to her and say "good dog!" and play with her. There's no bigger reward for a dog than to be reunited with her owner. Repeat this process at the next scheduled potty – you'll see your dog will catch on very quickly!

Remember to use biodegradable poop scoop baggies to clean up after your dog, especially if she toilets in a public area. You might want to leave some of her poop in your designated area to encourage her to potty in that spot again.

Some people have recommended getting poop from another dog and placing this in the designated area. I highly recommend that you *do not* do this: puppies that have not yet had their full course of vaccinations may be vulnerable to possible diseases lurking in another dog's poop.

Your Potty Training Checklist

- Take your dog to the designated area to potty shortly after your puppy wakes, plays, trains and drinks.
- Take your dog to the designated area to potty 30 minutes after eating.
- Confine your dog to a crate or exercise pen (x-pen) for short periods.
- Watch for your dog's potty signals, then gently and promptly take her to the designated potty area.
- Have a designated spot for potty.
- Do not punish your dog for accidents.
- Give lots of praise when your dog toilets in the designated area.
- As your dog beings to potty, say "potty" or another special word, so this command is reinforced.

How to Read The Breed Profiles

In this guide you'll find 32 profiles of dogs that make great companions for apartment dwellers. These profiles will help you decide which dog is suitable for your lifestyle, personality and experience with dogs. Each profile has the dog's picture with a tag line which captures the essence of the breed. I will then look at each of the following topics relating to each breed:

Picture

Most profiles will feature a photograph, so you get a clear idea of the breed's appearance. Some breeds come in different color, so this section will give you more information of what each breed looks like.

Breed Summary

Type–All dogs profiled in this guide are 'pure'. Pure means the dog is bred from parents of the same breed. When the lineage of a purebred dog is recorded, that animal is said to be 'pedigreed'. This means the breeder will give you a certificate identifying the breeds of the dog's parents and grandparents. If the dog is a mix, then each parent of the dog is a different breed from the other parent. Not all designer hybrid dogs are half of each purebred; rather it is common for breeders to breed multi-generational crosses.

Group - Kennel clubs classify breeds into different groups to identify their common overall purpose and qualities. The types and names of groups can differ between kennels, so for the purpose of this guide, groups defined by the American Kennel Club (AKC) will be used. According to the AKC, each breed will belong to one of the seven groups:

- Sporting: These dogs are used to hunt birds and game.

- Hound: These dogs are also used for hunting and are known for their scenting ability and stamina.

- Working: These dogs usually engage in some physically active task or work for people. There are a wide variety of tasks such as therapy and guarding; so many different types of dogs are included in this group.

- Terrier: These dogs were originally kept to hunt vermin, but are now mainly kept as companions and pets.

- Non-Sporting: These dogs are known as sturdy animals; the many dogs belonging to this group have diverse characteristics such as appearance, size, coat and personality.

- Herding: These dogs have the ability to control the movements of groups of other animals. Many of these dogs are kept as companions and have never actually herded farm animals; they can't help their instinct and so gently herd their owners and other family owners.

- Toy: These dogs are small and charming. Despite their size many are tough and feisty. Toys are popular with people who live in small apartments as they take up little space and require minimal exercise.

When you learn the group of the particular breed in which you're interested, please refer to the relevant descriptions above to gain a better understanding of the breed's qualities.

Average life span - Here, you'll be given the dog's approximate life expectancy in human years. In other words, how the long this breed usually lives. As with humans, factors such as diet, lifestyle, health and luck can all contribute to the dog's longevity. On average, dogs age seven years for every human year. For smaller breeds, the age ratio decreases, with the smaller dog ageing 5 years for every human year.

Cost - Costs can vary widely depending on where you buy your dog. The prices are a guide only and are indicative of what you might pay if you bought this breed from a reputable breeder. The cost is applicable across the United States, United Kingdom and Australia.

Height, Weight and Size - Each dog generally falls within a certain height and weight range for their breed. I have also included the following size classifications:

- Toy

- Small

- Medium

- Large

- Extra-Large

You'll be surprised that there are medium, and even large dogs, that are suitable for apartment living. However, size should be considered in terms of how much space your apartment has so you can decide which size can be accommodated.

Famous Owners

Here, I'll share which celebrities who own this breed.

Appearance

The overall look, available coloring and unique physical characteristics of each breed will be explained in vivid detail.

Temperament

Like humans, dogs are not perfect! So, in this section I'll explain the positive qualities of the breed as well as possible undesirable traits. Whilst no dog is perfect, early and effective training and socialization can minimize a dog's undesirable tendencies.

When it comes to hybrids, it is important to remember that the temperament will be influenced by the characteristics of the parent breeds.

Exercise

In her book entitled *Animals Make Us Human*, Temple Grandin says in order for dogs to be balanced and well-mannered they need 45 minutes to one hour per day of play and seeking. Dogs that are suitable for apartment living will often be happy with a set amount of exercise per day. In this section, I'll explain how much exercise and what type of exercise will satisfy this breed.

Special Talent

Each breed has a special talent! I'll share this with you, so you can unleash your dog's potential.

Children and Other Pets

Some breeds make suitable companions to other dogs and pets, whilst others require some work in that area. So, in this section I'll alert you to possible problems in this area so you can nip any issues in the bud.

Trainability

Each breed will get a rating between 0 and 5 stars. I'll also explain the reason for the rating.

★★★★★ 0 stars: A feral or undomesticated dog unsuitable as a pet.

★★★★★ 1 star: Not trainable and not motivated to please humans.

★★★★★ 2 stars: Difficult to train and require experienced dog handlers.

★★★★★ 3 stars: Requires consistent training by an experienced handler due to stubbornness or a need for variety.

★★★★★ 4 stars: Easy to train, likes to please, but can be distractible.

★★★★★ 5 stars: Intelligent, bright, attentive and motivated to learn.

Grooming

Some dogs need a lot of brushing and sprucing, whilst others require less attention. In this section, I'll pay particular attention to the breed's coat and teeth.

Diet

A good diet is essential for any breed. However, I'll address any special dietary requirements or sensitivities.

Barking

Often apartments are small enough to cause problems with neighbours if an occupant is noisy, so I'll focus on whether barking may be a problem for the breed.

Health

Every breed has particular issues to which it may be prone; I'll share what these are. Bear in mind that some health issues can be minimized or avoided and so I'll share ways in which you optimize your dog's health.

I'll also include information from The Canine Health Information Center (CHIC) relating to which conditions your dog should be tested for. CHIC is a centralized canine health database jointly sponsored by the AKC/Canine Health Foundation and the Orthopedic Foundation for Animals. CHIC's mission is to assist owners, breeders, and scientists breed healthy dogs.

Breed Clubs

Here, I'll list the websites of relevant breed clubs in the USA, UK and Australia.

Affenpinscher

The Affenpinscher is a cute little 'monkey' of a dog; this breed is amazingly playful, affectionate and amusing.

Breed Summary

- Type: Pure
- Group: Toy
- Average life span: 10-16 years
- Average cost: $1,000-2,000
- Height: 9.5-11.5 inches (24-29 centimeters)
- Weight: 7-9 pounds (3-4 kilograms)
- Size: Small

History

The Affenpinscher is related to the Brussels Griffon and possibly to the terrier group. The breed originated in Munich, Germany and France and is believed to be one of the oldest known toy breeds. During the 17th century, Affenpinschers were frequently kept as ratters around stables and farms. The Affenpinscher was later miniaturized and became a house pet during the 18th and 19th centuries, where they continued to serve as mice hunters. Today, the Affenpinscher serves as a fun companion dog, with good watchdog capabilities.

Famous Owners

There are no famous Affenpinschers or famous owners of this breed.

Appearance

The Affenpinscher is wiry-haired and terrier-like in appearance. The Affenpinscher has a refined, yet shaggy, appearance. This breed has an impish, monkey-like facial expression and her head is carried confidently. The tail is curved around gently up over the back.

Coat: The Affenpinscher's wire-haired coat is usually black, but can also be gray, silver, red, beige or black and tan. The texture of the coat is rough and harsh. Some dogs may have a black mask.

Temperament

Qualities

Highly intelligent and proud, this breed walks with the confident gait of a larger dog. The Affenpinscher is generally courageous, alert and curious. Highly affectionate, the Affenpinscher shows great loyalty and affection toward her owner. Although a Toy breed, the Affenpinscher shares many characteristics of the terrier group. This means they can be feisty, charming and have some pluck about them! Affenpinschers keenly observe their owner and are sensitive to their owner's moods.

Many hours of fun can be had with this playful, amusing breed.

Traits

In France this breed is known as 'Diablotin Moustachu' or mustached little devil; the Affenpinscher's charm and intelligence make them highly mischievous!

Exercise

An active bundle of joy, the Affenpinscher's exercise needs can be met with indoor play, making her an ideal apartment dog. Indoor play and a daily walk or frolic outdoors will keep the Affenpinscher happy.

Special Talent

The Affenpinscher is known to be an excellent mice hunter and a fearless watchdog.

Children and Other Pets

The Affenpinscher is not recommended for very young children as this breed tends to guard food and toys. Older children must be taught how to gently handle the Affenpinscher. The Affenpinscher enjoys being with her family and other pets, with whom she is properly socialized.

A mark of her terrier ancestry is the Affenpinscher's tendency to challenge, or become hyper-excited around, unfamiliar (sometimes larger) dogs. Take care to ensure the dog is socialized with other dogs as a puppy, so she is less likely to acquire this habit.

Trainability

3 stars: Requires consistent training by an experienced handler due to stubbornness or a need for variety.

Cheerful and mischievous, the Affenpinscher requires fun and variety in training sessions. Repetition will bore the Affenpinscher and slack handling will cause the dog to rebel. The Affenpinscher is capable of learning new commands and agility quickly.

Housetraining can be a challenge and so consistency is needed.

Grooming

The harsh coat of the Affenpinscher should never be clipped too short, as this ruins the coat for a long time. All that is required is a brush and comb twice a week, and a trim twice a year. A good groomer can trim the dog and it is possible for the owner to learn this skill. This breed sheds virtually no hair.

Diet

Affenpinschers do not have any special dietary requirements.

Barking

Although the Affenpinscher is generally a quiet and gentle dog, she is fearless when faced with a perceived threat and can therefore become hyper-excited and vocal.

Health

There are no major health concerns associated with the Affenpinscher, although some may be prone to fractures and a slipped stifle.

Like any short-nosed or brachycephalicbreeds, the Affenpinscher may suffer from breathing issues, especially in hot weather.

Watch for hair that grows around the corner of the dog's eyes, as this may cause irritation.

The   http://www.caninehealthinfo.org/breeds.html   recommends the Affenpinscher is tested for:

- Patellar Luxation
- Hip Dysplasia (Optional)
- Legg Calve Perthes (Optional)

Breed Clubs

America: http://www.affenpinscher.org/

United Kingdom: http://www.affenpinscherclubuk.com/

Basset Hound

The Basset Hound is the sweetest and gentlest of breeds. This hound is extremely affectionate with her family.

Breed Summary

- Type: Pure
- Group: (Scent) Hound
- Average life span: 8-13 years
- Average cost: $250-1,000
- Height: 12-14 inches (30-35 centimeters)
- Weight: 45-60 pounds (20-27 kilograms)
- Size: Medium

History

The Basset Hound's ancestors, that is, other basset types, were depicted on Egyptian tombs. The name Basset comes from the French word 'bas' meaning low; the Basset Hound is known for her short stature. The Basset Hound may have originated from dwarf dogs present in litters of other French hunting breeds. Because of her height, the Basset Hound was originally used in France to track small game. The Basset Hound became quite popular during the reign of Napoleon and was a favorite amongst French royalty. The Basset Hound was introduced to the United States when President George Washington was presented with Basset Hounds by a French aristocrat. It is believed the Basset Hound is a direct relation to the Bloodhound.

Famous Owners

- Elvis Presley's *Sidney*
- Marilyn Monroe's *Hugo*
- Emperor Napoleon III and President George Washington both owned Basset Hounds

Appearance

The Basset Hound has the longest ears of any breed and a long saber tail, which is held high. Although the Basset Hound has short legs, she will have a long, big, heavy body. Despite her short height, her long body makes her quite able to reach objects which would otherwise be out of reach of other dogs of similar height. This breed's skin tends to hang loose, especially around the neck (dewlap), which gives this dog a mournful, yet charming, look.

Coat: The Basset Hound's coat sheds constantly and is short, smooth and close. The coat can be tri-color combinations of black, tan, white or a bi-color combination of tan and white. The tan color can vary from reddish-brown, to red and lemon. A rare and desirable coat color for the Basset Hound is or blue. The Basset Hound usually has a white tipped tail (flag) -this allows hunters to find this dog through brush when trailing game.

Temperament

Qualities

This Basset Hound is sweet, gentle and docile. These hounds are peaceful creatures and they'll never start a fight. The Basset Hound makes a great family pet, making her an ideal companion for children. The Basset Hound is a loyal companion and enjoys the social interaction that a family can offer.

The Basset Hound has a fantastic sense of smell and tends to sleep a lot.

Traits

Basset Hounds can be well-behaved when trained well and also excel in competition obedience. However, a firm, consistent yet gentle approach to obedience is required as the Basset Hound can be stubborn.

The Basset Hound dislikes being left alone and will not do well with an owner who is away often.

The Basset Hound's reflexes are quite slow, so do not expect quick reactions.

Exercise

Despite a love of sleep, the Basset Hound requires a long daily walk. The Basset Hound can easily be distracted into following a scent, which makes off-lead walking a risky proposition; keep the Basset Hound on a leash to ensure she does not run away!

Exercise should not include jumping, which can be hard on this breed's legs (especially the front legs).

Special Talent

The Basset Hound is very good at hunting and tracking.

Children and Other Pets

The Basset Hound makes a great family dog. They are extremely affectionate with children and get along great with other dogs.

Trainability

★★★ 3 stars: Requires consistent training by an experienced handler due to stubbornness.

Basset Hounds can be stubborn, and so patient and positive handling is required. The best trained Basset Hound can be difficult to handle when she's picked up a scent!

Keep in mind that the Basset Hound has been known to excel in competition obedience, so good training does have a positive impact on this breed.

Housetraining can be a challenge.

Grooming

The Basset Hound sheds constantly. Having a short, smooth coat means a bath every 1-2 months is fine; however a daily brush with a hound glove is essential.

This breed's long floppy ears (leathers) mean air cannot circulate inside them. The ears may drag along the ground, which means they may pick up germs and bacteria. Also, the Basset Hound may accidentally bite her own ears whilst eating. This means the Basset Hound's ears may be prone to infection or ear mites; a weekly clean of both the inside and outside of the ears is recommended to counteract infection and disease. Some owners gently peg back the Basset Hound's ears whilst eating to prevent any accidental injury.

Diet

Basset Hounds tend to put on weight quickly, which places added strain on their legs and spine. Their large chests make them prone to bloat (gastric torsion); Basset Hounds should be fed two smaller meals a day, rather than just one large meal.

Barking

The Basset Hound is known to be quite vocal and has a deep musical bark. Basset Hounds may 'talk' to you by barking, howling, whining or murmuring when they want attention, food or feel edgy.

Health

The http://www.caninehealthinfo.org/breeds.html recommends the Basset Hound is tested for:

- Eye problems
- Thrombopathia (Optional)

Possible lameness and eventual paralysis may arise due to the Basset Hound's long, heavy body and short legs.

Breed Clubs

America - http://basset-bhca.com/

In the United States, special picnics and 'waddles' draw a loyal following of Basset Hound owners. Many of these events raise funds for local Basset Hound rescue organizations.

United Kingdom - http://www.bassethoundclub.co.uk/

Australia - http://www.bassethounds.org.au/

Beagle

The Beagle is a sweet, gentle and lively dog. Your heart will melt with those dark, soulful eyes!

Breed Summary

- Type: Pure
- Group: (Scent) Hound
- Average life span: 12-15 years
- Average cost: $450-850
- Height: 13-15 inches (33-38 centimeters)
- Weight: 20-25 pounds (9-11 kilograms)
- Size: Small

History

Dogs of similar size and purpose to the modern Beagle can be traced to Ancient Greece around 5th century B.C. The modern Beagle was developed in the 1830's and most likely began as a cross between the Harrier Hound and other hounds. Their small size, scenting ability and stamina meant the Beagle is ideal for hunting hare and rabbit.

Beagles have proved useful in quarantine services. Countries such as New Zealand, China, Australia and Canada have used Beagles to detect and prevent food and other illegal items (such as drugs or explosives) from entering their countries.

Because of their gentle nature and small build, Beagles are also frequently used as therapy dogs, visiting the sick and elderly in hospitals and aged care homes.

The Beagle is also one of the most popular breeds in the United States; according to the American Kennel Club, the Beagle was ranked 4th most popular breed in the United States. The Beagle has proved to be a wonderfully intelligent and sociable pet.

The miniature version of the Beagle is now extinct.

Famous Owners

- President Lyndon Johnson's *Him* and *Her*. President Johnson caused consternation when he was photographed picking *Him* up by the ears in front of a group of visitors at the White House.
- Barry Manilow's *Bagel* and *Biscuit*
- Charlie Brown's *Snoopy* is the most famous Beagle in the world

Appearance

The Beagle's overall look is that of a miniaturized Foxhound. Beagles have large, dark brown eyes and long, droopy ears. The Beagle's legs are short and their tails sit high. The white tipped tail (flag) allows the dog to be easily seen by her human hunting companions when she is following a scent.

Coat: The Beagle's coat is short, hard and is easy to groom. Their coats are commonly tri-color: black, tan and white. But both the tan and white, and lemon and white combinations are becoming more popular. The Beagle is a moderate shedder.

Temperament

Qualities

The Beagle is sweet, gentle lively dog who loves everyone she meets. The Beagle is generally cheerful and happy-go lucky in nature. They are also very sociable, brave and intelligent. Beagles love company and are keen to please their owners. Beagles are extremely loyal and are ideal for families, as Beagles are considered to be good around children.

The Beagle is a sturdy hunting dog with a personality that win anyone over.

Traits

Because Beagles are such sociable creatures, they may suffer separation anxiety if left alone for long periods. The Beagle's need for company makes them a more suitable breed for who can spend time with this dog.

Beagles can be a little excitable and so she will need to be taught to be calm in unfamiliar or rowdy situations, such as when visitors arrive or a lot of activity in the home.

Exercise

Beagles require a moderate amount of exercise. A good daily walk and some play sessions with the family should suffice.

Keep in mind that when walking a Beagle that she can be easily distracted into following a scent, which makes off-lead walking a risky proposition; keep the Beagle on a leash to ensure she does not run away!

Special Talent

The Beagle has the best developed sense of smell of any breed. The Beagle's specialty is therefore scent detection. That's why Beagles have been used in drug detection and quarantine services around the world.

Children and Other Pets

Beagles are typically good with other dogs as they were originally bred to hunt in packs. However, Beagles may not be good with other small pets due to their natural hunting instincts. The Beagle is excellent with children; she makes a lovely, merry and ever-ready play companion!

Trainability

★★★★ 4 stars: Easy to train, like to please, but can be distractible. Generally obedient, the Beagle is easily distracted by smells around her.

She also may be difficult to recall once she has picked up a scent.

Beagles require firm and patient training. The Beagle can be single-minded at times and it can be hard to hold her attention when she is carried away with a scent. Therefore, it is recommended training sessions are short and fun.

Grooming

The Beagle's weatherproof coat requires minimal grooming; they can be brushed occasionally with a bristle brush and bathed only when necessary.

This breed's long ears mean air cannot circulate inside them. This means the Beagle's ears may be prone to infection or ear mites; a weekly clean of both the inside and outside of their ears is recommended to counteract infection and disease.

Diet

The Beagle does not have any special dietary requirements. However, the Beagle is prone to weight gain, which can lead to heart and joint problems.

Barking

The Beagle can be a good watch dog as she has a tendency to bark or howl when confronted with unfamiliar people or situations. Beagles do like to bark and bay loudly when hunting. Although Beagles are noisy hunters, they tend to be quieter indoors.

Health

The http://www.caninehealthinfo.org/breeds.html recommends Beagles are tested for:

- Hip Dysplasia
- Musladin-Lueke Syndrome

The Center also recommends a cardiac, thyroid and eye examinations.

The Beagle can be prone to heart disease, epilepsy, chondroplasia (dwarfism) and disk (spinal) issues. Beagles may be affected by a variety of eye problems such as glaucoma, corneal dystrophy and cherry eye. The Beagle may occasionally 'reverse sneeze' which can sound like honking, snorting, or gagging. Although harmless, this behavior often manifests for very short periods but can be quite startling because the dog appears to be choking or gasping for breath. In actual fact, the dog is merely drawing air in through her mouth and nose simultaneously. The cause of this behavior is not known. Reverse sneezing can be brought on by over excitement, play, allergies, or upon waking up.

Breed Clubs

America: National Beagle Club of America Inc.
http://clubs.akc.org/NBC/

United Kingdom: The Beagle Club
http://www.thebeagleclub.org/

Australia:
The Beagle Club of NSW (Australia) Inc
http://beagleclubnsw.org.au/

Bichon Frise

The Bichon Frise is a well-mannered, sensitive dog. They are playful and affectionate with a wonderfully cheerful attitude.

Breed Summary

- Type: Pure
- Group: Non-Sporting
- Average life span: 15 years
- Average cost: $450-700
- Height: 9-11 inches (22-27 centimeters)
- Weight: 7-12 pounds (3-5 kilograms)
- Size: Small

History

Originating in the 13th century, the Bichon Frise's ancestors were the Barbet (medium sized French water spaniel) and Standard Poodle. Some sources say the Bichon Frise's name derives from the Barbet's diminutive, 'barbichon', however this is unlikely as the word 'Bichon' is older than the word 'barbichon'.

Transported and used as barter in various continents by Spanish sailors in the 14th century, the Bichon Frise later became a favorite amongst French royal courts. The breed was also favored by the painters of the Spanish schools, who often included them in their works. Enjoying sporadic popularity since, it was not until the late 19th century when the Bichon Frise became more common by accompanying the organ grinders of the middle and western coastal regions of North Africa (Morocco, Algeria, Tunisia and Libya), leading the blind and doing tricks in circuses. The Bichon became popular in Australia in the mid-1960s, largely due to a TV show which featured the breed. All Bichon Frise's in the United States today originate from two American breeders who acquired these dogs in 1959 and 1960.

Famous Owners

- Christina Aguilera's *Lucy*

Appearance

The Bichon Frise is a small and sturdy dog. Similar in appearance to the Miniature Poodle, the Bichon Frise's dark round eyes and inquisitive expression gives the breed a cute charm. The tail is long and curled gracefully over her back. Her ears are long and hang close to the head.

Coat: The Bichon Frise's coat is curly and dense, characteristics she shares with the Poodle. The breed's double coat consists of a textured outer coat and silky undercoat. This breed's coat is usually white, and may also have a smattering of buff, cream or apricot around her ears, paws and body. Other coat colors are apricot and gray. The Bichon Frise's coat sheds minimally.

Temperament

Qualities

Considered to be a small, attractive companion, the Bichon Frise is also a happy, friendly and affectionate dog. The Bichon Frise enjoys cuddles and playtime. This powder puff is also blessed with intelligence, making any owner proud of both her looks and brains!

The Bichon Frise is a well-mannered, sensitive and confident dog and is suitable for people who want a pet to accompany them on various outings.

This breed is considered good for allergy sufferers.

Traits

Bred to be a companion dog, the Bichon Frise may demand too much attention from her owner. Owners are encouraged to instil their dog with a sense of independence so she does not develop a tendency to shadow her owner or become clingy and needy.

Exercise

The Bichon Frise is an active little dog and needs a daily walk. In addition to her daily walk, playtime is a great way to ensure the Bichon Frise uses her energy. Off-leash play time in a safe open area with other dogs is also recommended.

Although not a retriever or water dog, the Bichon Frise's history with sailors and ships means she has an affinity with water and retrieval. Therefore, exercise that involves swimming and fetching will suit this breed.

Special Talent

Having served as a circus attraction in the past, don't be surprised if this little powder puff has a pageant for performing tricks!

Children and Other Pets

Bichon Frise's need regular human interaction and affection to be happy. They are very social dogs and love to be taken everywhere with the family. They do very well with other dogs, pets and children.

Trainability

5 stars: Intelligent, bright, attentive and motivated to learn. The Bichon Frise thrives with a fun, gentle training program.

The Bichon Frise ranks 45th in Stanley Coren's *The Intelligence of Dogs*, being of average intelligence in working or obedience.

Bichon Frise's are considered very intelligent and can be taught many little tricks that will impress any audience! The Bichon Frise is an easier dog to train because she is highly motivated to please her owner, although keep in mind that housetraining may take more time and patience.

Grooming

The Bichon Frise's coat requires regular grooming; therefore this dog is not suitable for people who do not want to spend money or energy on grooming.

Good grooming requires that the coat is trimmed on a regular basis as the Bichon Frise's coat sheds minimally and does not stop growing. If not trimmed regularly, the coat can become tangled and matted. The trim should show off the outline of the breed's body and give the body a rounded appearance from any direction. The coat on the head, beard, mustache, ears and tail is longer. In order to achieve this result, professional grooming is recommended. The eyes should be kept trimmed and cleaned to prevent staining and infection.

Diet

The Bichon Frise does not have any special dietary requirements.

Barking

The Bichon Frise is not known to bark unnecessarily.

Health

The   http://www.caninehealthinfo.org/breeds.html   recommends the Bichon Frise is tested for:

- Hip Dysplasia
- Patellar Luxation
- Legg Calves Perthes (Optional).

The Center also recommends the following tests or examinations:

- Eye
- Congenital Cardiac Database (Optional)
- Urinalysis to screen for diabetes, bladder infections, and crystals (Optional)
- Bile acid blood tests to screen for liver shunts (Optional). (A Bichon Frise who is underweight, the runt of the litter, or has negative reactions to food high in protein are likely to be suffering from a shunt).
- Standard veterinary blood panel including CBC, electrolytes, glucose levels, and liver and pancreatic enzymes - to screen for anemia, infection, cancer, bleeding or platelet disorders, kidney function, diabetes, liver function, and pancreatic function (Optional).

The Bichon Frise may also be prone to cataracts, watery eyes, skin and ear conditions and epilepsy. Their skin may also be very sensitive to flea bites.

Breed Clubs

America - http://www.bichon.org/

United Kingdom - http://www.bichonfriseclubofgb.com/

Australia - http://www.bichonfrise.com.au/

Bolognese

The graceful, intelligent, beautiful and charming Bolognese is the perfect companion dog.

Breed Summary

- Type: Pure
- Group: Toy
- Average life span: 12-15 years
- Average cost: $1000-2000
- Height: 10-12 inches (25-31 centimeters)
- Weight: 4-9 pounds (2-4 kilograms)
- Size: Small

History

The origins of the Bolognese are not entirely certain. The Bolognese's closest relative is the Maltese, however it is not certain which breed originated first. The Bolognese descended from the 'canes melitenses' mentioned by Aristotle (384 B.C. – 322 B.C.) and her existence has been documented since 1200. The Bolognese was later developed in the northern Italian city of Bologna (the breed's namesake). Because of her beauty and grace, the Bolognese was given as gifts and became a favorite of the nobility during the Renaissance. However, as the nobility faded, so too did this breed's popularity. The breed, near extinction, was revived by a breeder in Italy – Gian Franco Giannelli – and was later brought to England by Liz Stannard in 1990.

Famous Owners

This breed was once adored by European nobility. Two famous owners were:

- Catherine the Great of Russia (1729-1796), the most renowned and the longest-ruling female leader of Russia.

- Madame De Pompadour (1721-1764), member of the French court and official chief mistress of Louis XV from 1745 to her death.

Appearance

The Bolognese is compact and sturdy. Although small, the Bolognese is far from fragile-looking. The Bolognese has a square, stocky build – her length equals their height. The Bolognese's tail is long and curves over her back. The Bolognese has round eyes and long, hanging ears.

Coat. The Bolognese's white coat is long, dense, fluffy and woolly in texture. The Bolognese possesses a single coat, that is, she has no undercoat. The coat falls in loose open ringlets on her body, however the hair is shorter on her face. The Bolognese's coat sheds minimally.

Temperament

Qualities

The Bolognese possesses a calm disposition and happy nature. Graceful and charming, the Bolognese also sports a sense of clownish playfulness! Possessing what appears to be eternal youth, these dogs are known to behave like puppies well into their adulthood. The ultimate companion dog, the Bolognese shows great affection, loyalty and devotion.

Other qualities include: intelligence, enthusiasm, attentiveness and a willingness to participate in family activities.

Traits

The Bolognese thrives in the company of her owner and so can suffer from separation anxiety if left alone too often or for long periods.

Because of her history of being the preferred pet of nobility, there's a hint of superiority in the Bolognese's demeanor. Therefore, an owner should ensure the Bolognese is not spoilt or indulged as this will encourage her to transform into a bossy and arrogant creature.

Exercise

The Bolognese is the perfect apartment dog as she is happy to lounge around the house. Having said that, her youthfulness and zest means she loves a walk and some playtime every day. Owners will be pleased with the Bolognese's amazingly adaptable activity levels; she is quiet and calm when inside, and active and energetic when outside!

Special Talent

The Bolognese is an excellent watch dog.

Children and Other Pets

The Bolognese can get along well with children. As the Bolognese is small, it is recommended families with very young children take special care that no harm comes to this sensitive little dog. Although the Bolognese gets along with other dogs and pets, this breed will happily become a family's only pet.

Trainability

★★★★★ 5 stars: Intelligent, bright, attentive and motivated to learn. These intelligent dogs are relatively easy to train as they love to please their owners and find learning easy. As this dog is very intelligent, variety and fun should be central to any training session.

Like the Bichon Frise, the Bolognese can be challenging to housebreak.

Grooming

The Bolognese requires regular grooming. The coat should be brushed regularly; spend 15 minutes combing through the coat every day. The Bolognese is a low-shedding breed - any dead fur stays need to be brushed out or matting will occur.

This breed's long ears mean air cannot circulate inside them. The ears may therefore may be prone to infection or ear mites; a weekly clean is recommended to minimize the likelihood of infection and disease.

Diet

The Bolognese does not have any special dietary requirements.

Barking

The Bolognese is not known to bark unnecessarily; however, she makes a good watch dog as she will alert her owner to anything unusual.

Health

The Bolognese is a very hardy breed and has no known health problems at this time. The Canine Health Information Center has not recommended tests for the Bolognese.

Breed Clubs

America:
The Bolognese Club of America
http://www.boloclubofamerica.org/bca.htm

United Kingdom:
British Bolognese Club
http://britishbologneseclub.co.uk/new/

Boston Terrier

Boston Terriers are one of the best companions a person could ask for; they are alert, friendly, highly intelligent and affectionate.

Breed Summary

- Type: Pure
- Group: Non-Sporting
- Average life span: 15 years
- Average cost: $300-1,000
- Height: 15-17 inches (38-43 centimeters)
- Weight: 10-25 pounds (4-11 kilograms)
- Size: Small

History

The Boston Terrier, formerly the American Bull Terrier, was originally bred from pit-fighting bull and terrier dogs. These ancestors of the Boston Terrier were imported into the United States from Britain in 1865. The first Boston Terriers weighed up to 10 kilograms (44 pounds) and are one of the few breeds that were developed in the United States. They were gradually bred down in size and then crossed with French Bulldogs to produce the Boston Terrier (with their unique screw tail) we know today. By 1889, these dogs became very popular in Boston and the

American Bull Terrier Club was founded. In 1991 the breed was renamed to Boston Terrier, after the breed's birthplace. The Boston Terrier was the first non-sporting dog bred in the United States.

Famous Owners

- Joan Rivers' *Lulu*

- LeAnn Rimes' *Harley*

Appearance

The Boston Terrier is short-tailed, sturdy and compactly built, and with eyes that are wide apart, large, round and dark in color. The Boston Terrier has a short muzzle and small ears that are carried erect.

Coat: The Boston Terrier's has a short, smooth, bright and fine in texture. The Boston Terrier's color can be brindle, seal or black with white markings. White markings are usually located between the eyes and over the head (blaze), collar, and all or parts of the forelegs and hind legs. The Boston Terrier is an average shedder.

Temperament

Qualities

The Boston Terrier is known as 'the American Gentleman' due to a classy appearance, gentle disposition and love of companionship. The Boston Terrier carries an air of determination and strength. Boston Terriers are alert, lively, kind and friendly dogs.

Traits

Boston Terriers can get overexcited or rambunctious. The Boston Terrier is very sensitive to the tone of her owner's voice. They can also possess a stubborn streak.

Exercise

The Boston Terrier will need daily exercise. Time spent in an off-leash dog park or on a longer walk will be perfect. These dogs love to play and will burn off their energy quicker if they are exercised off-leash and have the chance to play with other dogs or chase after a ball. The Boston Terrier does well in an apartment because they don't need to roam around in a large space.

Special Talent

The Boston Terrier is the ultimate companion - her aim in life is to please her owner.

Children and Other Pets

Boston Terriers make great family pets - they are good with children, elderly people and strangers. The Boston Terrier is an affectionate breed and enjoys being treated like one of the family. Despite being 'terrier' by name, Boston Terriers are not 'terrier' by nature. As such, if socialized well, the Boston Terrier typically gets along with other household pets and dogs.

Trainability

★★★★★ 5 stars: Intelligent, bright, attentive and motivated to learn.

The Boston Terrier ranks 54th in Stanley Coren's *The Intelligence of Dogs*, being of average intelligence in working or obedience. The Boston Terrier wants nothing more than to please her owner, making her very trainable. These dogs are incredibly clever and quick to learn.

Boston Terriers can be challenging to housetrain.

Grooming

Moderate grooming is required for this breed. The Boston Terrier's smooth, short, easy to groom coat can be brushed occasionally. They are average shedders. Take care to clean her prominent eyes carefully on a daily basis. Debris may find its way into the Boston Terrier's open and erect ears; therefore check and clean her ears weekly.

Diet

The Boston Terrier possesses a sensitive digestive system, and so a good diet is necessary to help minimize the Boston Terrier's tendency for flatulence. However, a good diet does not guarantee success in this regard!

Barking

Boston Terriers make good watchdogs and bark only when necessary.

Health

The http://www.caninehealthinfo.org/breeds.html recommends the Boston Terrier is tested for:

- Congenital Deafness
- Patellar Luxation

Boston Terriers may suffer the following ailments:

- Trouble breathing when stressed, excessively exercised or enduring extreme weather conditions. Like the Pug and ShihTzu, the Boston Terrier is a brachycephalic breed, which means they have a short muzzle and can typically have breathing issues. Boston Terriers have a tendency to snore. They may also reverse sneeze; this behavior can be quite startling because the dog appears to be choking or gasping for breath. In actual fact, the dog is merely drawing air in through her mouth and nose simultaneously. The cause of this behavior is not known. Snoring and reverse sneezing is not considered life threatening.

- Difficulties giving birth because the breed's narrow pelvis and newborns' large heads. A 2010 UK Kennel Club survey revealed 90% of Boston Terrier litters are delivered by caesarean.

- A hereditary tendency toward heart and skin tumors.
- Eye injuries because of their prominent eyes.
- Eye conditions such as cataracts and cherry eye.
- Deafness
- Heart murmur
- Curvature of the back (roaching). This may be attributed to knee cap problems with the rear legs (causing the dog to lean forward onto her forelegs) or simply a physical characteristic of the dog.

Breed Clubs

America - http://bostonterrierclubofamerica.org/

United Kingdom - http://www.thebostonterrierclub.co.uk/

Australia - http://www.qldbostonterrierclub.com/

Cavalier King Charles Spaniel

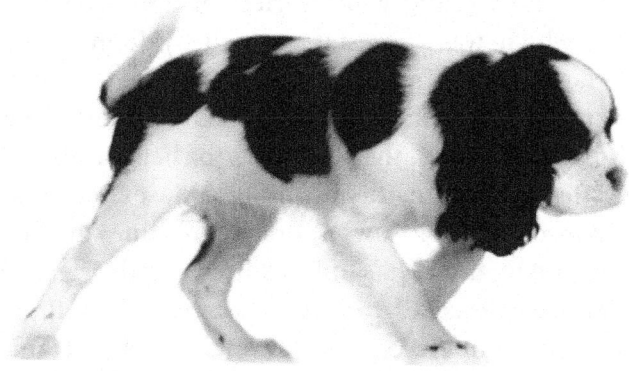

Extremely sweet-natured and friendly, the Cavalier dog greets everyone with great enthusiasm and a wagging tail!

Breed Summary

- Type: Pure
- Group: Toy
- Average life span: 9-14 years
- Average cost: $1,000-2,500
- Height: 12-13 inches (30-33 centimeters)
- Weight: 13-18 pounds (5-8 kilograms)
- Size: Small

History

The Cavalier King Charles Spaniel, namesake of King Charles II (1630-1685), originated in Great Britain. The Cavalier's predecessors, toy spaniels, were originally developed as hunters, later prized as house pets by English nobility. For centuries, these toy spaniels were depicted in paintings and tapestries along with their aristocratic families and so these toy spaniels became canine symbols of a family's wealth and privilege. Myths surround their utility, some believed the toy spaniels possessed the ability to keep fleas away and prevent some forms of stomach illness. In the late 1600's the long muzzle of the spaniels fell out of fashion, and shorter nosed breeds, particularly the Pug, became a favorite of the aristocracy. The toy spaniels were bred with such short nosed breeds, and possibly the Pug, which gave rise to the Cavalier we know today. The red and white variety of the Cavalier is named 'Blenheim', which was the estate owned by John Churchill, 1st Duke of Marlborough in the early part of the 18th century who owned many of these Cavaliers. By the 20th century there was a failed effort to restore the Cavalier to her original physical characteristics by breeding them with the now extinct Toy Trawler Spaniel. World War II saw a drastic decline in the breed's population, and by the 1940's only six breeding dogs existed. All of today's Cavaliers descend from these six dogs. The first Cavalier known to be living in the United States was brought from England in 1956 by W. Lyon Brown, who went on to co-found the Cavalier King Charles Club United States. In 1994, the American Cavalier King Charles Spaniel Club was also founded.

Famous Owners

- King Charles I of England's *Rogue*
- Former United States President Ronald Reagan and singer Frank Sinatra also owned Cavaliers
- Lauren Bacall's *Blenheim*
- Mickey Rooney's *Sir Digby*
- Princess Margaret's *Rowley*

Appearance

Although the Cavalier is one of the largest toy breeds, she is one of the smallest of the Spaniels. The Cavalier has large, soft and lustrous eyes with large, pendulous ears. A defining characteristic is the Cavalier's sweet, gentle and adoring facial expression. The Cavalier's chest is deep and the back is straight and level. The Cavalier's tail is carried horizontally with the ground and moves in a circular motion when the dog is active. The Cavalier's gait is elegant and carefree.

Coat: They have a distinctively beautiful, medium-length, silky coat that comes in four colors - Blenheim (chestnut and white), tri-color (black, white, and tan), ruby (solid red) and black and tan. The coat is very well feathered on the legs, chest, ears and tail. The coat is wavy, but not curly or woolly. The Cavalier is an average shedder.

Temperament

Qualities

The Cavalier is gentle, patient and sweet-natured. Loyal and affectionate, the Cavalier makes a great companion both in the home and during outings. At home, the Cavalier fits on the owner's lap perfectly as she is smaller than the typical Spaniel.

The Cavalier is quite a friendly breed and greets everyone with great enthusiasm and a wagging tail!

The Cavalier is a versatile dog as she is able to adapt to different families and lifestyles; families with children, couples and single people can all enjoy the company of this wonderful pet. Eager to please, the Cavalier does what she can to fit into any household and becomes a favorite amongst family members!

Traits

The Cavalier is said to possess boundless love for her owner. This means the Cavalier may not take kindly to being left alone for too long. Longs stints alone may lead to depression, separation anxiety and destructive behavior.

The Cavalier is quite sensitive to her owner's moods. A harsh tone or hollering may make the Cavalier nervous. If the Cavalier is constantly faced with such unpleasant behavior from her owner, the dog may develop a shy and insecure disposition.

As Cavaliers regard all strangers as potential friends, they do not generally perform well as guard dogs.

Exercise

The Cavalier is amazingly adaptable and so her activity level will naturally correspond with that of her owner. As such, Cavaliers do well with different people with different exercise needs such as active singles, busy families, as well as seniors and those with limited mobility.

Cavaliers are active dogs with boundless energy. Despite this, Cavaliers still make good apartment dogs as they enjoy playtime and lap time with their owner. Exercise and play each day will keep these dogs satisfied.

Cavaliers have a strong instinct to chase moving objects or animals, including vehicles on busy streets, and so they tend not to ever become streetwise. Therefore, care should be taken when walking these dogs - keep them on a leash when in open, public areas.

Special Talent

The Cavalier is endowed with special skills in competitive obedience.

Children and Other Pets

The Cavalier is an excellent companion for dogs and other pets in the family. As they love to chase, proper socialization is required so the Cavalier learns how to get along with her animal companions and not to give chase in the house. Cavaliers are a peaceful breed and will try to get along with any dog, even those of a larger size! Early socialization with other dogs will enable the Cavalier to harness her natural friendliness and confidence with other dogs.

Cavaliers are generally good with children, however these dogs can be especially fragile and should not be left alone with younger children who may accidentally harm them.

Trainability

★★★★★ 5 stars: Intelligent, bright, attentive and motivated to learn. The Cavalier's primary motivation is to please her owner and attract positive attention; this makes them great dogs to train in either obedience or tricks. The Cavalier ranks 44th in Stanley Coren's *The Intelligence of Dogs*, being of average intelligence in working or obedience. The Cavalier is intelligent, quick and very responsive making her easy to train. Positive methods coupled with consistency will serve the Cavalier well.

Grooming

As an average shedder, a Cavalier's coat requires moderate, but regular grooming. Dead hair, if not removed from the coat, will become matted and tangled. Grooming can be easily done in a short stint of ten minutes at least every second day. A stiff bristle brush and a grooming comb will suffice.

Carefully trim the long hair on the feet and between the pads with blunt edged grooming scissors. Gentle pressure on the top and bottom of the foot will cause the pads to spread apart, making it easy to clip and check for trapped debris.

Always check the ears for debris or signs of discharge and wipe with a warm, wet cloth. Also clean the area around the eyes with a damp cloth, using water only.

Diet

The Cavalier does not have any special dietary requirements.

Barking

The Cavalier is a friendly dog and so barking at strangers will not necessarily be an issue.

Health

The http://www.caninehealthinfo.org/breeds.html recommends the Cavalier is tested for:

- Hip Dysplasia

- Patellar Luxation

The Center also recommends regular eye examinations and cardiac evaluations.

Health concerns associated with the Cavalier also include mitral valve disease, chiari-like malformation and syringomyelia.

Breed Clubs

America- http://www.ckcsc.org/ and http://ackcsc.org/

United Kingdom - http://www.thecavalierclub.co.uk/

Australia - http://www.cavaliersa.com/

Chihuahua

They are very intelligent, loyal, devoted and spirited dog.

Breed Summary

- Type: Pure Breed
- Group: Toy
- Average life span: 15 years
- Average cost: $1,500-3,500
- Height: 6-9 inches (15-23 centimeters)
- Weight: 6 pounds (3 kilograms)
- Size: Small

History

There is no general consensus as to the Chihuahua's ancestry and so there are differing accounts of how this breed came to be.

Fennec Fox

There is speculation that the Chihuahua descends from the Fennec fox (*Fennecus Zerda*), a small animal from the deserts of Africa. Like these foxes, the Chihuahua likes to live in groups of her own kind (the Fennec differs from other foxes in regard), their prey of choice is small insects, rodents and lizards and they have poor dental health.

Asian Hairless Dogs

Some believe the Chihuahua descend from hairless dogs of Asia. These ancestors migrated from Russia into Alaska. Another story is that Chinese brought an early version of the Chinese Crested to the Americas in the 7th century B.C., which later became the Chihuahua.

The Mexican Connection

The Chihuahua may descend from the Xoloitzcuintli, a hairless breed which originated in Mexico.

Yet another theory suggests the breed did indeed come from Mexico, and rather being a descendant of the Xoloitzcuintl, the breed instead descends from the now extinct Toltec Techichi. The Toltec were a very small dog, possibly a rodent, whose likeness has been found amongst ruined stone carvings. Later, the Aztecs kept these sacred dogs as companions. Following the downfall of the Aztec civilization, the little dogs were left to fend for themselves. In 1850, some of these dogs were found in the ruins of a palace and brought to the United States.

Mexican peddlers were known to be selling them to tourists as early as 1884.

An Ancient Connection

Those that speculate the Chihuahua lived in Egypt 3,000 years ago, point to possible evidence, discovered in 1910, of the mummified remains of a little dog in an Egyptian tomb possessing a Molera, or opening in the top of the skull, much like that of a human infant, and a typical physical characteristic of today's Chihuahua.

The Recognition of the Breed

By the early 1900's Chihuahuas were recognized as a separate breed and, over time, their numbers grew. In 1923 the Chihuahua Club of America was formed. By 1952 long-coats and short-coats were officially recognized as separate varieties.

Famous Owners

- Paris Hilton's *Tinkerbell*
- Madonna's *Chiquita*
- Marilyn Monroe's *Choo-Choo*

Appearance

Chihuahuas walk swiftly and possess an alert demeanor. Chihuahuas are compact and small. Chihuahuas have oversized, apple-shaped heads, with prominent, luminous eyes and a saucy expression. The breed's eyes are generally dark, but light–colored Chihuahuas have ruby-colored eyes. Large, flared ears are a notable characteristic. The Chihuahua's tail is carried high and curled over their back.

Coat: There are two varieties of coats:

- Shorthaired coats are smooth, glossy, and are a little coarser than the long haired Chihuahua. The coat is a little longer in the body than the head and ears. Such Chihuahuas possess a furry tail and neck ruff.

- Longhaired coats are soft, and can be flat or wavy. Ears, feet, front and back legs are feathered with a plumed tail and neck ruff.

Chihuahuas are minimum to average shedders.

Temperament

Qualities

Chihuahuas make great watch dogs. They are known for only barking when something is hinky. If the Chihuahua barks, chances are there is something worth investigating.

Chihuahuas have no particular dietary requirements. But a good diet is highly recommended, as this will help combat dental issues to which the breed is prone.

Whether long or short-haired, this breed requires regular combing and brushing. The short coat will need to be brushed about once every week to remove dead fur and the long haired coat will need to be brushed about two to three times per week. Some people recommend daily brushing, especially the bib (long hair on the chest). Another area that can be a problem is the rear end, as fecal matter and other debris can become stuck in the fur. This area is usually clipped shorter or bathed more frequently.

The Chihuahua's large eyes tend to tear more that breeds with smaller eyes. This is so they can keep their eyes clean and clear of debris. The breed's watery eyes can cause tear stains.

Dental problems are a common in this breed, so keeping the Chihuahua's teeth clean is essential.

4 stars: Easy to train, like to please, but can be distractible. This breed will need a firm and consistent owner. Chihuahuas want to please their owners, so teaching them obedience and house rules can be a pleasure, if done well. The Chihuahua ranks 67[th]in Stanley Coren's *The Intelligence of Dogs,* being of fair intelligence in working or obedience.

The Chihuahua needs extensive socialization as puppies around people, dogs and children so she will be tolerant of others throughout her life.

As Chihuahuas are very loyal companions, they may show aggression towards others when in their owner's arms. This may seem funny and harmless at first, but this behavior should be firmly discouraged from the beginning. If allowed to develop, this behavior may result in the Chihuahua actually biting and nipping at anyone, even other family members. Once this behavior is ingrained it will be difficult to reverse.

The Chihuahua's most well-known characteristic is unrivaled loyalty and devotion.

Although small, Chihuahuas benefit from a walk daily. During outings, care must be taken that the Chihuahua does not challenge other dogs. This is because the Chihuahua is prone to behaving like a bigger, tougher dog!

This breed suits apartment living very well as they take up such little space; they enjoy the cozy family interaction an apartment affords.

Chihuahuas are possessive and will not like being separated from their owners. Chihuahuas are known to have a self-important outlook and walk with a purposeful strut. At times, Chihuahuas may shiver from fear or excitement. This may elicit sympathy from the owner, but beware the dog that employs this tactic for the sake of attention

Chihuahua may pick one member of the family and remain loyal to the person above all others. Chihuahuas love and crave human interaction.

intelligent, happy, spirited dogs. They make an affectionate lapdog. They have a good sense of reasoning skills. Chihuahuas are known for their loyalty and devotion. The Chihuahua may pick one member of the family and remain loyal to the person above all others. Chihuahuas love and crave human interaction.

Traits

Chihuahuas are possessive and will not like being separated from their owners. Chihuahuas are known to have a self-important outlook and walk with a purposeful strut. At times, Chihuahuas may shiver from fear or excitement. This may elicit sympathy from the owner, but beware the dog that employs this tactic for the sake of attention.

Exercise

Although small, Chihuahuas benefit from a walk daily. During outings, care must be taken that the Chihuahua does not challenge other dogs. This is because the Chihuahua is prone to behaving like a bigger, tougher dog!

This breed suits apartment living very well as they take up such little space; they enjoy the cozy family interaction an apartment affords.

Special Talent

The Chihuahua's most well-known characteristic is unrivaled loyalty and devotion.

Children and Other Pets

As Chihuahuas are very loyal companions, they may show aggression towards others when in their owner's arms. This may seem funny and harmless at first, but this behavior should be firmly discouraged from the beginning. If allowed to develop, this behavior may result in the Chihuahua actually biting and nipping at anyone, even other family members. Once this behavior is ingrained it will be difficult to reverse.

The Chihuahua needs extensive socialization as puppies around people, dogs and children so she will be tolerant of others throughout her life.

Trainability

★★★★ 4 stars: Easy to train, like to please, but can be distractible. This breed will need a firm and consistent owner. Chihuahuas want to please their owners, so teaching them obedience and house rules can be a pleasure, if done well. The Chihuahua ranks 67th in Stanley Coren's *The Intelligence of Dogs,* being of fair intelligence in working or obedience.

Grooming

Whether long or short-haired, this breed requires regular combing and brushing. The short coat will need to be brushed about once every week to remove dead fur and the long haired coat will need to be brushed about two to three times per week. Some people recommend daily brushing, especially the bib (long hair on the chest). Another area that can be a problem is the rear end, as fecal matter and other debris can become stuck in the fur. This area is usually clipped shorter or bathed more frequently.

The Chihuahua's large eyes tend to tear more that breeds with smaller eyes. This is so they can keep their eyes clean and clear of debris. The breed's watery eyes can cause tear stains.

Dental problems are a common in this breed, so keeping the Chihuahua's teeth clean is essential.

Diet

Chihuahuas have no particular dietary requirements. But a good diet is highly recommended, as this will help combat dental issues to which the breed is prone.

Barking

Chihuahuas make great watch dogs. They are known for only barking when something is hinky. If the Chihuahua barks, chances are there is something worth investigating.

Health

The http://www.caninehealthinfo.org/breeds.html recommends the Chihuahua is tested for:

- Congenital cardiac issues – Chihuahuas may encounter heart-valve issues such as mitral valve heart disease and heart murmurs
- Eyes issues - Chihuahuas may be prone to eye problems such as glaucoma and corneal dryness because of their protruding eyes
- Patellar Luxation – Chihuahuas may suffer from knee caps slipping out of place

Chihuahuas may also be prone to:

- Hypoglycemia

- Open Fontanelle
- Rheumatism
- Epilepsy
- Demodicosis
- Cystinuria
- Hemophilia
- Pulmonic stenosis
- Collapsing tracheas

Breed Clubs

America - http://www.chihuahuaclubofamerica.com/

United Kingdom - http://www.the-british-chihuahua-club.org.uk/

Australia - http://www.chihuahuaclubofsainc.com/default.asp

Chinese Crested

The Chinese Crested is good with tricks. They are sweet, lively, affectionate and tirelessly playful.

Breed Summary

- Type: Pure
- Group: Toy
- Average life span: 10-14 years
- Average cost: $500-1,000
- Height: 11-13 inches (27-33 centimeters)
- Weight: 12 pounds (5.4 kilograms)
- Size: Small

History

Despite the breed's name, it has been argued that the Chinese Crested is not, in fact, originally from China. Rather, the breed may have originated in Africa. Several 19th century texts refer to this breed as the African Hairless Terrier. The story goes that the breed was discovered by Chinese sailors and merchants used these dogs as ratters on their ships. The breed was brought back to

China and bred smaller and gentler, and then the breed was traded as the 'Chinese Hairless' or 'Chinese Crested'.

Some argue the breed did actually come from China and was traded with merchants in South America.

Some believe the Chinese Crested may be the result of the Aztec civilization crossing the Mexican Hairless Dog and the Chihuahua. There is genetic evidence that shows a shared origin with the Mexican Hairless (Xoloitzcuintli). The Aztecs may have used these dogs as companions, bed-warmers in colder months and even as a delicacy at special events.

In the 1800's the breed became known in Europe and North America and in the 1950s; Debora Wood created the 'Crest Haven' kennel where she bred and recorded their lineages. The Chinese Cresteds belonging to burlesque dancer Gypsy Rose Lee were given to Crest Haven upon her death. These two blood lines are the foundation of subsequent generations of this breed.

Debora Wood founded the American Hairless Dog Club in 1959, eventually renamed the American Chinese Crested Club in 1978. The Chinese Crested was recognized by the American Kennel Club in 1991.

Famous Owners

In the 1950s, Debora Wood created the 'Crest Haven' kennel where she bred the Chinese Cresteds. Burlesque dancer Gypsy Rose Lee also owned Chinese Cresteds.

The Chinese Crested has been featured in TV and movies, such as *Halston* in *Ugly Betty* and *Krull* in *How to Lose a Guy in 10 Days*.

Appearance

The Chinese Crested is an elegant, fine-boned Toy breed with her head resembling that of a fox. The Chinese Crested is refined in appearance with an alert and intense expression. The Chinese

Crested has almond shaped eyes and her ears are large and erect. The Chinese Crested's tail is long, slender, and may be carried slightly forward over the back as she is walking.

A distinctive feature of the Chinese Crested breed is her hare feet, which means she possesses elongated toes. The Chinese Crested therefore has an uncanny ability to grasp items such as food, toys and even their human companions! Other breeds have 'cat feet', which means shorter toes.

Coat: There are two varieties of Chinese Crested – the hairless and 'powder puff'. The hairless has no coat except for a flowing mane, hair on her feet, and plumed tail. In almost every litter, there are some hairy dogs that grow into luxuriantly coated adults resembling little sheepdogs; these are known as powder puffs. The powder puff variety is completely covered with a double coat. The coat is soft, silky straight, somewhat dense and long. The Chinese Crested may be any color or combination.

The powder-puff trait is carried by both varieties and so cannot be bred out. Every hairless Chinese Crested has the ability to produce powder puff dogs, however, there is no way to predict if this will happen or not. Having said that, powder puffs bred together can never produce hairless dogs, since they do not carry the hairless gene.

Temperament

Qualities

The Chinese Crested is sweet and lively. Highly affectionate and exuberant, this dog will suit a spirited, playful owner. Your affection will be rewarded with returned affection, particularly as her hare feet give this dog the ability to grip in almost human-like fashion – quite a charming quality! The Chinese Crested loves being close to her owner and will always welcome cuddles.

Loving, funny and intelligent, this dog is suitable for any individual and family as long as they can provide frequent companionship and attention. Busy households with little time for pets or long absences will not suit this breed.

Traits

Initially timid, the Chinese Crested will warm to new company, especially if properly socialized as a pup. The Chinese Crested needs lots of family time and will become destructive or misbehave if left alone for too long.

The Chinese Crested bonds for life; this dog may choose one or two people in the family and even when these people leave the house, the dog will continue to wait or look for them. As such, they can be difficult to rehome or adopt.

Although suitable for families, the Chinese Crested needs children who are gentle. Rambunctious children may harm or terrorize this sensitive dog.

Tirelessly playful, the Chinese Crested can be a little hyperactive. An attentive and energetic owner is therefore a better companion for this breed.

Exercise

Keeping the Chinese Crested active is important, especially as this breed is prone to weight gain. An owner can meet some of the Chinese Crested's exercise requirements very easily in an apartment setting with playtime, games, tricks or simply encouraging her to wander and run around the apartment. Surprisingly, they are quite agile and can climb too!

Small, and somewhat delicate, the Chinese Crested should not be roughhoused as there is a risk of injury. Also, avoid any activity which involves jumping certain heights; this will save joint issues down the track.

A daily walk is also recommended. The hairless variety needs protection from the elements; sunblock all year round and a coat in winter is recommended. Also, beware of bushes and heavy grasses that may break this dog's skin.

Special Talent

The Chinese Crested possesses excellent agility, loves performing tricks and is a good climber.

Children and Other Pets

Chinese Crested makes a friendly, entertaining and playful family pet. Because she is rather delicate, she does best with older or gentle children.

The Chinese Crested will happily play and interact with dogs, cats and other pets. The hairless variety may suffer some scratches as a result of such play, so monitor this carefully.

Trainability

★★★ 3 stars: Requires consistent training by an experienced handler due to stubbornness or a need for variety. This breed will need a firm, fun and consistent handler. The Chinese Crested wants to please her owner, so teaching her obedience and house rules can be a pleasure. The Chinese Crested ranks 67th in Stanley Coren's *The Intelligence of Dogs*, being of fair intelligence in working or obedience. This breed may be stubborn or headstrong, however, this attitude may pass with fair leadership. The Chinese Crested may be timid around new people, sudden noises and new experiences. Therefore, socialization and exposure to new places, animals and people from puppyhood is a must.

For advanced obedience and tricks, then look no further than the Chinese Crested! This dog is ideal for those wanting a pet that performs interesting tricks. Examples of such tricks include sitting up, walking on her hind legs and climbing ladders.

Grooming

The Chinese Crested is clean, relatively odor-free and less likely to suffer from fleas and ticks. Because of their cleanliness, the Chinese Crested will avoid soiling in the apartment. Therefore, this breed can be taught to use a litter box or dog pads.

Because of her hare feet, the Chinese Crested's quicks run deeper into the nails. Take care not to trim the nails too short to avoid bleeding and pain.

Because of her susceptibility to acne, dryness and sunburn, care of both varieties of the Chinese Crested should include the use of hypoallergenic or oil-free moisturizing cream and baby sunscreen. Avoid using lanolin-based products on the Chinese Crested's skin, as some have allergies to it.

Trimming or shaving may be required to remove excess hair growth.

Regular brushing will keep the powder-puff's coat from becoming matted. A bath every 3-4 weeks is recommended.

The Chinese Crested can have what is called 'primitive mouth' - most of her teeth are pointy (like the canine teeth). The hairless, in particular, is prone to missing or crowded teeth. As such, she may be prone to teeth decay or tartar build-up if proper dental hygiene is not observed. Powder-puffs do not suffer from such poor dentition.

Diet

The Chinese Crested does not have any special dietary requirements. The Chinese Crested adores food, her body feeling hotter to the touch after she has eaten. Prone to obesity, the Chinese Crested will require a sensible diet and active lifestyle to help keep her healthy. Food portions can be increased a little in the winter months, to help keep her warm.

Barking

While not a problem barker, the Chinese Crested may resort to other problem behavior if left alone for too long.

Health

The http://www.caninehealthinfo.org/breeds.html recommends the Chinese Crested is tested for:

- Congenital cardiac issues
- Congenital deafness
- Eyes issues – The Chinese Crested may be prone to a painful and blinding inherited eye disease called primary lens Luxation and progressive retinal atrophy which can lead to blindness as well. The breed may also inherit another eye disease called Keratoconjunctivitis sicca (dry eye syndrome).
- Patellar Luxation – The Chinese Crested may suffer from knee caps slipping out of place.
- Hip dysplasia/Legg Calve Perthes – The Chinese Crested may suffer from a degeneration of the femur causing joint immobility and pain.

Along with Kerry Blue Terriers, the Chinese Crested can develop canine multiple system degeneration. This is a progressive movement disorder that begins between 10 and 14 weeks of age. After 6 months of age, the affected dog develops difficulty instigating movements and may fall frequently.

Breed Clubs

America - http://www.chinesecrestedclub.info/

United Kingdom - http://www.thechinesecrestedclubofgb.co.uk/

Australia - http://www.thechinesecresteddogclubofnsw.asn.au/

Chow Chow

The Chow makes a great watch dog. Sturdy and loyal, the Chow is a wonderful bear-like companion, with a laid-back attitude.

Breed Summary

- Type: Pure
- Group: Non-Sporting
- Average life span: 15 years
- Average cost: $500-1800
- Height: 17-22 inches (43-56 centimeters)
- Weight: 40-70 pounds (18-31 kilograms)
- Size: Medium

History

The Chow is an ancient northern Chinese breed originally used for hunting, herding, pulling and protection. The oldest know dog fossils date back several million years and resemble those of the Chow. In fact, the Chow's DNA shows the breed was one of the first to become domesticated from wild wolves. There are images depicting the Chow on ancient Chinese pottery dating back as far as 206 B.C., meaning this breed has been a native of China for about 2,000 years. The Chow may have been the original 'Mastiff' of the Tibetan Lama, and is also referred to in early Chinese writings as the Tartar Dog and the Dog of the Barbarians. The Chow may share ancestry with the Chinese Shar-Pei, Spitz, Keeshond, Samoyed, Norwegian Elkhound and Pomeranian. Beginning in 1760, Chows were purchased by English merchants, who brought them back to Britain where they were also exhibited in a zoo. Speculation as to the origin of the breed's name is rife; their original name, however, is *Songshi Quan*, which literally translated is 'puffy lion dog'. One theory is that the breed's name may have originated from the English word 'chow-chow', a term referring to various bits and pieces bought back from the Far East. In 1905 this breed was exported from Britain to America. Today, the Chow is primarily a companion dog.

Famous Owners

- Martha Stewart's *Paw Paw*
- Sigmund Freud's *Jo-Fi*
- Janet Jackson's *Buckwheat*

Appearance

The lion-like Chow is a large, stocky dog with a flat skull, broad, rounded muzzle and small triangular shaped ears. The Chow's eyes are deep-set and almond in shape. They are commonly known by their blue-black tongue - a characteristic they share with bears. This bluish color extends to the Chow's lips and oral cavity; this is the only dog breed that enjoys this distinguishing feature - other dogs have a black or a piebald pattern skin in their mouths. The nose can be black, or in the case of a blue-coated Chow, solid blue or slate-colored.

Chows have practically straight hind legs which give them a unique, stilted walk. The Chow's head is carried proudly and large in proportion to the body size. The thick ruff behind the Chow's head is said to resemble a lion's mane. The Chow has a dignified, sober, scowling and thoughtful expression. They should have a strong muscular appearance. The Chow also has a curly tail.

Coat: The Chow's coat gives them the appearance of a little bear. Their heavy double coat means Chows enjoy cooler weather, and can withstand very cold weather conditions. Their dense coats can be either smooth or rough. However, the Chow can be sensitive to hot conditions. The Chow's coat can be solid red, black, tan, blue, cinnamon or cream, and is also occasionally found in white. They may have lighter shading in the ruff, tail and featherings. The Chow sheds heavily at least twice annually.

Temperament

Qualities

Despite being an affable, faithful and loyal companion, the Chow exhibits the independent nature of a cat. A willingness to please may be present in some dogs, but the Chow is more likely to be a somewhat autonomous pet. Therefore, Chows make ideal pets for people looking for a dog that is easy to care for and is not needy.

The Chow is typically aloof with strangers, but bonds very closely with one owner. The Chow is a robust dog and she can demonstrate strong loyalty. The Chow guards the owner well. Chows are known for their laid-back, yet majestic demeanor. The Chow should be socialized early and more often with both people and other animals to bring out her best.

The Chow makes a wonderfully self-assured, yet loving, pet.

Traits

The saying goes that the Chow will readily die for her master, but will not readily obey! Forcing a Chow to comply can make her aggressive. The Chow's dominant streak must be managed (with strong leadership), but never broken.

Completely loyalty to her family, the Chow will be somewhat aloof with strangers and unknown animals. Chows can become fiercely protective of their family and territory. Owning a Chow can raise the cost of homeowners' insurance, as some insurance companies consider them high-risk dogs. The *Journal of the American*

Veterinary Medical Association, reported that out of 238 dog-bite fatalities between 1979 and 1998, the Chow was responsible for eight.

Because of her small, deep set eyes, the Chow has limited peripheral vision. Approach this dog from the front, to avoid giving the Chow any surprises.

Exercise

The Chow is a laid back dog that only requires moderate exercise. Chows are not overly active, and so they can be suited to an apartment lifestyle. However, Chows still need daily exercise. This will help stave off restlessness and boredom as well as provide a much needed avenue for regular socialization, something this breed needs. Some Chows may not take kindly to a leash. If the Chow is not properly trained, then off-leash activities are not recommended in open areas as they tend to have a mind of their own.

Once the Chow realizes that a walk or other exercise will occur daily, she will tend to assert her desire for the owner to make good on this arrangement!

Special Talent

The Chow is an excellent, loyal watch dog.

Children and Other Pets

The Chow is typically good with children and other pets if they get to know them when they are young.

Trainability

★★ 2 stars: Difficult to train and require experienced dog handlers. The Chow's cat-like personality makes her less eager to please than other breeds. The Chow needs firm training from an experienced owner. Chows are naturally dominant in personality and will need their master to be consistent and firm. A forceful approach will only result in the Chow becoming more stubborn. Although very clever, the Chow's stubborn attitude may frustrate progress. Diligence and patience is therefore a must! On the other hands, begging, pleading or cajoling will not elicit the desired response. These dogs will not 'perform' for their owner, simply because the Chow has no inclination   to   please   others.

Socialization from an early age is also a necessity. As they were originally bred to be guard dogs, Chows naturally take a hard-line stance in new situations. Whilst this may not result in acts of aggression, the Chow must be taught to be more tolerant and accepting of the unfamiliar.

Grooming

Whilst the Chow's temperament makes her an easy dog to care for, the grooming requirements are somewhat more demanding. The good news is that this odor-free and clean breed actually enjoys grooming activities! Grooming serves the dual purpose of maintaining the Chow's lustrous coat and allowing dog and owner to heighten their bond.

Regular brushing with a stiff bristled comb or slicker brush twice weekly is recommended. Apply a coat dressing to keep static to a minimum and condition the coat. Due to the breed's dense and thick coat (which makes it hard to dry thoroughly) dry shampooing is preferable to wet baths.

The Chow sheds heavily at least twice annually.

Despite the temptation to shave the Chow's heavy coat in order to save her from discomfort in summer, this is not recommended as this can lead to sunburned skin. Instead, ensure dead hair is brushed out. Always brush all the way down to the skin so debris and moisture is not able to become trapped and cause skin problems.

This type of coat has a tendency to mat rather easily if not properly cared for.

Due to the Chow's thick coat, fleas can be an issue.

Diet

Chows do not have any special dietary requirements.

Barking

These dogs are not known to bark unnecessarily, however due to their relatively short muzzles, Chows often snore.

Health

The http://www.caninehealthinfo.org/breeds.html recommends the Chow is tested for:

- Eye issues such as entropion, glaucoma and juvenile cataracts
- Elbow and hip dysplasia
- Autoimmune thyroiditis
- Patellar Luxation

Chows also have a predisposition for stomach cancer, hot spots, ear infections, lymphoma, diabetes mellitus, canine pemphigus and skin melanoma.

Breed Clubs

America - http://chowclub.org/ccci/

United Kingdom - http://www.thechowchowclub.co.uk/

Australia - http://chowchowclubvic.com.au/

Chow clubs often organize agility and other similar activities as this breed tends to enjoy the stimulation that navigating obstacles affords.

Cocker Spaniel

The Cocker Spaniel is a cheerful and a sweet companion. They are respectful, lively, playful and obedient dogs.

Breed Summary

- Type: Pure
- Group: Sporting
- Average life span: 12-15 years
- Average cost: $400-1100
- Height: 15 inches (38 centimeters)
- Weight: 15-30 pounds (7-14 kilograms)
- Size: Small

History

There are two types of spaniels: the American Cocker Spaniel and English Cocker Spaniel, both of which are simply called *Cocker Spaniel* in their respective countries of origin.

The breed originated in Spain (the word 'spaniel' comes from *Espagnol*, meaning Spanish). Used in falconry, Spaniels were also first mentioned in the 14th century literature and later became known as the 'cocking' or 'cocker spaniel' in the 19th century. Prior to 1901, Cocker Spaniels were only separated from Field Spaniels and Springer Spaniels by weight. The American Cocker Spaniel has evolved differently in appearance from the breed now known as the English Cocker Spaniel. In addition, there is a second strain of an English Cocker Spaniel, a working strain which is bred to work.

Cocker Spaniels were originally bred as hunting dogs in the United Kingdom, with the term cocker coming from their use as hunters of small bird known as the Woodcock. When the breed was brought to the United States, she specialized in hunting other types of Woodcock. The American Cocker Spaniel was never used as extensively as a gun and hunting dog in the United States, although this breed is excellent in hunting game birds such as pheasants, quail and partridges.

The Cocker Spaniel becomes increasingly popular and was one of the most popular breeds of the 1940's. By this time, the breed was almost exclusively used as a companion dog. Currently, the Cocker Spaniel is considered the fifteenth most popular dog breed in the United States and continues to be a favorite around the world.

Famous Owners

- Actor, Mark Radcliffe, known for portraying *Harry Potter* owns a Cocker Spaniel

- Former President of the United States, Rutherford B. Hayes' *Dot*

Appearance

Cocker Spaniels, the smallest member of the Sporting Group, are compact, sturdy dogs with finely chiselled heads and a balanced body. The Cocker Spaniel's ears long, pendulous and well feathered. The eyes are round, with a warm yet cheeky twinkle in their eyes.

Coat: The Cocker Spaniel has a silky, medium length coat, which is relatively easy to care for. The coat of the Cocker Spaniel varies in length with the hair on the head short and sleek and the hair on the ears, neck and chest being moderately long and well feathered. The rest of the body including the legs is well feathered with a silky, fine and flat hair that is easy to care for and very silky to the touch.

Temperament

Qualities

The Cocker Spaniel is also called the Merry Cocker because of her wagging tail. They are exceptionally friendly, but some may like to sound the alarm when strangers approach. They make excellent companions and also make great hunting dogs.

Traits

The Cocker Spaniel can be left alone for short to moderate periods of time but do not do well when left alone for long periods. They need human contact and interaction to be happy and content. Without enough attention they may be prone to habits such as chewing, barking and other separation-related problems.

Exercise

The Cocker Spaniel has plenty of energy and stamina. Their adaptability means they can adjust to various levels of exercise; periods of inactivity do not phase this dog. As they are natural retrievers, Cocker Spaniels will love the game of fetch. Working lines of Cocker Spaniels actively used as hunting dogs are more athletic than the show lines and so require additional exercise. Her desire to hunt renders her a capable gun dog; she covers the territory speedily, flushing game and retrieving on command. She takes to water readily.

Special Talent

The Cocker Spaniel possesses exceptional agility, and can specialize in hunting, retrieving, sledding and tracking.

Children and Other Pets

The Cocker Spaniel is a happy, friendly and enthusiastic dog that is great with families and children. They are great dogs for families as well as single people and really love being with humans, they are typically good with children and other family pets. The Cocker Spaniel is not a timid dog; rather they are just easy going and willing to accept other dogs into their space. They love everyone they meet. Cocker Spaniels that are raised with cats and other animals, will be gentle, affectionate and generous companions, sharing their bed and toys.

The Cocker Spaniel loves to be active and does best with a family where there is moderate to high activity, especially when the dog is young. They enjoy interacting with children and are tolerant of even very young children.

Trainability

5 stars: Intelligent, bright, attentive and motivated to learn. Typically, Cocker Spaniels are not a dominant and are willing to learn. The Cocker Spaniel is a dog that aims to please her owner. Unlike some of the hunting breeds they do not have a strong streak of independence and are generally very compliant. They tend to be soft dogs that do not do well with rough or harsh training. Cocker Spaniels rank 20th in Stanley Coren's *The Intelligence of Dogs*, as they possess excellent intelligence in working.

Grooming

The Cocker Spaniel requires regular care; daily (or every other day) brushing is ideal. To groom the Cocker Spaniel start with a pin brush or wide toothed grooming comb and begin at either the neck or the rump. Brush in the direction of hair growth. Never brush against the grain. Follow with a slicker brush to remove fine tangles. Groom the head and ears with a soft bristle brush. Excessive clipping of tangles may result in an uneven looking coat.

When engaging in gundog activities, the Cocker Spaniel needs careful brushing and combing every day, and care must be taken to remove mud that may be caked in her paws and ears. If used for hunting, or in the summer seasons, many people clip the Cocker Spaniel in a 'sport' or 'puppy cut' for easy care.

The Cocker Spaniel's eyes require regular with a water dampened cotton cloth. Removing debris from the eye helps fight infections.

The ears should be checked for any sign of wax build up or foul smelling discharge that can indicate an ear infection. Always take care when cleaning the ear and never clean past the outer ear. A veterinarian can flush out the ear, if required.

Diet

Cocker Spaniel does not have any special dietary requirements.

Barking

Some Cocker Spaniels like to bark. Barking can become a problem so teach the Cocker Spaniel to only bark once or twice when sounding the alarm.

Health

The http://www.caninehealthinfo.org/breeds.html recommends the Cocker Spaniel is tested for:

- Congenital cardiac issues
- Eye issues - glaucoma, cataracts, entropion and ectropion and Progressive Retinal Atrophy (which results in eventual blindness).
- Hip Dysplasia

Some of the more serious health concerns are:

- Immune Mediated Hemolytic Anemia
- Skin-allergies, seborrhea, lip fold pyoderma all which can lead to irritations and skin infections as the dog scratches and rubs the area
- Otitis externa
- Phosphofructokinase deficiency
- Cardiomyopathy-heart conditions such as disease or muscle development problems

Breed Clubs

America - http://www.asc-cockerspaniel.org/

United Kingdom - http://www.thecockerspanielclub.co.uk/

Australia - http://www.cockerspanielclubvic.org/Links.html

Coton de Tulear

The Coton de Tulear is gentle, friendly, alert and affectionate.

Breed Summary

- Type: Pure
- Group: Non-Sporting
- Average life span: 14-16 years
- Average cost: $1,000-3,500
- Height: 9-13 inches (23-33 centimetres)
- Weight: 11-15 pounds (5-7 kilograms)
- Size: Small

The Coton de Tulear was developed on the island of Madagascar, more specifically on the port of Tulear. The Coton de Tulear is a Bichon, and is linked most closely to the Bichon Tenerife and Tenerife Terrier. It is believed that the Tenerife dog was brought to Madagascar by pirates or French troops in the 16th and 17th centuries, and mated with a dog on the island - the result was a small, athletic and uniquely coated dog that came to be known as the 'Royal dog of Madagascar' and is still the island's national dog.

This small, friendly dog caught the fancy of the Malagasy royalty and they were the only people allowed to keep these dogs. When Dr. Robert Jay Russell discovered the breed in Madagascar in 1973 and brought the first ones to America, he coined the phrase 'the Royal Dog of Madagascar' and the name stuck. Dr. Robert Jay Russell also formed the Coton de Tulear Club of America in 1976. The Coton de Tulear is a relatively rare breed that is steadily gaining more popularity around the world.

Famous Owners

- Welsh actress, Catherine Zeta Jones, once received Coton de Tulear for her birthday
- Jane Fonda's *Tulea* (named after the town in Madagascar where the breed originated, Tulear)
- Barbra Streisand's *Samantha*

Appearance

The Coton de Tulear is small dog of the Bichon family with soft, cottony hair, a black or dark nose, expressive eyes that are set wide apart. The ears are triangular, set high and the paws are small and arched. The tail is low set and tapering. Their short legs are straight and well-muscled.

Coat: The eyes of the mature Coton de Tulear will be covered with the long hair from the forehead. They have a medium to long hair that is more like hair than fur; their coat can range in length from 4-6 inches (10-15 centimeters) in length.

Temperament

Qualities

The Coton de Tulear is playful, affectionate, intelligent, happy and is known to have a habit of walking on her hind legs to please people. Although generally quiet, this breed loves meeting new people and can become very vocal (by grunting and barking) when having fun.

Despite her fluffy and toy-like appearance, this breed is very sturdy and enjoys fun time with family. These dogs are ideal for any type of home or family situation; they interact well with children or the elderly and can adjust to the amount of exercise that the home provides.

Coton de Tulears are very gentle, friendly, affectionate in nature. They seem to constantly be smiling, wagging their tails and wanting to be around the family.

Traits

The Coton de Tulear does not appreciate being left alone for long periods; therefore this breed can be susceptible to separation anxiety. This breed is not suitable for people will have a lifestyle where their dog is left alone for long periods or cannot be included in family activities.

Exercise

Being a natural retriever, the Coton deTulear enjoys fetch. Exercise is needed to stay fit and healthy, and so regular walks or joggingare suitable activities for this breed. As such, the Coton de Tulear is suitable for an active owner or family. They make an ideal apartment dog, as they can play and fetch just as easily indoors as they do outside.

Special Talent

Coton de Tulears are ideal jogging companions, and can perform tricks, if trained to do so.

Children and Other Pets

Coton de Tulears are very sociable dogs and they get along with children, as well as other animals or house pets. The Coton de Tulear is an excellent companion dog for either smaller or larger dog breeds.

Trainability

3 stars: Requires consistent training by an experienced handler due to stubbornness or a need for variety. As a companion dog, the Coton de Tulear is sensitive to her owner's wishes and is eager to please. They are eager to learn and love competition and being in the spotlight. Coton de Tulears are very pleasant to train, although they are occasionally a bit headstrong. They learn quickly and are eager to work; however, they need consistency as they pick up bad habits as quickly as they pick up good ones! Most Coton de Tulearsare clean dogs; puppies will almost house-train themselves, if given the opportunity to get outside when needed. Teaching the Coton de Tulear tricks and entertaining routines is relatively easy.

Grooming

Even though they are low shedding, the Coton de Tulear's coat requires daily grooming. Since the hair is silky and dry to the touch, it is typically easy to groom using a wide toothed grooming comb or a pin brush. Start at the neck and groom towards the back, following the direction of hair growth.

The Coton de Tulear usually only sheds hair when being groomed, much like a human loses hair when they brush. Excess hair from between the paw pads and any long hairs in the outer ear area should be trimmed to avoid irritation.

It is unnecessary to usually bathe Coton de Tulears often because their coat's texture keeps them relatively clean. Their coat should not be clipped and should be left natural. The ears need to be cleaned regularly to avoid ear infections.

Because they are low-shedding, many people say that they are good for allergy-sufferers.

Diet

Coton de Tulears do not have any special dietary requirements.

Barking

This breed is not known to have any issues with excessive barking.

Health

The http://www.caninehealthinfo.org/breeds.html recommends the Coton de Tulear is tested for:

- Eye problems
- Patellar Luxation
- Hip Dysplasia

The Coton de Tulear is generally a healthy breed with no known health problems. However, this breed can be afflicted with heart problems, liver shunts and back (disc) problems.

In the United States all Coton de Tulears must complete a blood chemistry test as well as a general health test to qualify for breeding status in the Coton de Tulear registry. The conditions that the health exams look for include Legg Calve Perthes disease.

Breed Clubs

America- http://www.cotonclub.org/

United Kingdom - http://www.cdtclubuk.org/

Dachshund

The Dachshund is a proud little breed; these dogs are lively, clever, courageous and devoted to their owner.

Breed Summary

- Type: Pure
- Group: (Scent) Hound
- Average life span: 12-15 years
- Average cost: $250-500
- Height: 14-18 inches (35-45 centimeters)
- Weight: 16-32 pounds (7-14 kilograms)
- Size: Small

History

Dachshund experts have theorized that the early roots of the Dachshund go back to ancient Egypt, where engravings depicted short-legged hunting dogs. The recent discovery by the American University in Cairo of mummified Dachshund-like dogs in ancient Egyptian burial urns might give credibility to this theory.

The first verified reference to the Dachshund, originally named them 'Dachs Kriecher' ('Badger Crawler') or 'Dachs Krieger' ('Badger Warrior'), came from books written in the early 18th century. The Dachshund is the creation of German breeders and includes elements of German, French and English hounds and terriers. Dachshunds have traditionally been viewed as a symbol of Germany. Due to the association of the breed with Germany, the

Dachshund was chosen to be the first official mascot - named *Waldi* - for the 1972 Summer Olympics in Munich. They have been kept by royal courts all over Europe, including that of Queen Victoria, who was particularly fascinated by the breed. Originally, they were bred to hunt badgers by trailing scent.

The original German Dachshunds were larger than the modern variety, weighing between 30 and 40 pounds (14 and 18 kilograms), and came in straight-legged and crook-legged varieties (the modern Dachshund is descended from the latter). Though the breed is famous for exterminating badgers and badger-baiting, Dachshunds were also commonly used for rabbit and fox hunting, locating wounded deer, and pack hunting large game such as wild boar and the fierce wolverine.

The flap-down ears and famous curved tail of the Dachshund have deliberately been bred into the dog. In the case of the ears, this is to keep grass seeds, dirt, and other matter from entering the ear canal. The curved tail has a dual-purpose: to be seen more easily in long grass and, in the case of burrowing Dachshunds, to help pull the dog out if she becomes stuck in a burrow.

Famous Owners

- John F. Kennedy bought a Dachshund puppy for his then-girlfriend Olivia, whilst touring Europe in 1937. The puppy, *Dunker*, never left Germany after Kennedy started getting terrible allergies.
- William Randolph Hearst's *Helena*
- Pablo Picasso's *Lump* (thought to have inspired some of his artwork. Pronounced *Loomp* which is German for 'Rascal'. *Picasso and Lump: A Dachshund's Odyssey* tells the story of Picasso and Lump.
- Andy Warhol's *Archie* and *Amos*, whom he mentioned frequently in his diaries and depicted in his paintings.
- Donald Rumsfeld's *Reggy*
- Kevin Smith's *Shecky*

Appearance

There are six varieties of Dachshund: Smooth-haired, Long-haired and Wire-haired, each occurring as both Standard and Miniature. The Dachshunds Standard weight is 16-32 pounds (7-15 kilograms), the Miniature is under 11 pounds (5 kilograms). Their standard height is 25-28 centimeters (10-11inches) and the miniature is 20 centimeters (8 inches).

A typical Dachshund is long-bodied and muscular, with short, stubby legs. The paws are unusually large and paddle-shaped, for powerful digging. Long coated Dachshunds have a silky coat and short featherings on their legs and ears. The skin is loose enough not to tear while tunneling in tight burrows. The Dachshund has a deep chest to allow enough lung capacity to endure long periods of hunting.

Coat. The smooth coat is short, smooth and shiny. The wire-haired coat consists of a uniform tight coarse outer coat with a fine, soft and longer undercoat. This variety of Dachshund has a beard and eyebrows. However, the hair is shorter and smooth on the ears. Their tails have thick hair and taper to a point.The longhaired coat has sleek hair, often with a slight wave. The hair is longer under the neck and on the chest, the underside of the body and on the ears and behind the legs. Their tails have the longest hair and are carried like a flag.

Dachshunds have a wide variety of colors and patterns; they can be single-colored, single-colored with spots, and single-colored with tan points plus any pattern. The most common color is red and the black and tan variety. Isabella is a silver/gray all over color with light translucent brown points or no distinct points at all. Two-colored dogs can be black, wild boar, chocolate, fawn, with tan 'points', or markings over the eyes, ears, paws, and a tail of tan or cream. Other patterns include piebald, in which a white pattern is imposed upon the base color or any other pattern, and a lighter 'boar' red. The reds range from coppers to deep rusts, with or without somewhat common black hairs peppered along the back, face and ear edges, lending much character and an almost burnished appearance; this is referred to among breeders and enthusiasts as a 'stag', 'overlay' or 'sable'. True sable in a Dachshund is when each single hair is banded with three colors: light at the base of the hair, red in the middle, black at the end. An additional striking coat marking is the brindle pattern with stripes over a solid background, usually red. If a Dachshund is brindled on a dark coat and has tan points, she will have brindle on the tan points only.

Temperament

Qualities

Dachshunds are full of verve - they are sprightly, curious, lovable and extremely playful companions. Outgoing in nature, the Dachshund requires a large amount of interaction and engagement. They require moderate exercise, and can adapt to most living environments. They are very protective and make excellent watchdogs – they will defend themselves and their family, if threatened.

Traits

Dachshunds think for themselves; this trait can easily be interpreted as a stubborn streak! They have a penchant for chasing small animals, birds, and thrown objects (such as balls) with great determination and ferocity.

Dachshunds are clever, but mischievous at times. They are brave to a fault; often not realizing how small they are, they take on some big challenges including bigger dogs!

If Dachshunds become bored, they can be destructive, so it's important to keep them stimulated when left alone.

Exercise

Dachshunds are bred for work and have a fair amount of energy. The Dachshund needs plenty of exercise to burn off their never-ending energy, and to keep them strong and prevent obesity. As young dogs, they are typically quite active, but can get lazy as they get older. Fetch may be sufficient to give the Dachshund proper exercise. They will do well in an apartment as they are small dogs that don't need too much space. However, they will also enjoy a walk and can get a good amount of exercise this way. Because of their short legs, they are not considered good running companions. Also, because of their long bodies, Dachshunds are not considered suitable for apartments with stairs; frequent use of stairs can cause back problems for the Dachshund.

Special Talent

Dachshunds are competitive, obedient and make excellent watchdogs.

Children and Other Pets

Dachshunds do best with children and other pets, but may be jealous and get irritated easily so they should be supervised until the owner has a true handle on how their Dachshund behaves around other pets.

Trainability

3 stars: Requires consistent training by an experienced handler due to stubbornness or a need for variety.

The Dachshund will need to be firmly and consistently trained. Leadership is key - as the Dachshund is a stubborn and clever breed that will do her best to get her way. Once trained, the Dachshund is a great companion dog and extremely loyal. The Dachshund ranks 49th in Stanley Coren's *The Intelligence of Dogs*, being of average working and obedience intelligence.

Grooming

Dachshund grooming requirements vary with the type of coat:

- The short-haired Dachshund is the easiest to groom, requiring only a weekly light rub down with a damp cloth and a hound's glove.
- The long-haired Dachshund has fine fur, which needs to be

brushed regularly to keep them free of mats and tangles.

- The wirehaired Dachshund should be professionally groomed at least twice a year to keep the coarse hair trimmed and neat.

Regardless of coat type, the breed's long ears are susceptible to infection, and should be checked and cleaned regularly. This breed is an average shedder.

Diet

Dachshunds do not have any special dietary requirements.

Barking

Dachshunds love to show off their surprisingly loud bark for a little dog.

Health

The http://www.caninehealthinfo.org/breeds.html recommends the Dachshund is tested for:

- Eye Examination problems
- Patellar Luxation
- Progressive Retinal Atrophy
- Autoimmune thyroiditis
- Congenital Deafness

The Dachshund's short legs are caused by a dominant gene which produces a condition known as chondrodysplasia; this is where the cartilage of the growth plates grows at a slow rate and can weaken the backbone. This means the long spine might be vulnerable to back problems, especially if the dog is obese, frequently uses stairs or is allowed to jump down from chairs or couches.

Dachshunds also have a tendency to become lazy and overweight as they age, causing extra strain on their back.

Dachshunds are prone to spinal disc problems also known as Dachshund paralysis, as well as heart disease, urinary tract problems and diabetes.

A new minimally invasive procedure called 'percutaneous laser disk ablation' has been developed at the Oklahoma State University Veterinary Hospital. Originally, the procedure was used in clinical trials only on Dachshunds that had suffered previous back incidents. Since Dachshunds are prone to back issues, the goal is to expand this treatment to Dachshunds in the wider population.

Other Dachshund health problems include hereditary epilepsy, granulomatous meningoencephalitis, dental issues, Cushing's syndrome, thyroid problems, various allergies and atopies, and various eye conditions including cataracts, glaucoma, Progressive Retinal Atrophy, corneal ulcers, non-ulcerative corneal disease, sudden acquired retinal degeneration and cherry eye.

Breed Clubs

America - http://dachshund-dca.org/

United Kingdom - http://www.dachshundclub.co.uk/

Australia - http://www.dachshundaustralia.org.au

English Bulldog

The Bulldog makes a great watchdog. They are also good in agility, guarding, hunting, tracking and weight pulling.

Breed Summary

- Type: Pure
- Group: Non-sporting
- Average life span: 8 years
- Average cost: $1,200-2,000
- Height: 12-16 inches (30-40 centimeters)
- Weight: 49-55 pounds (22-24 kilograms)
- Size: Medium

History

The English Bulldog descended from ancient Mastiffs that originated in Asia and were brought to Europe by nomads. Mastiffs were bred for ferocity in fighting, holding or bringing down aggressive prey. The Bulldog was bred in the early 13th Century for bull baiting. The short muzzle and wide lower jaw were needed for the dog to clamp itself to the bull's nose like a vise, and the nose had to be upturned so that the dog could still breathe while clinging to the bull. This breed is mentioned in many historical works, most notably, in Shakespeare's *King Henry VI*. When animal baiting contests were outlawed in England in 1835, these dogs were increasingly exported to America and also to Germany, where they helped create the Boxer. The last of the working Bulldogs in England were crossed with Pugs to create a stocky, docile, family pet-known today as the English Bulldog.

Famous Owners

- Adam Sandler's *Meatball*
- Brad Pitt's *Jacques*
- David Beckham's *Coco*
- Miley Cyrus's *Ziggy*
- Pink's *Elvis*
- Ozzy Osbourne's *Lola*

Appearance

English Bulldogs are medium, compact, wide dogs. This breed has wide shoulders and massive heads. A Bulldogs cheeks should extend to the sides of its eyes. The Bulldog is known for the dense folds on her head. The Bulldog has a short, black, broad nose with broad nostrils. The Bulldogs lower jaw is undershot and her eyes are dark, round and widely spaced. The Bulldog's ears are small and rose-shaped. The Bulldog's short tail is carried low. Bulldogs possess short stocky legs and square build; as such they walk with a characteristic waddle.

*Coat:*The English Bulldog's coat if fine, short and smooth.

Temperament

Qualities

The English Bulldog portrays power and strength, yet they are the gentlest of dogs. Bulldogs are known for being affectionate and dependable dog. They possess a great deal of courage and make outstanding watch dogs. Bulldogs definitely love interacting with their human companions; they crave attention and seek to please their owners.

Traits

Bulldogs can be stubborn and can be attention-seekers.

Exercise

The English Bulldog will need daily exercise. Playing by itself will not be sufficient; this dog requires a good walk or romp. They will do well in an apartment because they don't need much space, but outdoor activities will suit this breed.

Special Talent

The English Bulldogs are quite adept at agility, guarding, tracking and weight pulling.

Children and Other Pets

The English Bulldog is a lively character, with an affectionate and playful personality. They are sweet breed, with a keen desire for companionship. This dog will make a great pet; they are known to have good relationships with children and other pets.

Trainability

★★★ 3 stars: Requires consistent training by an experienced handler due to stubbornness. This breed will need firm and consistent training – the English Bulldog is a very stubborn breed who will need a patient owner.

Grooming

Bulldogs are easy to groom. Bulldogs should be brushed with a firm bristle brush. Bulldogs need to have their face washed daily with a damp cloth. Special attention needs to be taken to clean under the folds in their skin.

The following items are necessary to clean the English Bulldog's nose folds:

- Washcloth (damp) or cotton swabs
- Dry cloth
- Petroleum jelly
- Ear-wash (optional)
- Square gauze (optional)

Take these steps on how to clean the English Bulldog's nose folds with a damp washcloth:

1. Clean each side one side at a time.

2. Gently hold the English Bulldog's cheek in the left hand.

3. Hold up the skin by gently pulling it up toward the forehead or from the side of the English Bulldog's face. Lift the folds and look for redness, moist sores, rashes, or musty smells which may indicate infection.

4. Run the damp washcloth through the folds from one side to the other and around every wrinkle. Push the damp cloth all the way into the fold.

5. If there is any crusted debris that is hard to remove, use the washcloth to dab some more water to loosen the debris. A small amount of petroleum jelly on the washcloth can also help soften the debris. Do not try to scrub away stubborn dirt as this may hurt the English Bulldog.

6. Once no debris is visible on the washcloth, gently dry each fold individually with a clean dry cloth until the water evaporates so that bacteria and yeast do not build up.

7. To help keep the folds cleaner longer, spread a small amount of ear wash onto the gauze square and use it to wipe the folds on the English Bulldog's face.

Consult a veterinarian if thick, yellowish discharge with a foul odor, excessive amounts of black debris or moisture in the folds, or a bald spot or a rash is present in the English Bulldog's folds.

These could be signs of an infection and fungus that needs immediate attention.

Diet

Bulldogs do not have any special dietary requirements.

Barking

Bulldogs do not have a tendency to bark unnecessarily.

Health

Bulldogs have a tendency to breathing problems because of their short nose and some also have small windpipes which contribute to their breathing difficulties.

Bulldog dogs often have to be delivered by caesarean because of their large heads.

Bulldogs are prone to skin infections, poor eyesight and hip and knee problems.

Breed Clubs

America - http://www.bulldogclubofamerica.org/

United Kingdom - http://www.britishbulldogclub.co.uk/

Australia - http://www.aussiebulldogclub.com/

Havanese

The sweet Havanese is a playful, alert, gentle, responsive and intelligent dog.

Breed Summary

- Type: Pure
- Group: Toy
- Average life span: 14-15 years
- Average cost: $900-2,500
- Height: 9-12 inches (25-29 centimeters)
- Weight: 7-14 pounds (3-6 kilograms)
- Size: Small

History

The Havanese almost became instinct after the French, Cuban and Russian revolutions. Although native to Cuba, the Havanese is now very rare in that country. The Havanese was originally kept as a pampered lap dog of the higher class aristocrats in Cuba during the 18th and 19th centuries and was also used to herd poultry. The Cuban's crossed the French variety of the Poodle with the existing Blanquito de la Habana, also called the Havanese Silk Dog (now extinct), to create what was called the Bichon Havanese. Today the Havanese is kept as a family pet.

Some German breeders encountered litters that included puppies with shorter, flatter coats, with feathering on the skirts, tail, ears and legs. This came about as a The Havanese is an active and lively dog, but does not require vigorous exercise. She is small enough that many of her exercise needs can be met in the apartment, an environment which suits her well because she is generally a well behaved dog that does not take up much space. They can also get sufficient exercise from accompanying their owner on a daily walk. The Havanese is happiest indoors where she can be part of the family.

The Havanese can get very attached to her owner. As a result, the Havanese does not do well in a household where she will be left alone all day. Special efforts should be made to ensure this dog learns to spend time alone to avoid

The Havanese is a gallant and curious dog, and possesses are springy gait. The Havanese is very friendly, and typically welcomes strangers, but some may be more shy than others. These dogs are ideal apartment companions as they like to be indoors with their owners. Affectionate and loyal, these dogs love the companionship of their owners and also love to entertain visitors.

The Havanese is an ideal playmate. Despite the small size, the Havanese is not fragile and delicate and tends to be brave and robust. This dog is the perfect combination of friendliness, eagerness to please and playfulness. The Havanese is playful, alert, gentle, responsive, easy to please and intelligent.

The Havanese is highly adaptable to almost any environment, and is in tune with her owner's emotions. The Havanese is a curious dog and loves to sit up high and watch what is going on around her.

The Havanese is small, robust with a tail carried over her back. The Havanese is somewhat longer than she is tall, creating a rectangular overall shape. The Havanese is covered in long, silky, wavy hair which insulates them in hot weather. Unfortunately, the coat does not act as a shield against colder weather in the same way that it does against heat. This breed's eyesare large, almond-shaped and dark brown in color.

Coat: The coat is rich, long and silky and grows to about 6-8 inches (15-20 centimeters) in length. The Havanese's double coat protects them from the tropical heat. The coat is glossy and can have a pearly luster. The coat stands off the body slightly, and flows gracefully as the dog moves about.

- Venus Williams' *Harold Reginald*
- The family of an American business magnate, television personality and author, Donald Trump, owns two Havanese
- British musician, Seal, and American model, Heidi Klum have a Havanese
- American TV personality and style expert, Robert Verdi, owns a Havanese

will have these smooth coats. The short coated Havanese is now called the Smooth Coated Havanese (Shavanese).

The Havanese was first bred in the United States in the 1970s using Havanese dogs brought by Cuban families that immigrated to the United States; this dog has since grown in number and popularity.

result of a short haired recessive gene carried by some Havanese dogs. When Havanese which recessive genes are bred together, some of the puppies will have these smooth coats. The short coated Havanese is now called the Smooth Coated Havanese (Shavanese).

The Havanese was first bred in the United States in the 1970s using Havanese dogs brought by Cuban families that immigrated to the United States; this dog has since grown in number and popularity.

Famous Owners

- Venus Williams' *Harold Reginald*
- The family of an American business magnate, television personality and author, Donald Trump, owns two Havanese
- British musician, Seal, and American model, Heidi Klum have a Havanese
- American TV personality and style expert, Robert Verdi, owns a Havanese

Appearance

The Havanese is small, robust with a tail carried over her back. The Havanese is somewhat longer than she is tall, creating a rectangular overall shape. The Havanese is covered in long, silky, wavy hair which insulates them in hot weather. Unfortunately, the coat does not act as a shield against colder weather in the same way that it does against heat. This breed's eyesare large, almond-shaped and dark brown in color.

Coat: The coat is rich, long and silky and grows to about 6-8 inches (15-20 centimeters) in length. The Havanese's double coat protects them from the tropical heat. The coat is glossy and can have a pearly luster. The coat stands off the body slightly, and flows gracefully as the dog moves about.

Temperament

Qualities

The Havanese is a gallant and curious dog, and possesses are springy gait. The Havanese is very friendly, and typically welcomes strangers, but some may be more shy than others. These dogs are ideal apartment companions as they like to be indoors with their owners. Affectionate and loyal, these dogs love the companionship of their owners and also love to entertain visitors.

The Havanese is an ideal playmate. Despite the small size, the Havanese is not fragile and delicate and tends to be brave and robust. This dog is the perfect combination of friendliness, eagerness to please and playfulness. The Havanese is playful, alert, gentle, responsive, easy to please and intelligent.

The Havanese is highly adaptable to almost any environment, and is in tune with her owner's emotions. The Havanese is a curious dog and loves to sit up high and watch what is going on around her.

Traits

The Havanese can get very attached to her owner. As a result, the Havanese does not do well in a household where she will be left alone all day. Special efforts should be made to ensure this dog learns to spend time alone to avoid behavior problems related to separation-related anxiety.

Exercise

The Havanese is an active and lively dog, but does not require vigorous exercise. She is small enough that many of her exercise needs can be met in the apartment, an environment which suits her well because she is generally a well behaved dog that does not take up much space. They can also get sufficient exercise from accompanying their owner on a daily walk. The Havanese is happiest indoors where she can be part of the family.

Special Talent

The Havanese has outstanding abilities in agility and obedience.

Children and Other Pets

As much as the Havanese loves her owner, she is neither possessive nor aggressive when the owner expresses affection for other people and animals. In fact, the Havanese does quite well with other pets in the home and often makes chummy playmates of them!

This is a great family dog, because they are small enough to keep in the house, but they are not snappish or yappy like many other

Toy breeds. They love children and make very good playmates for them. Unlike other Toy breeds, they can tolerate a child's clumsy and rough play.

Trainability

5 stars: Intelligent, bright, attentive and motivated to learn. The Havanese is very intelligent and eager to please, which makes them quite easy to train. They have an exceptionally good sense of smell and will love to play games involving finding hidden items.This breed is clever and can be trained for basic obedience and tricks. They love performing tricks - these dogs are eternal performers! Because of their sensitivity to the owner's emotions, a gentle approach is needed.

Like many Toy breeds, the Havanese can be difficult to housebreak, but they can be trained to use a litter box, which can greatly reduce issues with housebreaking. Because of their small size and sensitivity to the cold, many owners choose to paper train their Havanese if they live in a very cold climate. This allows them to avoid sending the dog outside in cold weather and snow. Because the Havanese is cheerful and easy to train, this breed is often used for a variety of service jobs such as: therapy dog, assistant dog for the hearing impaired, tracking, and detection of mould and termites. They also compete in a variety of dog sports, such as: agility, fly-ball and musical canine freestyle.

Grooming

If not being used for show purposes, the Havanese coat can be kept short for easy maintenance. If the coat is kept long it should be brushed 2-3 times per week to keep from matting. The Havanese coat is designed to protect her from the heat, so do not click the coat very short as she will not be protected from hot weather.

The excess hair on the bottom of her paws and in-between the pads need to be trimmed regularly. The eyes and ears need to be cleaned regularly.

Diet

The Havanese does not have any special dietary requirements.

Barking

The Havanese is not prone to excessive barking, but they will bark to alert their owner that guests are arriving. The Havanese's sensitivity to the owner's emotions makes her an ideal watchdog, because once the dog observes that the owner is comfortable with a visitor, the Havanese will also be at ease.

Health

The http://www.caninehealthinfo.org/breeds.html recommends the Havanese is tested for:
- Hip Dysplasia
- Eye problems
- Patellar Luxation
- Congenital deafness

Overall, the Havanese is a very healthy long-lived breed. The Havanese is susceptible to dry skin and Progressive Retinal Atrophy.

The Havanese Club of America encourages Havanese owners to have their dogs tested for:

- Eye disease
- Congenital deafness
- Patella luxation
- Cardiac diseases
- Hip dysplasia
- Hip joint disorder (Legg Calve Perthes)
- Elbow dysplasia.

Breed Clubs

America - http://www.havanese.org/

United Kingdom - http://www.havaneseclub.co.uk/

Italian Greyhound

The Italian Greyhound is excellent with tricks. They are affectionate, playful, keen, well-mannered, very bright and makes an excellent companion-dog.

Breed Summary

- Type: Pure
- Group: Toy
- Average life span: 12-15 years
- Average cost: $400-900
- Height: 12-15 inches (32-38 centimeters)
- Weight: 8-10 pounds (3-5 kilograms)
- Size: Small

History

The Italian Greyhound is one of the oldest Greyhound lines, it is believed to have originated more than 4,000 years ago in the countries now known as Greece and Turkey. A similar dog has been found in the Egyptian tombs of over 6000 years ago and was depicted in the ancient artifacts of Pompeii, Italy and has since become a popular dog throughout the royal families in Europe.

This breed was brought to Europe by the Phoenicians and was later developed and trained by the Romans. The name of the breed is actually a reference to the breed's popularity during the Renaissance period in Italy.

The Italian Greyhound has often appeared in old paintings and artefacts, has been favored by famous historical individuals like: Catherine the Great of Russia, Anne of Denmark and Queen Victoria.

The Italian Greyhound is such an endearing dog and has the notorious power to win a person's heart. Frederick the Great of Prussia liked his little Italian Greyhound so much, he even took his dog to war with him! When his Italian Greyhound died, Frederick buried his dog with his own hands on the grounds of his Sands Souci Palace. In 1991, Frederick's family granted his dying wish and transferred his remains to Sans Souci, and placed them beside his little Italian Greyhound. A 19th century African chieftain was so taken with these graceful dogs that he offered 200 cattle in exchange for one dog!

These dogs are popular as companions, but have also been used for hunting.

Famous Owners

- James I of England - James VI and I was King of Scotland as James VI from 24 July 1567 and King of England and Ireland as James I from the union of the English and Scottish crowns on 24 March 1603 until his death.
- Catherine the Great of Russia's favourite Italian Greyhound *Zemira* was buried in Peterhof Park and a porcelain figurine of the hound kept in the Grand Hall of the Peterhof Palace
- Anne of Denmark (Danish: Anna; 12 December 1574 – 2 March 1619), Queen consort of Scotland, England, and Ireland as the wife of James VI and I.

Appearance

The Italian Greyhound is an elegant, miniature fine-boned Greyhound with a long head thinning gradually to a pointed muzzle. Their eyes are large, dark and expressive. She has a thin coat, dark nose, thin lips and an arched back. The fine narrow ears fold back along the head, but rise perpendicular to the head when the dog is alert, anxious or excited. The neck is long and thin. The tail is straight ending in a slight curve. She is the smallest and most petite of the sight hounds.

Coat: The Italian Greyhound has an easy-care short, sleek coat in solid gray, slate gray, cream, red, fawn, black, or blue - often broken up with white markings on the chest and feet, or white with color markings. A flecked version also exists.

Temperament

Qualities

Italian Greyhounds are affectionate, playful, keen, well-mannered and bright. These dogs are very active, extremely fast and great climbers. The Italian Greyhound is a gentle, submissive and affectionate dog.

Traits

Italian Greyhounds become very attached to their masters and can be reserved with strangers. As such, care should be taken to teach this dog to be independent, otherwise this dog may develop separation issues.

Exercise

Italian Greyhounds are active little dogs who need a good, daily walk; they also love to run free and play. Play with groups of other Italian Greyhounds should always be supervised to prevent accidental injury, especially when the dog is young. Play with large dogs is not recommended. Italian Greyhounds can make a good jogging companion for short distances, but they do better as a walking companion.

These dogs enjoy playing fetch and finding hidden items. They do enjoy hunting by nature, and can look forward to a game of hide and seek.

Italian Greyhounds do not play well in cold weather unless they   are   kept   warm   and   well   protected.

Special Talent

Italian Greyhounds have a special ability to perform tricks.

Children and Other Pets

Italian Greyhounds are typically good with children and other pets if allowed to socialize with them when young. They get along well with other Italian Greyhounds and some recommend that you keep more than one of this breed.

Trainability

5 stars: Intelligent, bright, attentive and motivated to learn. The Italian Greyhound is a very quick learner but they are not good all weather dogs and making sure training takes place indoors is best. These dogs take direction and instruction well, and will be especially obedient after proper training. The Italian Greyhound ranks 60th in Stanley Coren's *The Intelligence of Dogs*, being of fair intelligence in working or obedience. These dogs are intelligent and will learn new skills fairly easily.

The dog needs to be trained on how and when to climb furniture, and they should not be left unsupervised on a bed or couch. They do have a tendency to leap out of cars or vehicles if they are not properly restrained.

Grooming

The Italian Greyhound is one of the easiest dogs to groom, with an extremely short, odorless coat. Since the Italian Greyhound has such a short coat and silky coat, it is very easy to maintain the coat's luster and shine. All that is needed to keep the fine, silky coat gleaming is a rubdown with a piece of towelling or chamois. Only bathe when absolutely necessary, such as when the dog is dirty. A wipe-down with a damp cloth is recommended after walks as seeds, burrs and dust can get into the coat and irritate the skin.

Diet

Italian Greyhounds do not have any special dietary requirements.

Barking

The Italian Greyhound is not known to bark unnecessarily.

Health

The   http://www.caninehealthinfo.org/breeds.html   Center recommends the Italian Greyhound is tested for:

- Hip Dysplasia
- Eye problems
- Autoimmune thyroiditis
- Patellar Luxation

As an adult, the Italian Greyhound is not too delicate, but are quite fragile until eighteen months old (their bones are quite fragile and they can break a leg or tail quite easily). Italian Greyhounds are prone to slipped stifle, fractures, Progressive Retinal Atrophy and epilepsy. These health problems may also be found in this breed: von Willebrand disease, color dilution alopecia, cataracts, vitreous degeneration, liver shunts, autoimmune hemolytic anemia, periodontal disease, gum recession, early tooth loss, bad tooth enamel, hypothyroidism and autoimmune thyroid disease (Hashimoto's disease).

Females whelp easily and are well-suited to motherhood.

As the Italian Greyhound hassuch low body fat, she may be quite sensitive to barbiturate-based anesthetics.

Breed Clubs

America - http://www.italiangreyhound.org/

United Kingdom - http://www.theitaliangreyhoundclub.co.uk/

Japanese Chin

The Japanese Chin is a very intelligent, charming and sensitive companion dog.

Breed Summary

- Type: Pure Breed
- Group: Toy
- Average life span: 10 years
- Average cost: $200-1,200
- Height: 20-25 inches (7-10 centimeters)
- Weight: 4-15 pounds (2-7 kilograms)
- Size: Small

History

There are two theories on the origin of the Japanese Chin or Japanese Spaniel. One is that this breed derives from Pekingese-like dogs brought to Japan by Zen Buddhist monks in the 500's A.D. and the other is that the breed descends from a lapdog sent as a present in 732 A.D. to the Emperor of Japan from Korea. For more than 1,000 years this little dog was a favourite of Japanese emperors who decreed that the breed should be worshipped. It is believed that smaller Japanese Chins were sometimes kept in hanging cages like pet birds. It has been suggested that Portuguese sailors introduced the breed to Europe in the 1600's.

Some of these dogs became the pets of Buddhist Monks, who nurtured and mated various types in their sheltered monasteries, giving them gifts to travelling dignitaries. They quickly assumed their rightful position in the Imperial palaces, where they were closely kept and guarded for the Imperial family by private eunuchs who were charged with looking after the little dogs' needs. Mere peasants were not allowed to own them as the small dogs became treasures, deemed more valuable than gold.

It was two hundred years later when an American naval officer, Commodore Perry, helped to make this dog famous in England. A breeding pair of Japanese Chins was presented to Queen Victoria by Commodore Perry, an American naval commander, on his return from the Far East in 1853. Commodore Perry is also credited with bringing the breed to America when he gave another pair to the President of the United States.

The name Japanese Chin is actually a misnomer for the breed origins lie not to Japan, but in China. It has long been surmised that the Japanese Chin and Pekingese were once the same breed with the Pekingese having been bred out to create the short, bowed-legged, long-back, pear-shape bodied breed of dog known today. Far Eastern works of art dating from the 17th to 20th century suggest that an early small Japanese dog resembled the old Continental Toy Spaniel of Europe. That Chinese Japanese Chin was the flat-faced, straight-legged called the 'Imperial Japanese Chin' was blended with the Continental Toy Spaniel of Europe to bring about the Japanese Chin of today.

By 1858, a full trade treaty had been negotiated between America and Japan. An exodus of the small Imperial dogs soon followed - given as gifts or sometimes stolen by Palace personnel and then sold to sailors. The long ocean voyage was difficult, arduous and taxing to the small frail dogs. Many perished en-route. Their bodies wrapped in silk as they were buried at sea. Those who did survive helped to establish the breed in England and America.

They became not only pets in castles and palaces throughout the western world, but also beloved treasures for the sailors' wives, mistresses and girlfriends. The Japanese Chin lorded over his environment and cared not whether it was a hundred-and-fifty room palace or a three room cottage: her concern was only that she was considered to be the most important within her domain.

Famous Owners

- Queen Alexandra's *Punch* and *Facey*

Appearance

Japanese Chins have an alert, intelligent and inquisitive expression. The Japanese Chin is a small and lively aristocratic little dog. They have a well-balanced and square body. The Japanese Chin's tail is plumed and carried over their back with a slight curve toward either side, set high on the back. They have large wide-set eyes giving them their distinctive Oriental expression. The Japanese Chin's feet are hare-shaped and point straight forward or have a very slight outward turn. The ends of the toes contain a slight feathering in mature dogs.

Coat: They have a soft, straight coat with a silky texture. It is black in most Japanese Chins, but may also have a red and white coat. The red coat includes all shades of red, orange, lemon and sable. They may have a white muzzle and blaze on the head but the marking should be symmetrical.

Temperament

Qualities

The Japanese Chin is an intelligent, charming, loving and sensitive companion dog. Japanese Chins are affectionate towards their owners and can be affectionate with those that she knows and trusts. The Japanese Chin is a happy, lively, intelligent, devoted, alert and independent breed.

The Japanese Chin was bred for the purpose of loving and entertaining her masters. While typically a calm little dog, they are well known for performing many enjoyable antics such as the 'Japanese Chin Spin', in which they turn around in rapid circles; dancing on their hind legs while pawing their front feet, clasped together, in the air; and, some even 'sing', a noise that can range from a low trill to a higher sound, almost operatic in quality.

Other cat-like traits include their preference for resting on high surfaces such as the backs of sofas and chairs, their ability to walk across a coffee table without disturbing an item, and some of the surprising places in which their owners often find them. They are often used as therapy dogs.

Traits

While this breed often loves everyone she is familiar with, she is also known to be somewhat aloof with strangers. She can also be somewhat reserved when she is in unfamiliar situations or locations. Even though the Japanese Chin is a loving and kind breed, she does have a mind of her own and likes to be the center of attention. When this attention is not given to her, the Japanese Chin can become jealous and brooding.

The Japanese Chin wants to be part of the family at all times and if this dog is left alone often, she will become depressed.

Exercise

Japanese Chins do not need a great deal of exercise but should be taken on a daily walk. They definitely enjoy a nice outdoor walk in good weather. Like other flat-nosed breeds, she should not be over-exerted in hot weather lest she suffer breathing difficulties.

The Japanese Chin Japanese can enjoy playtime within an apartment; this can be quite suitable for owners who are not active.

The Japanese Chin is well suited to learning tricks and this can suffice as exercise.

Special Talent

The Japanese Chin is great at performing tricks.

Children and Other Pets

The loyal Japanese Chins are good with children. The Japanese Chin makes a great family pet but is not recommended for boisterous children because of the breed's diminutive size and frailty. Japanese Chins do not like to be treated roughly as these dogs are quite delicate.

The Japanese Chin is quite a peaceful breed and will usually get along fine with other animals once she has had a chance to be around them in a safe environment.

Trainability

3 stars: Requires consistent training by an experienced handler due to stubbornness or a need for variety. The Japanese Chin is very intelligent and willing to please her owner. They are relatively more obedient than other toy breeds and they love to learn new tricks. Even so, the Japanese Chin can be stubborn and defiant at times.

The Japanese Chin ranks 62nd in Stanley Coren's *The Intelligence of Dogs*, being of fair intelligence in working or obedience. This breed is quickly becoming known for her excellent learning ability in the agility. The Japanese Chin is very capable of simple agility exercises such as jumping. Agility training is best begun when the dog is at least two years old.

Grooming

The Japanese Chin requires a little grooming, except for a daily brushing with a pure-bristle brush and the idea is that the hair should be brushed with a lifting motion so that it stands up in a soft plume. It would only take a few minutes each day to keep that coat looking wonderful. While the Japanese Chin is shedding it is a good idea to brush them more frequently. The breed is an average shedder. The hair between the pads of the feet should be trimmed when it becomes long.

The eyes should be clean every day and check the ears regularly for any signs of possible infection. For ear cleaning use baby oil and a cotton ball. Gently wipe around the outer ear and remove any debris that you may find. In the event the dog is scratching her ears more often than usual or shaking her head vigorously, take the dog to the veterinarian as this may be an indication of ear infection. The face should be occasionally wiped with a damp cloth and the folds cleaned with a cotton swab.

Use dry shampoo occasionally and bathe the animal only when necessary and a cream rinse will provide extra luster and softness. Extra conditioning will prevent tangles, making the coat easy to comb. They can be blow dried on a cool setting.

Diet

Japanese Chin does not have any special dietary requirements.

Barking

As small as this breed may be, they will make great watchdogs because they have the instinct to protect their beloved owners. The Japanese Chin will bark for the purpose of alerting the household to the arrival of a visitor or something out of the ordinary, but are otherwise very quiet.

Health

The http://www.caninehealthinfo.org/breeds.html recommends the Japanese Chin is tested for:

- Eye problems
- Patellar Luxation
- Congenital Cardiac Issues

The Japanese Chin, like other breeds with short noses, has a tendency to wheeze and snore. They also have a tendency to have eye and respiratory problems. Japanese Chins can also suffer from heat exhaustion if left in hot areas during the summer months.

It is estimated that 35% of Japanese Chins over the age of 12, and about 5% of dogs in middle age, may encounter endocardiosis.

The oversized eyes are easily scratched, and ulcerations can result. Mild scratches benefit from topical canine antibacterial ointment specifically for eye application; more serious injury or ulcerations require urgent medical care.

The Japanese Chin may also be at a risk of hypoglycemia when under the age of 6 months; this concern can continue in Japanese Chins that mature at 4 to 5 pounds (2-3 kilograms) or less.

Some Japanese Chins have seasonal allergies. Generally speaking, this is normal and should not cause alarm. However, if symptoms intensify or continue for prolonged periods, consult a veterinarian.

Breed Clubs

America - http://japanesechinonline.org/

United Kingdom - http://www.japanesechinclub.co.uk/

Canada - http://www.japanesespanielclubofcanada.com/

Lhasa Apso

The Lhasa Apso is a beautiful and robust dog with a friendly and assertive manner.

Breed Summary

- Type: Pure
- Group: Non-Sporting
- Average life span: 15 years
- Average cost: $400-2,600
- Height: 10-11.5 inches (25-29 centimeters)
- Weight: 13-18 pounds (5-8 kilograms)
- Size: Small

History

The Lhasa Apso is named after the sacred city of Lhasa in Tibet from where the breed originates. Referred to in Tibet as the Bearded Lion Dog, the Lhasa Apso's primary function was that of a guard of the homes of Tibetan nobility and Buddhist monasteries, particularly in or near the sacred city of Lhasa. The Lhasa Apso was often given to visiting foreign diplomats by the Dalai Lama. The Lhasa Apso first appeared in the western world in 1901 when several dogs were transported to England.

Famous Owners

- Ellen DeGeneres's *Olivia*
- Selma Blair's *Carol*

Appearance

The Lhasa Apso looks like a small version of the Old English Sheepdog. Their hair flows from the head over their small, dark, deep-set eyes. They have a dark beard and mustache, heavily feathered ears. The Lhasa Apso's neck has an abundant scarf of hair and the tail is feathered and carried over the back. They have short legs.

Coat: The Lhasa Apso has a long, heavy, double coat, cascading over her entire body to the floor. Gold, cream, and honey are the most popular colors, but the coat also comes in smoke, dark-grizzle, slate and a multi-color assortment of brown, white and black. Their coat can change color as they grow.

Temperament

Qualities

The Lhasa Apso is an independent, companion dog who wants to please her owner, yet she may be suspicious of strangers. Their unique personality characteristics have gained them a reputation as being a very emotional breed that can also be quite fearless. They often show happiness by rubbing their heads on their owners, running and rolling around, or sitting on their owner's feet.

The Lhasa Apso is happy, usually long lived, adaptable, spirited, devoted little dogs and good with children. They are affectionate and can be very obedient with their owners. Lhasa Apso's are people oriented and do not like to be left alone for long periods of time.

A favorite pastime would be quietly napping next to her owner. As such, the Lhasa is calm and makes a wonderful lap dog for all ages.

However, they can be quite active and entertaining when in a playful mood.

Traits

The Lhasa Apso is a breed that will need an owner who is patient and show leadership. They can be a stubborn. Although they are known to be independent at times, the Lhasa Apso is not a breed that can be left at home too often because they will become lonely and depressed.

They are wary of strangers while being loyal to those closest to them. Remember to respect their instinct of being wary of strangers. They can be aggressive to strangers, if not socialized well.

Exercise

The Lhasa Apso will need exercise every day as they have a moderate energy level. Trips to an off-leash dog park or a longer walk are ideal. These little dogs are known to be quite playful during the day so will not need excessive exercise in the evening. The Lhasa Apso does well in an apartment because they are small and don't need much space. The Lhasa Apso can also play indoors thus meeting her exercise needs while having fun. Nonetheless, they do enjoy some good exercise outdoors.

Special Talent

The Lhasa Apso is an outstanding, affectionate lap dog and travel companion.

Children and Other Pets

This breed is an excellent pet, but should be monitored around younger children. These little dogs are playful and full of energy and will play well with gentle, energetic older children.

Trainability

★★★ 3 stars: Requires consistent training by an experienced handler due to stubbornness or a need for variety. The Lhasa Apso is known to be quite stubborn, strong willed with a mind of her own. When the Lhasa puppy has been fully vaccinated, extensive socialization will make the Lhasa Apso a very friendly pet. Bringing the Lhasa puppy to various places involving different sounds, smells and sights will eventually put her at ease on walks and whilst traveling. Be careful when introducing them to new people by not overwhelming them with too much at one time. Lhasa Apso ranks 66th in Stanley Coren's *The Intelligence of Dogs*, being of fair intelligence in obedience.

Grooming

The long coat of the Lhasa Apso parts at the spine and falls straight on either side. When in full coat, they need to be brushed about once a day to keep their coats from matting. The coat must be cut short for easier grooming. They are an average shedder.

The feet should be checked for matting and for foreign matter. Eyes should be cleaned carefully to avoid tear stains.

If Lhasa Apso's are not kept properly groomed they can develop skin   problems.

Regular bathing is important but do not over bathe; once a month is sufficient. Dry shampooing is also an option. The Lhasa Apso has glands that secrete natural oil which coats the surface of the skin and keeps it supple and moist.

Diet

The Lhasa Apso does not have any special dietary requirements.

Barking

The Lhasa Apso is alert with a keen sense of hearing and a rich, sonorous bark that betrays her small size. The Lhasa Apso has a loud, persistent bark.

Health

The http://www.caninehealthinfo.org/breeds.html recommends the Lhasa Apso is tested for:

- Hip Dysplasia
- Eye problems
- Patellar Luxation

Overall, the Lhasa Apso breed is very healthy. Sometimes they would have skin problems if the coat is not kept free of parasites. They do have a slight tendency to get kidney problems, eye problems and bleeding ulcers.

Ear infections can occur if the ears are not dried properly after bathing, or kept free of unnecessary hair in the ear itself. Their eyes may tear if the hair is not kept out of their faces. A skin condition known as Sebaceous adenitis causes irritations of the skin resulting in Hot Spots (localized skin infections), hair loss, flaking of the skin and itching.

The Lhasa Apso can suffer from genetic kidney problems; these problems seem to be in certain breed lines rather than the whole breed.

Breed Clubs

America - http://www.lhasaapso.org/

United Kingdom – http://www.lhasa-apso-club.org.uk/

Maltese

The Maltese are very affectionate and happy dog, with a pageant for acting the clown.

Breed Summary

- Type: Pure
- Group: Toy
- Average life span: 15-18 years
- Average cost: $300-1,200
- Height: 8-10 inches (20-25 centimeters)
- Weight: 4-7 pounds (1-3 kilograms)
- Size: Toy

History

In about 25 A.D., the Greek historian Strabo reported: "There is a town in Sicily called Melita whence are exported many beautiful dogs called Canis Melitei", raising the possibility of Italian origin for the breed. It is also believed the breed originated on the Isle of Malta, but there has been other evidence that the breed may come from Italy or Asia. In England, many had tried to make the breed smaller and this almost led to the breed being wiped out. Eventually the practice of breeding them smaller was stopped and the breed was revitalised. In the mid 1800's, the breed was imported to the United States.

This ancient breed has been known by a variety of names throughout the centuries. Originally called the 'Canis Melitaeus' in Latin, she has also been known in English as the 'ancient dog of Malta', the 'Roman Ladies' Dog', and the 'Maltese Lion Dog'. The origin of the common name 'Cokie' is unknown, but is believed to have originated in the mid-1960s on the United States East Coast and spread in popular use. This breed has been referred falsely as the Bichon, as that name refers to the family ('small long-haired dog') and not the breed.

Famous Owners

- Halle Berry's *Willy* and *Polly*
- Heather Locklear's *Harley*
- Elizabeth Taylor's *Sugar*
- Anna Nicole Smith's *Marilyn*
- Eva Longoria's *Jinxie*
- Lindsay Lohan's *Chloe*

Appearance

Maltese are small, fine-bonded, but sturdy dogs. The ears are heavily feathered, long, and low set on the head. The Maltese has dark, round and alert eyes with black rims, giving them what is called a 'halo' effect. Their nose is black, though may fade and become brown or pink during the winter, referred to as a 'winter's nose'; it will turn back to black with more exposure to the sun.

Coat: Maltese have no undercoat, and have little to no shedding. The Maltese's silky all-white, single-layered coat can therefore become quite long. Some dogs may have kinky, curly, or woolly hair.

Temperament

Qualities

The Maltese is the most gentle-mannered of all little dogs. They are very affectionate, playful, loving and cheerful. They are full of personality, enthusiasm and energy. These dogs are ideal for first-time owners, as these lovable companions want nothing more than to be with their owner. Adoring and devoted to their owners, they are eager to please, and can be very protective.

The breed fares well in apartments and townhouses.

The Maltese is known for being a very affectionate and happy that is often described as a 'little clown'. They are a playful little breed and often become a treasured family member.

They were bred purely for human companionship and are great dogs for people who want a small pet that can be taken anywhere. They are energetic dogs that maintain their happy-go-lucky personality throughout their life. This breed is extremely affectionate and love to be carried around which gives them the reputation for being spoilt!

Traits

They are very intelligent, courageous spirit, bold and stubborn.

If they feel other animals or people may possibly be a threat to you, or their territory, they will frantically bark and possibly try to nip the intruder. They behave like they have no fear; they act like big dogs trapped in a little dogs' body.

The Maltese needs a lot of companionship and do not like being left alone for long periods of time as they can suffer separation issues. As a result the Maltese can become quite destructive and vocal, constantly barking in frustration. This dog is not a breed for people who do not intend to spend a lot of time with their dog.

Exercise

The Maltese is an active breed that requires daily, although minimal, exercise. Generally, a good walk plus off leash exercise is sufficient. In addition, the small size of the Maltese makes it very easy to exercise them inside, simply with a good game of fetch down a hallway. The Maltese exercise requirements are very minimal, mostly due to their size. Indoor games, a romp in a courtyard or a short walk on leash is more than enough then to keep them fit. They can become overweight very easily; it is important that they get regular exercise. One should wait until they are at least 8 months old to start jogging, or any long-distance walking.

They love to play outdoors and jumping in puddles and mud, so they can make a mess of themselves!

They make a great choice for the elderly or disabled person, or those with limited space, such as apartments.

Special Talent

The Maltese is very competitive, obedient, easy to train with tricks and can be a great watchdog.

Children and Other Pets

They usually get along with everyone but they are not recommended for homes with small children since they can be snappish and can be easily hurt by children. The breed is exceptional with other pets and dogs.

Trainability

★★★★★ 5 stars: Intelligent, bright, attentive and motivated to learn. Lively and spirited, they are fairly easy to train and highly intelligent, quick to learn tricks and commands, but may be difficult to housebreak. The Maltese ranks 59th in Stanley Coren's *The Intelligence of Dogs*, being of fair intelligence in obedience. Standoffish by nature, they need to be provided with enough socialization and exposure to different people, places, and animals at a young age. With a tendency to bark, they should be taught that excessive barking is not acceptable.

Grooming

The Maltese is a relatively difficult breed to groom. Owners wanting to keep the dog in full coat should expect a reasonable amount of work. The dog will need to be brushed on a daily basis to remove matting and dirt. Dead hair needs to be brushed and plucked out, as the breed does not shed; the coat will become matted if the dead hair is not removed.

The hair around the ears, feet and anus will need to be trimmed regularly to prevent matting. The coat should be parted down the center of the back from nose to tail and the hair allowed to lay flat on either side. To part the hair, one should stand directly behind the dog to ensure the part is straight. Using a metal comb, start at the beginning of the neck and run it straight down the spine. The coat will fall to either side of the spine, you can just comb straight through to the ground. Owners can also opt to wrap the long hair to keep it from matting and snarling up. The long hair on the head is made into a topknot held together with rubber bands, bows, or ribbons to allow the Maltese to see.

Many owners opt to clip the coat on a monthly basis to limit the amount of work required to maintain the Maltese's coat. Some owners will keep them in a 'puppy cut'.

They should be bathed on a regular basis. Some Maltese owners find it easier after washing using shampoo, adding a leave-in conditioner will loosen knots and snarls while combing. It is very important that all shampoo and conditioner residue is completely gone from the coat, as the coat will fray very easily. Towel-dry the coat until damp and then finish with a hand dryer on a cooler setting (using high heat will ruin the coat by causing the hair to break). Thoroughly dry each section of the dog's hair using a pin or slicker brush.

Maltese often have tear stains; the dog's eyes water excessively and turn the hair around the eyes a dark brown-black color. The face will need to be washed nearly every day to keep the coat white.

They need to get professionally groomed about once every month and a half.

Diet

Some may have a weak stomach and have trouble digesting most types of food.

Barking

They are suspicious to noises and strangers, and tend to be yappy.

Health

The   http://www.caninehealthinfo.org/breeds.html   recommends the Maltese is tested for:

- Hip Dysplasia
- Eye problems
- Patellar Luxation

The Maltese needs to have a diet of dry dog food and dental biscuits or chews to help their teeth stay strong and healthy. They may suffer from the following health issues: hypoglycemia, slipped stifle, problems with anesthetics and White Shaker Syndrome. Some minor issues may also be: open fontanel, hydrocephalus, distichiasis, entropion, teeth and gum issues, eye infections, liver problems and low thyroid.

Maltese are susceptible to 'reverse sneezing' which can sound like honking, snorting, or gagging. Although harmless, this behavior often manifests for very short periods but can be quite startling because the dog appears to be choking or gasping for breath. In actual fact, the dog is merely drawing air in through her mouth and nose simultaneously. The cause of this behavior is not known. Reverse sneezing can be brought on by over excitement, play, allergies, or upon waking up.

Breed Clubs

America – http://www.americanmaltese.org/

United Kingdom – http://www.themalteseclub.co.uk/home.html

Miniature Pinscher

The Miniature Pinscher, also known as 'Min-Pin', is energetic and playful. This spirited little breed is happiest in the company of her owner.

Breed Summary

- Type: Pure
- Group: Toy
- Average life span: 15 years
- Average cost: $400-850
- Height: 10-12 inches (25-30 centimeters)
- Weight: 8-10 pounds (3-4 kilograms)
- Size: Small

History

The Miniature Pinscher was developed in Germany, and although the history of this breed can only be traced back several hundred years, this breed is seen as one of the oldest breeds in existence today. The Miniature Pinscher is a German Breed, unrelated to the Doberman Pinscher, though they look nearly identical. The breed was developed from terrier breeds, including the German Pinscher and Italian Greyhound for the purpose of hunting rats in stables.

These dogs have been pictured in paintings for centuries, but the breed has only been documented for 200 years. Development of the breed outside of Germany began in 1895, when the German Pinscher Club was formed and created the first breed standard. The Miniature Pinscher first came to the United States in 1919.

Famous Owners

There are no known famous Miniature Pinschers or famous owners of this breed.

Appearance

Although small, the Miniature Pinscher is athletic in appearance with a square and compact body, with a deep chest (similar in look to a small greyhound). They are well-balanced and muscly. This breed has a wedge shaped head and small ears that are naturally folded and set high on the head. The Miniature Pinscher's eyes are oval and dark in color, with a clear and bright appearance. The Miniature Pinscher's long tail tapers to a point.

Coat: The coat of the Miniature Pinscher is short, smooth, shinyand lustrous. It lays flat against the dog and is slightly rough in texture. They can be found in several colors including black with rust red markings; solid red (a rich dark color) and stag red (where the red has black hairs intermingling throughout the coat); chocolate and chocolate and tan.

Temperament

Qualities

The Miniature Pinscher is known as the 'King of the Toys.' The Miniature Pinscher is a proud breed best described as spirited, fearless and mischievous. The Miniature Pinscher is an energetic, playful and friendly dog that thrives on being around her owner at all times. This intelligent breed is always alert and is often looking for something new to get into!

Traits

Even though the Miniature Pinscher is a sweet and gentle dog, they can be demanding. Owners should be certain not to spoil their dog, or they may become difficult to live with. They have a lot of energy and spirit.

Miniature Pinschers love to climb - especially when unsupervised. For this reason, owners should take care with what they leave on countertops and tables.

Exercise

These dogs will be perfect for people that live in apartments as they take up very little space. However, the Miniature Pinscher will need about a half an hour of outdoor exercise per day. Trips to a dog park would be excellent for these dogs so they can have a large amount of space in which to run and frolic.

Since this breed is prone to obesity, owners must ensure the dog gets regular exercise. However, it's also important to remember that they do not handle very hot or very cold temperatures very well, so outdoor exercise should be done in moderation during weather extremes.

Special Talent

The Miniature Pinscher is a competitive, obedient, agile little dog. They have a special ability to climb furniture.

Children and Other Pets

Miniature Pinschers can sometimes be aggressive with other dogs, so introduce them to other pets from an early age. They are fairly suspicious of strangers by nature, but with proper training at a young age, they will do quite well with visitors in the home once they have known that you are comfortable with them.

They are usually very loyal with their family and will usually lavish affection on anyone in their family but they can appear rather reserved, especially towards strangers. The breed is very good with children and can be good with other dogs, id socialized with them well.

They are not recommended for homes with small pets since the Miniature Pinscher has a strong prey drive and may attack or menace smaller animals.

Trainability

4 stars: Easy to train, likes to please, but can be distractible. Miniature Pinschers require socialization at an early age, to prevent them from being wary of human strangers and to prevent them from being aggressive with other dogs and animals. Puppy classes, where the puppies are introduced to each other and learn to share toys and water bowls would be perfect for this breed.

Because they are very self-absorbed, wilful and demanding by nature, Miniature Pinschers require early and consistent training. However, they are also quite intelligent and eager to learn. Once leadership is established, Miniature Pinschers will be eager to please their owner.

The Miniature Pinscher ranks 37th in Stanley Coren's *The Intelligence of Dogs*, being of above average intelligence in working or obedience.

Grooming

The Miniature Pinscher does not require a lot of maintenance and can be kept tidy with only one brushing each week. They only require a bath every 1-2 months. In between baths, the Miniature Pinscher can be kept clean with a damp cloth. Ears should be cleaned on a weekly basis and nails should be trimmed once or twice a month. This is a very easy breed to groom. They are average shedders, but their short hair is very easy to keep looking nice. Brush them with a firm bristled brush a couple of times a week, and use a damp towel occasionally to wipe off excess hair.

Diet

Miniature Pinschers do not have any special dietary requirements. However, Miniature Pinschers can be prone to obesity. Obesity in dogs creates some of the same problems as in humans; Miniature Pinschers with weight issues may therefore be more prone to heart disease, joint problems and a shorter life expectancy.

Barking

This is a moderately protective dog; they will certainly bark to alert you.

Health

The   http://www.caninehealthinfo.org/breeds.html   recommends that the Miniature Pinscher is tested for:

- Congenital cardiac issues
- Congenital deafness
- Eyes issues
- Patellar Luxation
- Hip dysplasia/Legg Calve Perthes

Overall, the Miniature Pinscher is a very healthy breed, with no specific common Health issues. However, they are not good at regulating their own food intake, so it's important not to overfeed them.

Breed Clubs

America - http://www.minpin.org/

United Kingdom - http://www.miniaturepinscherclub.co.uk/

Australia - http://www.minpinvicoz.com/

Miniature Schnauzer

The Miniature Schnauzer is a very determined, well-mannered, intelligent and alert dog.

Breed Summary

- Type: Pure
- Group: Terrier
- Average life span: 15 years
- Average cost: $700-900
- Height: 12-14 inches (30-36 centimeters)
- Weight: 11-15 pounds (5-7 kilograms)
- Size: Small

History

All three variations (Giant, Standard and Miniature) of the Schnauzer were developed in Wurttemburg and Bavaria in Germany. The original size of the Schnauzer was the Standard Schnauzer which dates back as far as the 15th century. It was from the Standard Schnauzer that the other two variations were created. It is believed that the original Schnauzer was created by crossing the German Poodle, the Wirehaired Pinscher and the German Wolfspitz.

Schnauzers were originally part of the Terrier Group from 1899 to 1945 because of the similarities between the two. The Schnauzer was transferred to the Working Group after it was discovered that the Schnauzer had originally served as cattle herders and guard dogs.

The Miniature Schnauzer was first recognized as a separated breed in Germany in 1899. The first Miniature Schnauzer came to America in 1925.

Famous Owners

- Avril Lavigne's *Sam*
- Janet Jackson's *Madison*
- Bob and Elizabeth Dole's *Leader*

Appearance

The Miniature Schnauzer is a small, robust dog, nearly square in proportion. The head is rectangular in shape, and is accentuated by the long, thick beard, and heavy eyebrows. The eyes are deep-set, small, dark brown, and oval shaped. Their ears are small, v-shaped and folded close to the head. The feet are small and round, with arched toes.

Coat: The Miniature Schnauzer's coat is made up of two layers: a hard wiry outer coat, and a soft undercoat. Coat colors include: salt and pepper, black, white or black and silver. The undercoat ranges between light gray and black. The muzzle, legs, and eyebrows are kept longer than the rest of the coat

Temperament

Qualities

The Miniature Schnauzer is both energetic and gentle. The Miniature Schnauzer is alert, spirited, friendly, intelligent and willing to please. They are often aloof with strangers until their owners actually welcome these new people. The Miniature Schnauzer is a very perky and bright-eyed companion. They are quite loving, affectionate and playful. The Miniature Schnauzer enjoys time and companionship from her owner.

Traits

Some can be reserved with strangers, but most love everyone. Without proper leadership, the Miniature Schnauzer can be feisty and reactive with other dogs. They require a lot of attention and affection on a regular basis as the breed tends to become depressed if neglected.

Exercise

Regular exercise is a must for all Miniature Schnauzers. They gain weight very easily, which can result in major health problems. They enjoy playing off-leash outdoors, where they can track and follow game trails, well away from busy traffic. The Miniature Schnauzer can also be taken to an off-leash dog park or regular walks as they need a moderate amount of exercise to burn off their energy. During the day these dogs play so after work they will not need too much exercise to tire them out.

This breed is perfect for apartments because of their size and will not need a back yard, but access to one would be a plus.

Special Talent

The Miniature Schnauzers are competitive, obedient, good in hunting, tracking, tricks and an excellent watchdog.

Children and Other Pets

The Miniature Schnauzer has an uncanny ability recognize when to be gentle and calm around children. They are generally good with children, but should be supervised with small children.

They make good companions, family pets, excellent guard dogs and mouse catchers.

Care should be taken to socialize this breed with other dogs when still a puppy as this breed can be reactive with other dogs if not socialized well or the owner lacks proper leadership.

Trainability

★★★ stars: Requires consistent training by an experienced handler due to stubbornness or a need for variety. Training a Miniature Schnauzer requires consistency and leadership. They are a very intelligent breed that must be taught at a young age that they are not the leader of the household. The Miniature Schnauzer is a clever breed and ranks 12th in Stanley Coren's *The Intelligence of Dogs*, being of excellent intelligence in obedience. The Miniature Schnauzer will need a lot of socialization, especially with other dogs; they can become dog aggressive.

Grooming

The Miniature Schnauzer has a thick coat that should be brushed or combed on a daily basis or at least once a week to avoid tangles and knots. A maintenance clipping must be done twice a year, especially during autumn and spring, to keep the coat in uniform length. The coat can be plucked or stripped to maintain the wiry texture instead of clipping. Clipping will destroy not only the texture but the peppery part of the salt and pepper hairs, leaving the dog a lighter shade of gray.

The Miniature Schnauzer almost never sheds hair. Before bathing and clipping, they need to be thoroughly brushed in case of any mat-build-ups. Brushing in an upward direction will help to avoid missing any mats. Start by brushing the leg hair in an upward direction, first from the top and work down. Do not to forget the armpits, belly hair, and in between the toes, as these areas tend to mat up easily. If a mat is found, owners must place their hands between the mat and skin to minimize the discomfort of removing the mat. Their eyebrows are to be combed forward, while the beard should be combed from the flat of the muzzle down and the underneath combed forwards. It is a good idea to run a brush down their back to help stimulate the skin, and remove any build-up of dirt and natural oils.

The Miniature Schnauzer should only be bathed when necessary. Over bathing can result in their body producing more oils than necessary to help replace those that have been washed away, leaving the coat dirty and greasy.

Check the ears on a regular basis for signs of infection. If the ears are overly hairy, a pair of haemostats or tweezers can be used to pull out any unnecessary hair. Brown waxy build-up, and/or redness, may be signs of an infection. Dogs with uncropped ears are at higher risk for ear infections due to lack of air flow.

Diet

If they seem to be suffering from itchy skin, this may be overcome by changing the dog's diet. They may tend to be allergic to corn and soy.

Barking

They will often express themselves vocally, and may bark to greet their owner, or to express joy, excitement or displeasure.Schnauzers tend to bark a lot, but they do not have a yappy bark. It sounds like a low howl.

Health

The http://www.caninehealthinfo.org/breeds.html recommends the Miniature Schnauzer is tested for:

- Eye problems
- Heart problems
- Myotonia Congenita

The Miniature Schnauzer is usually a healthy breed. Although some are prone to suffer from kidney stones, liver disease, skin disorders, von Willebrand's disease, diabetes, liver ailments, cysts and hereditary eye problems. They are also at high risk for heart murmurs, urinary infections, allergies, anemia, Cushing's disease and Schnauzer Comedone Syndrome or Schnauzer bumps. This breed may be susceptible to weight gain and obesity if overfed or given an unhealthy diet.

Breed Clubs

America - http://amsc.us/

United Kingdom - http://www.the-miniature-schnauzer-club.co.uk/

Australia - http://www.schnauzerclubnsw.org.au/

Norfolk Terrier

The Norfolk Terrier is a loving and a playful little dog that is known for having a big heart and lots of courage.

Breed Summary

- Type: Pure
- Group: Terrier
- Average life span: 12-16 years
- Average cost: $2,000-3,000
- Height: 9-10 inches (22-25 centimeters)
- Weight: 10-12 pounds (4-5 kilograms)
- Size: Small

History

In the 1880s, sportsmen developed a working terrier in eastern England, the Norwich Terrier. Now known as the Norfolk Terrier, these dogs were believed to have been developed by crossing various local terrier-like dogs, Irish Terrier breeds and other small red terriers used by the Gypsy ratters of Norfolk.

They were first called the Cantab Terrier when they became fashionable for students to keep in their rooms at Cambridge

University in England. Later, they were called the Trumpington Terrier, after Trumpington Street where the breed was further developed at a livery stable. Just prior to World War I, a prominent Irish horse rider - Frank Jones - sold many of these short-legged terriers to the United States, where they were called Jones Terriers. It was Jones who said the terriers were from Norwich.

Originally, the Norfolk Terrier was used for hunting a number of different rodents and vermin. The breed is known as an 'earth dog', which is a type of dog that follows an animal into its burrow and flushes it out. The Norfolk Terrier was cherished for her ability at hunting foxes and quickly gained popularity soon after development.

The popularity of the Norfolk Terrier is gradually increasing worldwide as these dogs become ideal for competitions and events requiring speed, agility and intelligence. They are avid hunters and chasers due to their history of being bred for these attributes, and these characteristics are still evident in the breed today.

Famous Owners

There are no known famous Norfolk Terriers or famous owners of this breed.Appearance

The Norfolk Terrier is compact and sturdy. This breed possesses short legs and a medium length tail. A curious and intelligent expression and brown eyes nicely compliment the Norfolk Terrier's fox-like face. She also has noticeable whiskers and eyebrows. Her medium sized ears are set high on the head, and are perky and folded. Originally bred as a vermin hunter, this breed is small enough to get into the smallest of spaces (including burrows), but is stocky enough to hold her own. No longer used for its original purpose, the dog makes a perfect small sized pet for homes with a limited amount of space.

Coat: TheNorfolk Terrier's short coat is coarse, with a waterproof outer coat and a soft, dense, thick undercoat which completely covers the body. There is a mane of thicker hair on the neck and shoulders. The Norfolk Terrier has small bushy eyebrows. Their color can be grizzle with dark points, wheaten, red, black and tan, as well as tan and grizzle.

Temperament

Qualities

Norfolk Terriers are considered to have the softest of temperaments, yet an assertive attitude. These dogs thrive on human attention and love to be included in the owner's activities. The Norfolk Terrier is loving and playful and is known for having a big heart and lots of courage. This is an energetic breed that is active and loyal. They can be quite self-sufficient and so have no problems finding something to do. They, along with Norwich Terriers and Border Terriers, have the softest temperaments of the Terrier group. Outdoors, they are natural hunters with a strong prey drive for small vermin. A Norfolk Terrier's general temperament is happy, spirited and self-confident.

Traits

Loving attention as they do, this terrier breed can have episodes of bossiness or jealousy but this is rarely a predominant characteristic. They can also be quite mischievous.

It is recommended the Norfolk Terrier be kept on a leash at all times during walks or in open spaces. It is not uncommon for instinct to kick in when this dog spots a squirrel or other small prey and give chase without regard for the owner's calls for the dog to return.

Exercise

Although a great indoor dog, the Norfolk Terrier requires plenty of activity. The Norfolk Terrier is an active breed but their small size makes them easy to exercise. The Norfolk Terrier loves to play fetch and chase after small object; a game of fetch down a hallway will give them ample exercise but should still be given a good walk each day. The Norfolk Terrier enjoys a high level of exercise but can also tolerate a day or two of occasional relaxation. They are great dogs for joggers and have boundless energy for those families with younger children.

Special Talent

The Norfolk Terrier has excellent agility, brilliant in hunting, tracking and is a great watchdog.

Children and Other Pets

As companions, they love people and children and make good pets. They generally share well with other household pets when introduced as a puppy. In the field, they worked as pack animals and therefore still want to be involved, making them great companions for households with children or older persons who can shower them with affection. The Norfolk Terrier is usually very playful and patient with children. They are good with other dogs and cats, but smaller animals such as gerbils, guinea pigs or even rabbits can trigger their strong prey drive and are not a good match for this breed. Little pets should be kept in cages at all times, preferably kept separate from the Norfolk Terrier.

Trainability

★★★★ 4 stars: Easy to train, likes to please, but can be distractible. The Norfolk Terrier is ranked 56th in Stanley Coren's *The Intelligence of Dogs*, being of fair intelligence in obedience. These dogs are notorious for being more difficult to house train, but a gentle, firm and persistent approach will eventually bring about positive results. A consistent training routine with rewards involving praise is the perfect motivator for a dog that thrives on attention.

Grooming

The Norfolk Terrier is easy to care for; expect to brush this dog only two or three times a week. The coat can be clipped and trimmed, but full clipping is not recommended. The coat needs to be hand stripped two or three times a year to keep their coat healthy. They are average shedders and will have a heavier shed in the spring and autumn, requiring extra grooming to keep the coat in good condition as well as to prevent dog hairs being left all over the household.

Only bath this dog once a month as more frequent bathing will strip natural oils from the coat. However, ears should be cleaned on a weekly basis.

Diet

Norfolk Terriers do not have any special dietary requirements.

Barking

Norfolk's can be barkers and are very vocal. The Norfolk Terrier is quite intellectual, and combined with their alertness, they make wonderful watchdogs.

Health

The   http://www.caninehealthinfo.org/breeds.html   recommends the Norfolk Terrier is tested for:

- Congenital heart problems
- Eye problems
- Patellar Luxation
- Hip Dysplasia
- Ichthyosis

Generally, the Norfolk Terrier is a very healthy breed. Common genetic disorders for the Norfolk Terrier are mitral valve heart disease and epilepsy.

Breed Clubs

America - http://www.norfolkterrierclub.org/

United Kingdom - http://www.norfolkterrierclub.co.uk/

Papillon

The Papillon breed is highly affectionate, energetic and obedient.

Breed Summary

- Type: Spaniel
- Group: Toy
- Average life span: Up to 16 years
- Average cost: $350-1,200
- Height: 7–11 inches (18-28 centimetres)
- Weight: 7-10 pounds (3-4 kilograms)
- Size: Small

History

The Papillon was portrayed in paintings dating to the 16[th]century. Famous painters like Rembrandt portrayed the Papillon in various artworks, usually accompanying their loving mistresses. The little spaniels were favorite companions of court ladies throughout Europe. Traders carried them in baskets on mules through France, Italy, and Spain.

The early toy spaniels from which the Papillon descended had drop ears, but in the 17th century court of Louis XIV a small spaniel with upright ears was developed and given the French name for butterfly - Papillon – as the dog's ears were said to resemble the outstretched wings of a butterfly. A Papillon with dropped ears is called a Phalène (French for moth).

Besides the ears, the only other major change in the breed's appearance was the color. Originally the little spaniels were solid in color, but in the modern times they are white with patches of color.

Famous Owners

- American singer and actress, Christina Aguilera, owns Papillons and has been photographed walking them
- King Henry II at allegedly spent upwards of 100,000 crowns on his Papillons

Appearance

The Papillons ears are large and fringed, giving them a wing-like appearance. Papillons' nose, eye-rims and lips are all black. The Papillon's high-set and plumed tail is long, well-fringed and arched over the back. Paw pads vary in color from black to pink, depending on the dog's coloring.

Coat: The Papillon's coat is full, long, fine and silky. The Papillon's coat lies flat on both the back and sides. There is no undercoat. Papillons are parti-colored or white with patches of any color. A blaze (area of white extending down between the eyes) and noseband may also be present. The Papillon's hair is simple and straight.

Temperament

Qualities

The Papillon is a happy, friendly, adventurous dog. They are not shy or aggressive. The Papillon loves to hunt and flush out butterflies, moths and mice. Papillons are obedient and have excellent agility skills. They are very devoted to their owners, and are a very high-spirited dog with a happy and lively personality.

Traits

The Papillon was raised to be a companion dog. Therefore, the owner must be mindful that this type of dog will require regular attention.

Exercise

The Papillon is a bundle of high energy. Papillons need a daily walk or run. Play will also take care of a lot of their exercise needs. Papillons can enjoy a good romp in a safe open area off lead, such as a courtyard.

Special Talent

The Papillon is a very intelligent and can easily learn new tricks.

Children and Other Pets

The versatility of the Papillon is hard to beat: they have the energy to keep up with active families, and are also calm enough to be happy with sleeping in the arms of an affectionate and less active owner. The Papillon can be socialized to be good with children and strangers, but are generally reserved around new people. Papillons are quite small and fragile and can be easily injured, so small children should not be allowed to handle them unless directly supervised. They can also be socialized to get along well with other pets, but care should be taken with rambunctious pets with claws who may injure the petite Papillon.

Trainability

★★★★★ 5 stars: Intelligent, bright, attentive and motivated to learn. Papillons are highly intelligent and can be easily trained. Papillons rank 8th in Stanley Coren's *The Intelligence of Dogs*, being one of the brightest dogs in obedience. They thrive on motivation, obedience work, agility trials, dog therapy, trick performance, and anything that allows them to use their intelligence and still be close to their human owners.

Grooming

The Papillon requires a shampoo that is clear, blue, or white shampoos. Other shampoos will eventually yellow their coat. For Papillons with red or sable colors, a slight bit of a cream rinse will helps as their hair tends to be a bit drier than the other colors (which is why red Papillons grow less fringe on their ears). Cream rinse used on other colors may have a tendency to look oily and stringy.

Rinsing the Papillon's coat properly is extremely important as a faint bluish tinge has been known to remain in the dog's coat if not rinsed well. Human shampoos for platinum blondes or for silver hair may be good for the Papillon. The whitening shampoos, if used, do not drain any color off the tri-color, black, or deep sable colors. However, whitening shampoos on the red hair will wash out its color with prolonged use.

To dry a Papillon's hair more quickly, the fur can be blown against the grain. When brushing the Papillon, never use a slicker brush as it will break the silky hair, leaving split ends. Use a comb, but never use it on wet hair.

Papillons have a higher tolerance for heat, but get cold faster. This is because Papillons' fur is light and they have thin coats.

Diet

The Papillon does not have specific dietary requirements, however, they are known to have dental issues and so a diet specifically formulated for dental health is recommended.

Barking

Like some toy breeds, the Papillon can be yappy.

Health

The http://www.caninehealthinfo.org/breeds.html   recommends the Papillon is tested for:

- Eye problems – one such eye problem is Progressive Retinal Atrophy
- Patellar Luxation
- Congenital heart problems.

The Papillon may also suffer from seizures, dental problems they may be at risk for intervertebral disk disease, and allergies.

Breed Clubs

America - http://www.akc.org/breeds/papillon/

United Kingdom - http://www.eurobreeder.com/breeders/united_kingdom_dog_breeders.html

Pekingese

The intelligent and courageous Pekingese is sometimes affectionately called 'Peke'. This dog carries herself with dignity and pride.

Breed Summary

- Type: Pure
- Group: Toy
- Average life span: 10-15 years
- Average cost: $400-750
- Height: 6-9 inches (15-22 centimeters)
- Weight: 8-10 pounds (3-4 kilograms)
- Size: Small

History

The Pekingese were believed to be a close relative of the Lhasa Apso and Shih Tzu. The Pekingese was an ancient breed believed to have developed over 2,000 years ago in China. Recent DNA research confirms the Pekingese is one of the oldest dog breeds. There is evidence that the Pekingese was a beloved breed of Chinese nobility. The breed was so beloved by the Chinese that commoners would bow to the dogs. Originally only part of Chinese society, the Pekingese was eventually discovered by British in 1860, when British troops invaded the Imperial Palace in China and discovered a number of these dogs within the grounds. At the Palace, the Pekingese served two purposes: as a companion breed and palace guard. Once the breed arrived in England, they became a favorite companion for many nobles. Initially, the breed remained rare, but by the early 1900's the Pekingese gained more popularity worldwide.

Famous Owners

- Shirley Temple, an American film and television actress, singer, dancer, and former United States ambassador to Ghana and Czechoslovakia
- Barbara Cartland, an English romance novelist
- Loretta Swit, an American actress best known for her portrayal of Major Margaret "Hot Lips" Houlihan on M*A*S*H
- Elizabeth Taylor, a British-American actress, known for as being one of the brightest stars of Hollywood's Golden Age.
- Betty White, American actress, comedienne, singer, author, and television personality
- Jennifer Gray, an American actress known for her roles in the 1980s films *Ferris Bueller's Day Off* and *Dirty Dancing*

When the famous ship Titanic went down, only two dogs survived and one of them was a Pekingese.

Appearance

The Pekingese is muscular, small, broad-chested, with a body that is low and wide to the ground. They are called 'The Lion Dog' because their overall shape is like that of a small lion. The Pekingese's legs are short and bowed. The Pekingese has a broad head with flat, long heart-shaped ears. This breed's eyes are large, round and wide set and they have a flat, wrinkled muzzle. The heavily-feathered tail of the Pekingese is long and carried up over her back. They have a distinct relaxed, rolling walk.

Coat: The Pekingese has a heavy coat with thick, frilled scarf around the neck. The Pekingese has a double coat with a short, dense undercoat and long, straight topcoat. This little lion will have, what appears to be, a little mane around her neck! The majority of Pekingese are gold, red or sable. Pekingese also come in other colors such as: cream, black, white, fawn, brindle, sables, black and tan and occasionally 'blue' or slate grey. Pekingese with the latter color often has poor pigment and light eyes. They can be both solid in color or parti-color. Some dogs will have a black 'mask' too. Albino Pekingese (white with pink eyes) are also known to exist but they can come with various health issues.

Temperament

Qualities

The Pekingese was said to combine the nobility of the lion with the grace and charm of the marmoset. Despite her small size, the Pekingese is independent and courageous. The Pekingese can be friendly and outgoing, but wary of strangers. They make great lapdogs, and are quite content to sit in their owner's lap. The Pekingese can be a loyal and loving friend. The Pekingese is an excellent guard dog and can be quite protective of those in the home.

Traits

Obstinacy and jealousy can be part of a Pekingese's makeup. The Pekingese will often become attached to one person, and can become demanding and jealous of their chosen owner. Although small, this breed often displays the attitude and courage of a bigger dog.

Exercise

A walk a day is sufficient for the Pekingese. They can tire themselves out with just playing and exploring so not too much additional exercise is needed. Due to their size and minimal exercise requirement, this dog suits an apartment lifestyle.

Some Pekingese will not like walks, and will just tolerate them.

The Pekingese is brachycephalic, and so exercise is hot weather is not recommended because they may be prone to overheating. A walk in cooler weather or in cooler parts of the day in the summer months is much more to their liking.

Short legs give some Pekingese difficulty with stairs; older dogs may not be able to go up or down stairs alone.

Special Talent

The Pekingese is an outstanding watchdog, in line with their heritage as palace guards!

Children and Other Pets

With people they know, Pekingese are very affectionate and they love spending time with their owners. They are particularly loyal and protective. The Pekingese can be very stubborn and therefore may be snappy with younger, precocious children. However, older and gentler children make a good match for this breed. For the Pekingese to accept other pets (including dogs) generous and ongoing socialization is required, preferably from puppyhood.

Trainability

★★★ 3 stars: Requires consistent training by an experienced handler due to stubbornness or a need for variety. The Pekingese's stubborn attitude can pose a challenge for owners; firm and consistent training with small sessions and repetition will keep this dog on track for success. This breed does really well in agility.

Grooming

The level of difficulty associated with grooming a Pekingese mainly depends on whether the dog is kept in a 'show coat' or 'dog coat'. If keeping a dog coat, have her clipped every six to eight weeks. Brushing only needs to be done on a weekly basis and bathing should be done only when necessary. If you are keeping the dog in a 'show coat', expect a lot of work. Brushing should be done on a daily basis to remove matting and you will need to pin up the hair above the eyes.

The Pekingese is a heavy shedder. The coat will need to be bathed regularly, usually once every month or two and you will have to trim the hair around the feet, ears and backside to prevent matting.

The face should be washed on a daily basis and ears should be cleaned weekly. A damp cloth should be used to wipe away excess dirt and moisture around the eyes and wrinkles. Any signs of redness or swelling in the ears should be a cause for concern. Contact a veterinarian if you notice anything unusual. Foul smelling ears could be a sign of a yeast infection.

A spray bottle of grooming spray or distilled water should be kept handy so that the coat can be lightly misted. This will help to cut down on the formation of mats and also help keep the coat healthy.

Diet

Pekingese do not have any special dietary requirements.

Barking

The Pekingese barks at anything out of the ordinary, and so can be excellent watchdogs in order to protect their family.

Health

The   http://www.caninehealthinfo.org/breeds.html   recommends the Pekingese is tested for:

- Hip Dysplasia
- Eye problems
- Patellar Luxation

The Pekingese is considered to enjoy average health. Due to their short face, the breed is prone to heat exhaustion and breathing problems. Pekingese may also be prone to skin allergies; therefore watch for any excessive scratching.

The Pekingese's long backs, relative to their legs, make them vulnerable to back and spinal injuries. Therefore, special care should be taken when picking up these dogs, by giving adequate support to the back with one hand under the chest, and the other under the abdomen.

Breed Clubs

America - http://www.thepekingeseclubofamerica.com/

United Kingdom - http://www.thepekingeseclub.co.uk/

Pomeranian

The Pomeranian is a very independent, alert, curious, intelligent, lively and vivacious companion.

Breed Summary

- Type: Pure
- Group: Toy
- Average life span: 15 years
- Average cost: $250-1,100
- Height: 7-12 inches (17-30 centimeters)
- Weight: 3-7 pounds (1-3 kilograms)
- Size: Small

History

This Pomeranian breed is a member of the Spitz family, which originated in the Arctic Circle. The then larger Pomeranian derived from the white Spitz that existed in Pomerania, northern Germany, from about 1700 and were used to herd sheep. During the late 1800s, Queen Victoria became a devotee of this dog, founding her own kennel for breeding. The Queen helped to boost the breed's popularity in England, and also purportedly contributed to the breed's smaller size as her love of smaller dogs made other breeders selectively breed for a smaller size. The Pomeranian that we know today was not in existence until the 1800's.

Famous Owners

- Marie Antoinette, Queen of France from 1774 to 1792
- Mozart, Australian composer of the classical era
- Michelangelo, Italian artist and sculptor
- Thomas Edison, American inventor

Appearance

As one of the smallest breeds in the world, the Pomeranian is an active, compact, sturdy, short, small dog with a soft, thick undercoat and harsh, bushy outer coat. The plumed tail is set high and lies flat on the back. Their small ears are erect and mounted high on the head, much like a fox. They have a very large ruff around the neck. Their alert and bright expression is accentuated by their dark, almond-shaped eyes.

A Pomeranian weighing less than 3 pounds (1 kilogram) is colloquially referred to as a 'teacup Pomeranian'. Beware: these Pomeranians are likely just the runt of the litter or have health problems.

Coat: The Pomeranian has a double coat. The coarse outer coat is long and straight and soft undercoat is soft and dense and sheds constantly. The Pomeranian's coat is thick and stands at length making the dog look larger than she really is. The coat on the head and legs is tightly packed and shorter than that on the body, with the legs being typically well feathered.

Temperament

Qualities

The Pomeranian is an extroverted breed, and is inquisitive, alert, cocky and somewhat demanding. Vivacious and buoyant, the Pomeranian is also friendly, and independent. They love to be around their owners and can be quite protective of them.

Their small size makes them convenient travel companions and they enjoy outings with their owners.

Traits

The Pomeranian can suffer from separation anxiety as she can become quite attached to her owner. Despite being bold and vivacious, most Pomeranians have a tendency to be moody. Some Pomeranians may also have also an irritating high pitched bark.

Exercise

Although small, the Pomeranian will need daily exercise; this breed will enjoy a daily walk and can tolerate longer walks. Pomeranians are very small dogs and will do very well in an apartment because they take up such little space.

Special Talent

The Pomeranian loves performing in front of others either as a show dog or trickster.

Children and Other Pets

The Pomeranian is loyal to her family and will typically get along well with other dogs and pets.

The Pomeranian's moodiness may make them unsuitable for very young children; too much annoying attention may make them snap. Pomeranians are ideal for older, respectful children and the elderly.

Trainability

★★★ 3 stars: Requires consistent training by an experienced handler due to stubbornness or a need for variety. Leadership is required to curb the Pomeranian's propensity for bossiness and obstinacy. The Pomeranian is an intelligent dog that is eager to learn. The Pomeranian ranks 23rd in Stanley Coren's *The Intelligence of Dogs*, being of excellent intelligence.

Begin socializing the Pomeranian with people early as possible, as she can be quite suspicious of strangers. This will help stave off the Pomeranian's desire to bark excessively at unknown people.

Because of their small size, Pomeranians can be seriously injured if the owner accidentally steps, or sits, on them. Therefore, Pomeranians must be taught not to get caught underfoot.

Pomeranians are also hard to housebreak.

Pomeranians love to perform tricks and can be quite proficient at this   skill.

Pomeranians are suitable for many types of tasks; they have been used for search and rescue and therapy dogs, and companion dogs for the hearing impaired.

Grooming

The Pomeranian's double coat requires regular grooming as they shed constantly; starting at the head, part the coat in sections and brush those sections forward and allow it to fall neatly back into place. Their coat should be trimmed only to give the coat a clean outline. Pomeranians are prone to dry itchy skin, so the use of dry shampoo over regular shampoos which can cause loss the coat to lose its natural oils.

Diet

Pomeranians have a propensity for dental issues, so a healthy diet is recommended. They can also be fussy eaters.

Barking

Pomeranians may bark excessively when a stranger approaches, especially as they are alert and protective of their domain; therefore it is important to teach the Pomeranian to limit their barking when visitors arrive, when they sense changes in their environment or encounter unfamiliar noises.

Health

The   http://www.caninehealthinfo.org/breeds.html   recommends the Pomeranian is tested for:

- Eye problems - Pomeranians are also prone to dry eyes, tear duct disorders and Cataracts, all of which can cause blindness.
- Congenital heart problems – some Pomeranians may have Patent ductus arteriosis.
- Patellar Luxation
- Hip Dysplasia (Optional)
- Legg Calve Perthes (Optional)
- Autoimmune thyroiditis (Optional)
- Pomeranians may also be prone to slipped stifle, black skin disease, collapsing trachea and to early onset dental decay and gum issues.

Breed Clubs

America - http://www.americanpomeranianclub.org/

United Kingdom
http://www.southofenglandpomeranianclub.co.uk/

Australia - http://www.pomclubnsw.com/links.htm

Pug

The Pug is very playful, affectionate and loves being the center of attention and is often described as a little clown.

Breed Summary

- Type: Pure
- Group: Toy
- Average life span: 12-15 years
- Average cost: $950-1,500
- Height: 10-14 inches (25-35 centimeters)
- Weight: 13-20 pounds (5-9 kilograms)
- Size: Small

History

The Pug is one of the oldest breeds. This breed was believed to have originated as early as 400 B.C. somewhere in Asia. The Pug is possibly a descendant of a short-haired Pekingese. Another theory is that the Pug resulted from the crossing a small Bulldog with another small dog. Others believe the Pug is a miniature form of the rare French Mastiff, Dogue de Bordeaux.

Pugs were kept as pets in Tibetan monasteries and later were brought to Japan. Later, Pugs then made their way to Europe, where they were commonly kept as pets by the royalty of several countries. Pugs even became the official dog of the House of Orange in Holland after one had saved the Prince's life by alerting him to the approaching Spaniards in 1572 at Hermingny.

According to historic accounts, Napoleon's wife, Josephine, sent him secret messages hidden under the collar of her Pug while she was in prison. Pugs then made their way to England after the British invasion of the Chinese Imperial Palace in 1860, where British troops discovered several Pugs and Pekingese. Today, the Pug remains a very popular companion dog.

Famous Owners

- Jessica Alba's *Sid*
- Billy Joel's *Fionula*
- Rudolph Valentino's *Margot, Maude, Monty, Molly, Milton and Maggie*

Appearance

This breed is short, compact, square and muscular. The Pug is one of the largest breeds in the Toy group. The Pug's head is large and round, with prominently large, dark and bold eyes. The ears are black, thin, small, and soft with a feel of velvet. The ears are either rose or button in shape. (Button ears fold over with the fold being level with the top of the skull but the tips does not hang pass the corner of the eyes). The Pug has large and deep facial wrinkles, with the color making the wrinkles more prominent by being darker on the inside rather than outside. Over the nose should be one large, major wrinkle. The slight roll of the hindquarters is typical of the Pug's gait is confident and cheery. The Pug's high-set tail may have one or two tight curls.

Coat: The Pug's is coat is fine, glossy, short, dense, smooth and straight with no curls or waves. The Pug's coat – which is usually three quarters of an inch to one inch long - consists of a short undercoat and slightly longer topcoat. The hair is smooth with a slightly hard texture. The Pug can be found in either silver, fawn, apricot and black. No matter the coat's color, all Pugs will have a black mask on the muzzle, ears and around the eyes. The coat is short, dense and one length with an overall smoothness over the body.

Temperament

Qualities

The Pug is playful, charming, dignified and loving. They are the extravert of the dog world - they are mischievous, self-confident, and cheerful. Pugs are not nervous or highly strung and are not known to display aggression.

The Pug's strength lies in their adaptable nature: they can be quiet, docile and yet vivacious and charming. Pugs are known as little clowns – yet they make the sweetest of companions. Many pugs are curious about strangers, and will be generally friendly towards new people.

Traits

They are often described as being a spirited breed but and may demonstrate bouts of stubbornness or mischief. Pugs can be somewhat wilful and so strong leadership from their owner is required.

Even though Pugs are suitable for families with children, they will not tolerate constant play and running with children for long periods of time.

Exercise

The Pug breed is an active breed that requires daily exercise in order to retain muscle tone. Walks and off leash exercise make suitable activities for this breed. It is important to ensure the Pug does not overheat during exercise. When exercising the Pug, listen to her breathing to ensure it does not get labored as this may be a sign or fatigue or overheating. The ideal temperature for exercise is 30 to 70 degrees Fahrenheit (1-21 degrees Celsius).

Special Talent

The Pug can be taught to some great tricks.

Children and Other Pets

Pugs typically get along with other dogs, pets, children of all ages and visitors. Affectionate and gentle, the Pug tends to welcome others into the family home. Other pets like cats, rodents or birds will tend to be met with gentle curiosity.

They tend to love children and are robust enough to play with the more rambunctious ones!

Trainability

★★★ 3 stars: Requires consistent training by an experienced handler due to stubbornness or a need for variety. Intelligent and eager to please, the Pug makes a fun student. Pugs rank 57th in Stanley Coren's *The Intelligence of Dogs*, being of fair intelligence in obedience. However, owners must be mindful of the Pug's tendency to be mischievous, stubborn and headstrong.

Grooming

The short, smooth coat of the Pug is easy to groom. They should be brushed with a firm bristle brush and be bathed only when necessary. They should be dried quickly and thoroughly after a bath to prevent chill.

A typical part of the Pug's look is her nose roll — the deep folds of skin over her muzzle. This roll wiggles whenever the Pug sniffs. Taking care of a Pug's wrinkles and nose roll forms part of the owner's grooming responsibilities. When their wrinkles are filled with debris, it can make Pugs feel very uncomfortable.

The nose roll and wrinkles should be cleaned on a regular basis to prevent foul odor and infections. The wrinkle right above the nose tends to accumulate the most debris. Some Pugs have larger nose rolls than others, but even the smaller ones need to be cleaned regularly to keep the Pug looking, feeling, and smelling, her best.

The following items are necessary to clean the Pug's wrinkles and nose roll:

- Washcloth (damp) or cotton swabs
- Dry cloth
- Petroleum jelly
- Ear-wash (optional)
- Square gauze (optional)

Washing the Pug's Face

Take these steps to clean the Pug's wrinkles and nose roll with a damp washcloth:

1. Clean each side one side at a time.

2. Gently hold the Pug's cheek in the left hand.

3. Hold up the skin by gently pulling it up toward the forehead or from the side of the Pug's face. Lift the folds and look for redness, moist sores, rashes, or musty smells which may indicate infection.

4. Run the damp washcloth through the roll from one side to the other and around every wrinkle. Separate the wrinkle and push the damp cloth all the way into the fold.

5. If there is any crusted debris that is hard to remove, use the washcloth to dab some more water to loosen the debris. A small amount of petroleum jelly on the washcloth can also help soften the debris. Do not try to scrub away stubborn dirt as this may hurt the Pug.

6. Once no debris is visible on the washcloth, gently dry each fold of the wrinkle individually with a clean dry cloth or hold each wrinkle until the water evaporates so that bacteria and yeast do not build up.

7. To help keep the wrinkles cleaner longer, spread a small amount of ear wash onto gauze square and use it to wipe the wrinkles and folds on the Pug's face and nose.

6. Clean the smaller wrinkles under the eyes the same way.

Consult a veterinarian if thick, yellowish discharge with a foul odor, excessive amounts of black debris or moisture in the folds, or a bald spot or a rash is present in the Pug's wrinkles. These could be signs of an infection and fungus that needs immediate attention.

Diet

Care should be taken not to overfeed the Pug as this breed will generally overeat, causing them to become obese.

Barking

The Pug does bark but is not considered a yelper. They may alert you to the presence of a stranger, however their barking may be muffled by their lips and short, flat muzzles.

Health

The   http://www.caninehealthinfo.org/breeds.html   recommends the Pug is tested for:

- Hip Dysplasia - According to a survey conducted by the Orthopedic Foundation for Animals nearly 64% of Pugs suffer from this condition. The breed was ranked the second worst-affected by this condition out of 157 breeds.
- Patellar Luxation
- Eye problems
- Pug Dog Encephalitis - This typically affects Pugs between 2 to 3 years of age. Pug dog encephalitis is a condition that is being researched because it seems to be related to genetics. Its symptoms are seizures, circling, blindness, coma and death. It is a rapid degenerative disease that can be fatal in a matter of weeks. Pugs can suffer from Epilepsy and these seizures can be totally unrelated to

encephalitis. There is no cure as the cause is still unknown.

Pugs are usually healthy and hearty dogs, but they can suffer from the following ailments:

- Colds
- Chronic breathing problems and snoring
- Keratites which is an inflammation of the cornea and ulcers
- Skin problems and allergies
- Weeping eyes
- Seasonal allergies, with symptoms such as weepy eyes and sneezing
- Demodectic mange, also known as "demodex". This condition is caused by a weakened immune system and is a problem for many young Pugs. It is easily treatable, but some are especially susceptible and presented with a systemic form of the condition. This vulnerability is thought to be from a result of their genetics and inbreeding.
- Eye prolapse - a common problem among Pugs and other brachycephalic breeds caused by a trauma to the head or neck, or even by the owner using a tight leash instead of a harness. While the eye can usually be pushed back into its socket by the owner, veterinary attention is advisable. If the prolapse happens on a regular basis, the Pug might require surgery, or in a worst case scenario, have the eye removed.

Due to their elongated soft palates and pinched nostrils, be particularly aware of the Pug's breathing when the weather is hot, humid, and cold.

Pugs typically have to have Caesarean Section to give birth.

372   The Best Dogs for Apartment Living

Breed Clubs

America - http://www.pugs.org/

United Kingdom - http://pugdogclub.org.uk/

Australia - http://www.pugclubvictoria.com/

Puli

The Puli is an intelligent breed and cheerful little dog. They are usually affectionate and happy too!

Breed Summary

- Type: Pure
- Group: Herding
- Average life span: 12-15 years
- Average cost: $500-1,500
- Height: 16-17 inches (41-43 centimeters)
- Weight: 25-35 pounds (11-16 kilograms)
- Size: Small

History

The accepted theory of the Puli's origin is that the breed was brought to Hungary by Magyar tribes that settled in the area. Since the 9th century, nomadic shepherds on the Steppes of Hungary have utilized two kinds of sheep dogs. One is the familiar large, white guard dog (Komondor) that was used to protect the flock at night. The other was a small active herding dog, the Puli (Pulik in *plural*), and it was this little bundle of energy that actually herded the sheep by day. These ancient shepherds were impressed with the Puli's intelligence and willingness to work. For these reasons, Pulik were highly regarded and respected by these ancient nomads. The shepherds did not cross breed the two types and through the centuries the unique characteristics of each became firmly fixed and it has remained that way to present day. The breed did not become well known in the rest of the world until the 1800`s, but by that time, the breed had already dwindled in Hungary and was close to extinction. The breed managed to survive, thanks to Dr. Emil Raitsits and Adolf Lendl, who re-established the Puli with their own breeding kennel in 1912. The beginning of the 20th century was a real turning point for the breed as they became house dogs after her utility as a shepherd was no longer widely needed. The breed was again almost extinct during World War II and is still considered rare to this day. The Puli was imported to the United States in the 1930's.

Famous Owners

- Mark Zuckerberg's *Beast*

Appearance

One of the most unique looking breeds, the Puli is a robust, hardy and compact medium sized dog. Pulik have a sturdy build that is square in proportion, with the length equalling the height. A side view reveals the Puli's head is egg shaped. The breed's medium sized ears hang down the side of the head. The breed is fairly muscular and strong while at the same time being somewhat fine-boned.

Coat: The Puli has a wonderful and unique corded coat that makes this breed one of the most unusual. The coat can grow long and will grow out as the animal ages; a full adult coat can reach the ground. Pulik have a double coat; the undercoat is short and dense and soft in texture and the top is a corded coat. Generally, the coat begins to cord when the dog is about 8 months of age. The coat hangs flat either side of the dog with a long part down the spine. The cords are hard in texture and are fully formed by the time the dog is 5 years of age. This breed has little to no shedding.

The original breed was multi-colored. It has only been through years of specialized breeding that the color variations were eliminated. By the 1940's black was believed to be the only purebred Pulik. However,Pulik can be found in several solid colors, the most common color is black. Other less common coat colors are white, gray or cream (off white or fakó in Hungarian) and apricot (with or without a black mask). The white Pulik are often blue-eyed and called Roxies.

Temperament

Qualities

Pulik are a chipper, lively breed who enjoy the company of their owners. This breed is capable of big, joyful expressions of love. The Puli is an excellent choice as a family pet. They will adapt to most surroundings and circumstances easily, but they do better with this if they are brought into the home at an early age. Pulik are reasonably intelligent, agile dogs.

They are devoted and form close bonds with their owners. The Puli is sensitive, fun loving, courageous, but also at times tough and headstrong. They are loyal to their owners and wary of strangers. They are highly active and keep a playful, puppy-like behavior their entire life.

As a working dog, the Puli is very obedient, focused and determined. Some of them are used as police dogs. As a livestock guarding dog they are fiercely protective of their territory and flock, and, despite their relatively small size, will fearlessly try to scare and drive any intruder away, however they very rarely inflict any real injuries.

Their responsibilities as a herding dog in the past may have added to their sense of independence today.

Traits

Pulik tend to be reserved with strangers, but once they get to know someone, they become very friendly and affectionate.

Exercise

The Puli is energetic, lively and needs a lot of exercise. They will love to join their owner's activities or enjoy a romp in a park. They will happily play with their owners and with other dogs who are a part of the family or with whom they are familiar.

Many of these animals love to swim, but it should be noted that not all Pulik are good at swimming and they should not be allowed to go into water unsupervised.

When being walked Pulik should be on a leash as they may decide to run off to explore something they see (which is a trait associated with their past as a herding dog).

Special Talent

Pulik are excellent in competition, obedience and herding. If trained, they can specialize in police work.

Children and Other Pets

Pulik make an excellent family pet. They can do well with older children, but may not have much patience for younger, boisterous children. Pulik also do well with other dogs and pets as long as they are raised with them and properly socialized.

Trainability

★★★★★ 5 stars: Intelligent, bright, attentive and motivated to learn. This breed has long been used as a working herd animal and that long history of working has made the animal very receptive to training. The Puli ranks 27th in Stanley Coren's *The Intelligence of Dogs*, being of above average intelligence in working and obedience. Obedience training is important for the Puli since this is an extremely intelligent dog, which makes him easy to train, but also gives him the chance to think on their own.

Pulik are valued for their energy and determination, which is a result of their sheepdog history. Pulik are natural shepherds, and instinctively know how to herd a flock of sheep or livestock, even if they have been raised as a family dog and have never been formally trained in herding. Despite their bulky appearance and very thick coat they are very fast and able to change directions instantly and are obedient enough to train for athletic competition.

Grooming

When Puliks are young, all that is needed is a weekly brushing and the dog will only need to be bathed when necessary.

When the Puli reaches about 6-8 months of age, the cords will begin to form - it is very important to keep the Puli clean at this stage since any dirt or dampness can cause discoloring of the coat. Once cords begin forming, it is the owner's responsibility to maintain the integrity of the cords throughout the dog's life. This means separating the cords on a weekly basis, as well as checking the skin for any problems. Each coat is unique, but generally, the sections should not be made thinner than the width of a pencil. Once this dog has cords, she should never be brushed. Not only will brushing destroy the unique character of the coat, but the brushing will be very uncomfortable to the dog.

Learning how to take care of the Puli's cords may take time and practice, but Pulikoften finds this type of care to be relaxing.New owners of the Puli may wish to attend a dog grooming class to learn the proper method for separating the cords.Once the dog is full grown, the cords will be 5 to 6 inches (13-15 centimeters) in length.

The coat should be bathed on a regular basis to keep the cords clean and to minimize the breed's typical doggy odor; the coat should be dried completely otherwise mildew will form in the cords.Use an electric dryer, but monitor the heat setting. Even with the dryer this can take a long time, up to two hours. However, if left to air dry the dog can remain wet for up to two days.

The hair between the pads of the feet should be trimmed regularly.

Diet

Pulik do not have any special dietary requirements.

Barking

This breed is not known to bark unnecessarily.

Health

The http://www.caninehealthinfo.org/breeds.html recommends the Puli is tested for:

- Hip Dysplasia
- Eye problems
- Patellar Luxation
- Degenerative Myelopathy
- Congenital Deafness (Optional)
- Congenital heart problems (Optional)
- Elbow Dysplasia (Optional)

The Puli is generally a healthy and robust breed; she suffers from few health problems, some being Progressive Retinal Atrophy, Cataracts and Hip Dysplasia.

Pulik may also be prone to eye inflammations caused by hair getting under their eyelids.

Breed Clubs

America - http://www.puliclub.org/

United Kingdom – http://www.hungarianpuliclubofgb.co.uk/

Australia – http://home.vicnet.net.au/~puli/

Shih Tzu

The Shih Tzu is highly energetic, intelligent, affectionate and outgoing.

Breed Summary

- Type: Pure breed
- Group: Toy
- Average life span: 12-16 years
- Average cost: $300-2,000
- Height: 10-11 inches (25-28 centimeters)
- Weight: 9-16 pounds (4-7 kilograms)
- Size: Toy

History

The Shih Tzu, also known as the 'Chinese Lion Dog', 'Chrysanthemum Dog' (because her face resembles a flower), or 'Shih Tzu Kou' (which translates to 'Lion Dog', giving the dog a revered status in Buddhism) originates in Tibet as far back as the 1600's. The Shih Tzu we know today was primarily developed in China during the reign of Chinese Empress Dowager Cixi in the late 1800's, likely from crosses of the Pekingese and Lhasa Apso.

The breed survived even when their number declined during the British colonization, but was generally not distinguished from the Lhasa Apso until 1934, when the smaller, shorter nosed variety was reassigned her original Chinese name. The Shih Tzu was recognized by the American Kennel Club in 1969 and has continued to climb in popularity to this day. Crossbreeds between Shih Tzu and other toy breeds are also increasing in popularity, particularly crosses with the Poodle and Bichon Frise.

Famous Owners

- Nicole Richie's *Honeychild*
- Rebecca Mader's *Bella*
- Geri Halliwell's *Harry*

Appearance

The Shih Tzu is a compact, yet robust toy sized dog covered with an attractive mop of hair, and large, well-rounded eyes. The Shih Tzu carries her head high and has an undershot bite. The dog's long tail iscarried high, and curled over the back. The head of the Shih Tzu is round with a brachiocephalic muzzle that is short and square. The long ears of the Shih Tzu hang down the side of the dog's face.

Coat: The Shih Tzu's undercoat is dense, short and soft. The top coat is very long, reaching the floor, silky, abundant and elegant. The dog's facial hair is quite long, with a beard and mustache common to the breed; often owners will have the hair on top done up with bows or clips. The Shih Tzu can be a range of colors including black, red, white, cream, brown and gray. They can be solid in color as well as multi-colored, tri-colored and have shading.

Temperament

Qualities

Upbeat and playful, the Shih Tzu is a happy, alert, outgoing, affectionate, friendly and spunky little dog. They are extroverted, trust everyone and will even offer strangers unconditional affection. They are courageous, vivacious and loyal. The Shih Tzu makes an ideal companion dog.

Traits

This dog's sense of self-importance and dignity may occasionally spill over into arrogant attitude, as well as stubbornness. As they can be quite owner-orientated, these dogs may suffer separation-related issues, if left alone for long periods.

Exercise

Shih Tzus don't need much exercise, but daily exercise and play is sufficient. They love to play games and can be kept inside for activities, such as fetch and other dog games. This is an ideal dog for apartments because they are small, love the company of their owner and can be exercised indoors. They also enjoy outdoor play in good weather.

Special Talent

They can be a great watchdog.

Children & Other Pets

The Shih Tzu makes a great family pet. They need with an active, busy owner or family; these dogs love to be where the action is! Surprisingly tough, these dogs do well with children. The Shih Tzu also make great companions to other pets; always supervise introductions to ensure a smooth start to their friendship.

Trainability

★★★ 3 stars: Requires consistent training by an experienced handler due to stubbornness or a need for variety. Due to their short attention span, the training sessions should be short, frequent and fun. They are a highly intelligent dog, with a stubborn streak. The Shih Tzu ranks 70th in Stanley Coren's *The Intelligence of Dogs,* being of fair intelligence in working or obedience. The Shih Tzu can be challenging to housebreak.

Grooming

The Shih Tzu requires daily brushing with a bristle brush as this will keep the coat from matting. Some Shih Tzu owners like to keep the coat trimmed to make maintenance easier. The nails needs to be kept trimmed to prevent curling. The ears need to be kept clean and dry; check them daily to keep ear infections at bay. Shih Tzu's eyes can be very sensitive; keep them clean and healthy. They shed little to no hair.

Diet

Shih Tzu's should not be overfed as this breed tends to gain weight quickly. The Shih Tzu can be a picky eater.

Barking

Shih Tzu's are typically quiet in the house but do like to bark.

Health

The   http://www.caninehealthinfo.org/breeds.html   recommends the Shih Tzu is tested for:

- Hip Dysplasia
- Eye problems
- Patellar Luxation

Some ShihTzu's are prone to ear, eye, and respiratory problems. They may have back problems and spinal disc disease due to their long back and short legs. The ShihTzu's have poor dental health and require veterinary attention as their teeth tend to be lost early.

The ShihTzu is a brachycephalic breed, which means they are prone to breathing difficulties.

Breed Clubs

America - http://www.americanshihtzuclub.org/

United Kingdom - http://www.theshihtzuclub.co.uk/index.php

Australia - http://tzuclub.webs.com/

Toy Poodle

The Toy Poodle is very intelligent and truly shines in any type of training.

Breed Summary

- Type: Pure
- Group: Toy
- Average life span: 12-15 years
- Average cost: $1,000-2,000
- Height: 14-18 inches (35-45 centimeters)
- Weight: 16-32 pounds (7-14 kilograms)
- Size: Small

History

The Toy Poodle shares a history will all the other sized Poodles. It is not clear where the breed originated since two countries - France and Germany - have claimed this breed as their own. Although exactly which breeds went into the Toy Poodle's development is unknown, it is believed that the Spanish Water Dog, North African Barbet, German Water Dog, Hungarian Water Dog and the Portuguese Water Dog are all part of the Poodle's genetic makeup.

The main consensus is that the Poodle was developed in Germany, roughly in the 1500's in an effort to create a versatile hunting dog.

From Germany, the Poodle was quickly adopted by the French where the breed was refined into what we know today. The first Poodle to be developed was the Standard Poodle, however, it wasn't too long before the Miniature and Toy versions of the breed were created.

In France, the Poodle is known as the 'Caniche', or duck dog, and has been regarded as the national dog of France, where she was commonly used as a retriever as well as a travelling-circus trick dog.

The breed has been around for at least 400 years throughout Western Europe. The Poodle's distinctive looks made the breed a popular subject for paintings, dating back to the 15th century. In the 18th and 19th centuries, the Poodle could be seen in circuses throughout Europe and America performing a variety of tricks. The English word Poodle comes from the German 'Pudel', meaning to splash in the water. Their coat is moisture-resistant, which helps their swimming. All of the Poodle's ancestors were acknowledged to be good swimmers.

This breed has become one of the most popular dog breeds ever. Poodles are retrievers or gun dogs, and are still used by hunters in that role, however, they also make a great companion dog.

Famous Owners

- John Steinbeck's *Charley*
- Patrick Swayze's *Derek*
- Winston Churchill's *Rufus*
- Mary Tyler Moore's *Diswilliam*
- Vanessa Hudgens' *Shadow*

Appearance

Toy Poodles are elegant, yet squarely built and well proportioned. The eyes are very dark, oval in shape and have an alert and intelligent expression. Ears hang close to the head, set at, or slightly below eye level. Toy Poodles are compact and robust while having a refined and delicate look. This athletic looking dog has a medium length tail with a high curve to it.

Coat: Poodles have a single layer coat which is dense and curly that sheds minimally. They do not have an undercoat. The coat texture ranges from coarse and woolly to soft and wavy. They only come in solid colors such as silver, blue, red, cream, gray, cafe-au-lait, white, black, brown and apricot.

Temperament

Qualities

The Toy Poodles intelligence is well known; they can be taught all different tricks through various skill levels. They enjoy performing and entertaining their owners. They are one of the easiest and brightest breeds to train. They are alert, responsive, playful, and eager to please. They tend to love children interaction with their owners. They don't seem to be a destructive type when left alone.

The breed has a good sense of humor and is often described as being clown-like in nature.

Traits

The Toy Poodle is usually a very playful breed and they can often be too smart for their own good which often leads them into trouble. While the standard Poodle has a high playfulness with other dogs the Toy poodle is a little less enthusiastic. They can be shy with strangers and should be socialized as a puppy.

Exercise

The Toy Poodle is very active for a small dog who needs the regular daily walks. Play will also be able to consume their energy and will keep them balanced and happy. They enjoy running around in dog parks or in a secured area. Not only is walking a great way to exercise Toy Poodles, but indoor games work well too.

Retrieving is natural to most Toy Poodles. Water retrieving may be also be suitable, and is also a great way for the Toy Poodles to get exercise. Interaction is a must for these dogs like playing games, or learning new tricks is a great way to keep these dogs in good spirit.

Special Talent

Toy Poodles are obedient, poised, good at retrieving, good with tricks and make an excellent watchdog.

Children and Other Pets

The Toy Poodle is incredibly even tempered and does well with children. They are usually good with other dogs and pets but they do much better if they are properly socialized. The Toy Poodle can make a brilliant watch dog since they are naturally suspicious of strangers and will usually be reserved with them.

Trainability

★★★★★★ 5 stars: Intelligent, bright, attentive and motivated to learn. Toy Poodles are extremely intelligent and exceedingly responsive that they are one of the most trainable dog breeds. The Toy Poodle ranks 2nd in Stanley Coren's *The Intelligence of Dogs*, being of excellent intelligence in obedience. Their ability to learn almost anything has done a lot to keep their popularity high throughout all these years.

Grooming

The Toy Poodle can be quite a task to groom, even though she is a low shedding breed which makes them a great option for allergy sufferers. Their thick curls can become matted very easily and it is recommended that Toy Poodles are brushed on a daily basis. In addition to brushing, the ears should be cleaned on a weekly basis and the eyes should be washed on a daily basis to prevent tear stains.

Frequently tidy up the coat with scissors or it can be clipped into a number of coat patterns that were originally designed for hunting. Bathing should be done on a monthly basis and nails should be trimmed once or twice a month.

There are various types of clipping styles for Toy Poodles such as the puppy clip, English saddle clip, continental clip and sporting clip.

Diet

Toy Poodles do not have any special dietary requirements.

Barking

They will bark to defend or alert their owners, but tend to be more reserved than other small toy breeds.

Health

The http://www.caninehealthinfo.org/breeds.html recommends the Toy Poodle is tested for:

- Progressive Retinal Atrophy
- Eye problems
- Patellar Luxation

The Toy Poodle is considered to enjoy average health. They are susceptible to a number of health problems including sebaceous adenitis, Addison's Disease, von Willebrand's disease, hyperadrenocorticism, legg perthes disease, hypothyroidism, epilepsy, gastric torsion (bloat) and optic nerve hypoplasia. A number of Toy Poodles may be more prone to eye diseases such as cataracts, glaucoma and retinal disease.

Breed Clubs

America - http://www.poodleclubofamerica.org/

United Kingdom – http://miniaturepoodleclub.weebly.com/

Australia – http://www.poodleclubnsw.com/

Welsh Corgi

The Welsh Corgi is an intelligent, devoted dog with a bold, regal spirit!

Breed Summary

- Type: Pure
- Group: Herding
- Average life span: 12-15 years
- Average cost: $600-1000
- Height: 10-12 inches (25-30 centimeters)
- Weight: 25-38 pounds (11-17 kilograms)
- Size: Small

History

There are two distinct breeds that are recognized for the Welsh Corgi: the Pembroke Welsh Corgi and the Cardigan Welsh Corgi, with the Pembroke more common. Welsh Corgi is a small type of a herding dog that originated in Wales. Both of these breeds originated from the Swedish Vallhunds brought to the areas around Wales in the 800's.

Cardigan

Brought to Wales by the Celts around 1,000 B.C., the Cardigan is an ancient breed. The Cardigan used to work cattle, using their short stature to their advantage by nipping at their heels without getting kicked. These dogs have been employed for centuries by Welsh farmers for herding livestock to new grazing areas and driving the neighbor's cattle away.

Pembroke

The Pembroke is believed to have been introduced the Pembrokeshire area of Wales by Flemish weavers about 920 or 1,100 B.C. Another possibility for the Pembroke's origin is that they were developed by breeding the Cardigans and Swedish Vallhunds, a Spitz-type dog resembling the Pembroke and brought to Wales by Norse invaders. Some surmise that the short legs and stature occurred from breeding with Pomeranians.

The Pembroke became a popular dog, especially in the United Kingdom, when Queen Elizabeth II started breeding and raising them. The Pembroke has been used in many commercials worldwide. Their primary purpose is no longer that of the herding dog, rather they are now considered an ideal companion dog in either an outdoor or indoor environment.

The Pembroke and the Cardigan were not recognized as separate breeds until the 1940's. Welsh folklore says the Corgi is the preferred mount of fairy warriors. Some folk legend says Corgis were a gift from the woodland fairies, and that the breed's markings were left on its coat by fairy harnesses and saddles. Corgis usually have a marking, a white stripe, that runs from the nose, through the eyes, and up into the forehead; this marking is referred to as a 'blaze'. Since the two Corgi breeds developed in the Welsh hill country, in areas only a few miles apart, there is evidence of crossbreeding between the two that accounts for the similarities

Famous Owners

Pembroke

- Queen Elizabeth II has owned more than thirty Corgis in her lifetime, including *Susan*, who was a gift for her eighteenth birthday in 1944
- Hilary Swank's *Karoo*
- Jennifer Aniston's *Norman*
- American novelist, Stephen King, owns a dog called *Marlow*. Corgis have also featured in King's books, such as the character *Horace* in *Under the Dome* and *Daisy* in *The Regulators*

Cardigan

There are no known famous owners of the Cardigan.

Appearance

There are two breeds of Welsh Corgis, the Cardigan and the Pembroke, each named for the county in Wales where each breed originated. The differences between the two breeds include bone structure, body length and size.

Cardigan

The Cardigan is a long-tailed, low set, heavier-boned, with a deep chest. These dogs can be any color and may have white markings. Cardigans are larger than the Pembrokes, with full rounded ears. Overall, the Cardigan has a long body with short legs, culminating in a low-set, fox-like tail. The Cardigan is a handsome, powerful small dog, with a sturdy build.

Coat: The Cardigan is a double-coated dog where the outer coat is dense, slightly harsh in texture, and of medium length. The Cardigan's undercoat is short, soft, and thick.

Pembroke

The Pembroke is sturdy and has short and powerful legs. They have the square shape and solid build. Their eyes are dark, alert and bright. The Pembroke features pointed ears, and are somewhat smaller in stature than the Cardigan. Many people would say that the Pembroke looks like a fox. They are low-set, intelligent, strong and sturdy with stamina sufficient to work a day on the farm. The dog's head is fox-like and the tail short. Historically, the Pembroke was a breed with a stumpy tail. If you come across a Pembroke with a tail at all, it is usually curly.

Coat: The Pembroke's short to medium coat is clean, very thick and water resistant. The outer coat is quite coarse and they have a soft inner coat. They can come in many different colors including fawn, tan, sable, black and red and often there are white markings on the face, chest and legs.

Temperament

Qualities

The Cardigan is an intelligent, devoted dog. The Cardigan is a devoted family dog, and makes an excellent watch dog.

The Pembroke is outgoing, happy, friendly and loyal to the family. They can be somewhat aloof with strangers. Pembrokes are active dogs, breeders suggesting they are more outgoing and excitable than the reserved Cardigans. They are affectionate and accepting of children though may be suspicious of strangers. They are quite active, not docile lap dogs. Pembrokes tend not to be as stubborn or independent as some other herding breeds.

These Corgis are easy to train and they work with enthusiasm.

Traits

The Pembroke is instinctively a herding dog, a heeler, and may display this tendency by nipping at people's heels. If you get the Pembroke as a puppy, you may wish to train this tendency out of them.

The Cardigan is less sociable and more territorial than the Pembroke variety. As such, the Cardigan might be possessive of her own things with other dogs.

Welsh Corgis are loyal, devoted, protective and suspicious of strangers, and they make fine watch dogs.

Exercise

The Cardigan is more active than the Pembroke.

The Pembroke is a very active dog that craves long and frequent bouts of exercise. The Pembroke can live in an apartment, but the owner must be prepared to schedule regular, prolonged exercise. They may well enjoy hikes and jogging, provided the dog is used to such exercise. Otherwise, the dog should be trained to gradually become accustomed to such exercise. The Pembroke is extremely agile and can quickly change directions or drop and roll. In herding, such agility was useful when avoiding the kicking hooves of animals they were herding. The Pembroke is quite a hardy breed and therefore enjoys romping with children, games of tug of war, hide and seek and even tag.

Exercise for the Welsh Corgi should not include jumping up or down, even onto furniture as this type of activity can potentially cause injury to the dog's back or legs.

Daily exercise is recommended for both varieties, as inactivity may lead to obesity. Heavy dogs are more likely to have back and spinal problems.

Special Talent

The Welsh Corgi is often used in herding competitions and will need little formal training in that skill.

Children and Other Pets

The Welsh Corgi is intelligent, obedient, willing to please, affectionate, loving with the family. In the early settlements these dogs were prized family members, helping hunt game and guarding children. They generally also do well with other pets.

Playful and lovable, they are good with kind, gentle children, particularly if they are socialized with them from an early age.

If you have more than one dog, these dogs will run and play with the other dog, which is great for exercise. They will also do well with cats and other pets if raised together from a young age.

Trainability

★★★★★ 5 stars: Intelligent, bright, attentive and motivated to learn. Easily trained, they are excellent show and obedience dogs.

Pembrokes rank 11th and Cardigans rank 26th in Stanley Coren's *The Intelligence of Dogs*, being excellent working dogs. These dogs are highly intelligent and learn quickly. Naturally dominant, these dogs need strong leadership from their owner.

Grooming

Grooming requirements for Welsh Corgis are moderate.

The Cardigan has a plush double coat, and so requires regular brushing with a firm brush to remove dead hair and dirt. The Cardigan is a moderate shedder; they molt twice a year, in spring and autumn. It is at this time that more attentive grooming is required.

The Pembrokes short to medium coat is easy to maintain – a brushing twice a week with a wire brush or pin brush is sufficient.

The Pembroke sheds heavily during the spring and summer and so more frequent brushing is required during those periods.

The Pembroke tends to clean herself, therefore she is quite a clean dog. The Pembroke has a water resistant coat and so bathing is only recommended when necessary.

Diet

The Welsh Corgi does not have any special dietary requirements.

Barking

Welsh Corgis make excellent watch dogs; they will sound the alarm when others approach the family home. Barking can be a problem, especially if these dogs are left alone for long periods. A great training exercise is to teach this breed to both bark and be silent on cue. In this way, barking will be less of a problem.

Health

The http://www.caninehealthinfo.org/breeds.html recommends the Welsh Corgi is tested for:

- Congenital cardiac issues
- Eye issues - The Corgi is susceptible to glaucoma and Progressive Retinal Atrophy.
- Canine Hip Dysplasia

The Cardigan and Pembroke are among the long-lived and healthiest dogs in the herding group. Both types are genetically predisposed to encounter canine hip dysplasia, canine degenerative myelopathy and progressive retinal atrophy. The Pembroke is also susceptible to inter vertebral disc disease and epilepsy.

Since all Welsh Corgis are dwarfs they are prone to a series of skeletal problems. Choose a compact and well-proportioned animal if possible. Unusually long bodied Welsh Corgis are more prone to slipped discs in the middle of the back.

Breed Clubs

America - http://www.cardigancorgis.com/

United Kingdom - http://www.cardiganwelshcorgiassoc.co.uk/

Australia - http://www.corgiclubvic.com/links.html

West Highland White Terrier

The West Highland White Terrier is adaptable, versatile, athletic and quite adventurous.

Breed Summary

- Type: Pure
- Group: Terrier
- Average life span: 12 to 14 years
- Average cost: $500-2,000
- Height: 10–11 inches (25-28 centimetres)
- Weight: 15–24 pounds (7-11 kilograms)
- Size: Toy/Small

History

The West Highland White Terrier, also known as a 'Westie', is probably closely related to the other terriers of Scotland, including the Cairn, the Dandie Dinmont, the Scottish and the Skye. They were bred to be a working terrier, scouring the ground to take on rats, rabbits, badgers and foxes.

Originally known by several different names, this breed came to be known as the West HighlandWhite Terrier in the early

20thcentury. An imported female named Sky Lady, born in 1906 in England, was the first dog to be officially registered as a 'West Highland White Terrier'. The first Westie came to America in about 1905. By the end of the 20thcentury, the Westie was among the most popular of all dog breeds.

Famous Owners

There are no known famous owners of this breed.

Appearance

West Highland White Terriers have bright, deep-set, almond-shaped eyes that are dark in color. Their ears are pointed and erect. They have a deep chest, muscular limbs and with paws that are slightly turned out in order to give it better grip when climbing on rocky surfaces. In young puppies, the nose and footpads have pink markings, which slowly turn black with age.

Coat: West Highland White Terriers have a soft, dense, thick undercoat and a rough outer coat, which can grow to about 2 inches (5 centimeters) long. Their fur fills out their face to give a rounded appearance. As they develop into adults, the coarse outer coat is normally removed by either hand-stripping (the preferred method of dog showers), or otherwise clipping.

Temperament

Qualities

West Highland White Terriers are quite independent, self-assured and confident. They have a spunky, bold and adventurous personality. The West Highland White Terrier is loyal and active. They tend to be happy, curious and affectionate. The Westie is a very intelligent dog they love human companionship both indoors and outdoors. Introduce them gradually to the little newcomers, making sure they are not ignored or pushed back.s

Traits

West Highland White Terriers are known as the most affectionate of the terrier group, and may be prone to jealousy or separation issues. They can also be quite wilful and are known to be quite stubborn.

Exercise

The West Highland White Terrier is a high energy breed and enjoys regular, daily walks. Because of her terrier heritage, this dog enjoys chasing moving objects. Therefore, be careful of open areas when on walks with the West Highland White Terrier; you may have to keep this dog on a leash unless she is well-trained to return on command. An insatiable curiosity and a liking of the chase make games like fetch and hide and seek very suitable for the breed's temperament.

Special Talent

The West Highland White Terrier is both hardy and athletic.

Children and Other Pets

West Highland White Terriers make great family pets they are good with children, elderly people and strangers. The West Highland White Terrier is an affectionate breed and enjoys being included in the family activities.

Despite evolving into great companion dogs, West Highland White Terriers have still retained their terrier nature. As such, this breed typically does not get along with other smaller household pets, such as gerbils, hamsters and guinea pigs.

Trainability

★★★ 3 stars: Requires consistent training by an experienced handler due to stubbornness or a need for variety. The West Highland Terrier is intelligent, bold, independent and stubborn. The West Highland White Terrier ranks 47th in Stanley Coren's *The Intelligence of Dogs*, being of average intelligence in obedience. If the West Highland Terrier's owner does not show appropriate leadership, this breed will quickly develop the ability to gain the upper hand, and if allowed to progress to extreme, the bossiness of the West Highland Terrier may degenerate into dominant behaviors such as snapping.

Grooming

A thorough brushing is required once a week to keep the West Highland White Terrier's coat clean. The coat will either need to be clipped or hand stripped; stripping makes the coat harder and coarser, while clipping the coat makes it softer and sometimes wavy. Clipping is easy and quick. However, if the dog is being used in dog show, stripping is the preferred method.

Diet

West Highland White Terriers have no specific dietary requirements.

Barking

This breed loves to bark, showing off their independence and wilful attitude.

Health

The http://www.caninehealthinfo.org/breeds.html recommends the West Highland White Terrier is tested for:

- Hip Dysplasia
- Eye problems
- Patellar Luxation

The breed is predisposed to conditions found in many breeds, such as abdominal hernias. Puppies may be affected by craniomandibular osteopathy, a disease also known 'lion jaw'. The disease is an autonomic recessive condition and so a puppy can only be affected by it if both its parents are carriers of the faulty gene. It typically appears in dogs under a year old, and can cause difficulties in chewing or swallowing food.

The West Highland White Terrier is prone to skin disorders, such as atopic dermatitis (a heritable chronic allergic skin condition).

An inherited genetic problem that exists with West Highland White Terrier is globoid cell leukodystrophy and 'White Dog Shaker Syndrome'.

Breed Clubs

America - http://www.westieclubamerica.com/

United Kingdom - http://www.southernwesthighlandwhiteterrierclub.co.uk/

Australia-http://www.dogzonline.com.au/breeds/breeders/west-highland-white-terrier.asp

Yorkshire Terrier

The Yorkshire Terrieris the ultimate fashion accessory. Beautiful and compact, the 'Yorkie' can be carried in a bag and serve as an adorable travel companion.

Breed Summary

- Type: Pure
- Group: Toy
- Average life span: 12-15 years
- Average cost: $300-1000
- Height: 10-14 inches (25-36 centimetres)
- Weight: 5-7 pounds (2-3 kilograms)
- Size: Toy

History

The Yorkshire Terrier originated in Yorkshire and Lancashire in Northern England about 100 years ago. They have been used for hunting small animals and baiting rats, the Yorkshire proved a useful ally for men working in mines and wool mills. Yorkshire Terriers were also quite adept at penetrating badger and fox burrows. The Yorkshire is said to have been made from crossing the Paisley Terrier (a smaller version of the Skye Terrier) and the now extinct forerunner of the Manchester Terrier, the Black and

Tan Terrier. The Maltese Terrier and Dandie Dinmont are also possible ancestors.

The Yorkshire Terrier was introduced in North America in 1872, however, the breed's popularity declined in the 1940s. Interest in this breed was revived as a result of a Yorkshire Terrier known as *Smoky*, a World War II hero and TV star.

The Yorkshire is seen in many different sizes and people often think there are two varieties, miniature and standard. In fact, the Yorkshire should not exceed 7 pounds (3 kilograms), making it one of the world's smallest dogs. There are, however, many larger specimens that are ideal as pets. The Yorkshire is suited to town or country living, and like most small terriers, they are fearless.

Famous Owners

- Joan Rivers' *Spike*
- Gisele Bundchen's *Vida*
- Bruce Willis' *Wolf* and *Fishbein*

Appearance

shedding and considered a good alternative for people with allergies.

Yorkshire Terriers are small, compact and carry themselves confidently.The muzzle is medium-sized and they have a small, flat head.The Yorkshire Terrier's eyes are medium-sized, round and dark. Her small, v-shaped ears are carried erect.

Coat: A newborn Yorkshire Terrier dog is born black with tan points on the muzzle, above the eyes, around the legs and feet and toes, the inside of the ears, and the underside of the tail. It may take three years or more for the coat to reach its final color. As an adult, the Yorkshire's coat is long and silky with a steal bluish and tan color. Often the hair on top of the head is worn up with bows to keep it out of the dog's eyes. This breed is non-

Corporal Smoky (c. 1943–21 February 1957), is a famous Yorkshire Terrier who served in World War II by participating in 12 air-sea rescue and photo reconnaissance missions. She is also credited as being the world's first therapy dog by accompanying nurses to greet the wounded. *Smoky* learned numerous tricks, which she performed for troops with the Special Services and in hospitals in Australia and Korea. *Smoky* was officially promoted to Corporal and has 6 memorials in her honor. After the war, she performed numerous outstanding tricks in TV shows, including walking a tightrope while blindfolded. Her owner, Bill Wynne, wrote a book of his experiences with Smoky called *Yorkshire Doodle Dandy: Or, the Other Woman Was a Real Dog*.

Temperament

Qualities

The Yorkshire Terrier is a brave, adventurous, loyal and affectionate. They can be curious, and fearless as a watchdog. They have a great sense of hearing and can usually hear someone coming long before they get to the door. They are devoted to their owners. They are busy, inquisitive and bold. They can be aggressive towards animals so it is always a good idea to introduce with caution.

Though small, the Yorkshire Terrier is active, overprotective and attention-seeking. The Yorkie does not display the overly soft temperament seen in other lap dogs.

Traits

Without the owner's strong leadership and proper socialization, Yorkshires may show aggression toward other dogs or small animals.

At times, Yorkshire Terriers can be domineering and may challengetheir owners. Sometimes, this dog will demand plenty of attention.

The Yorkshire Terrier can be somewhat aloof with strangers.

The Yorkshire is very active and adventurous indoors and fits comfortably into the smallest of households. They can get plenty of exercise inside because of their small size. They love room to run. They do not require a lot of exercise but do enjoy walks. It is always a good idea to keep various toys around for them to play

Exercise

with. They will mostly enjoy any game that involves interaction with their owners.

Special Talent

The Yorkshire special talent is being a watchdog. The Yorkshire Terrier can be suspicious of strangers and will therefore sound the alarm by barking if people not known to the dog visit.

Children and Other Pets

Yorkshire Terriers make great family pets but do best with older children; this is because older children can be taught to treat the Yorkshire Terrier with respect. Yorkshires may snap if surprised, frightened or teased by exuberant younger children.

They can be aggressive with others dogs, if not socialized at a young age.

Trainability

3 stars: Requires consistent training by an experienced handler due to stubbornness or a need for variety. Yorkshire Terriers are very intelligent, easy to train, but may prove stubborn at times. Some may be difficult to potty train. The Yorkshire Terrier ranked 27th in Stanley Coren's *The Intelligence of Dogs*, being of above average intelligence in working.

Grooming

Yorkshire Terrierpuppies do not need much grooming at first, but it is a good idea to start young so they can become accustomed to it. It may take up to 6 months for the Yorkshire puppies to grow long hair.

Daily or weekly brushing is needed to ensure the Yorkshire Terrier's coat remains glossy and silky. The coat may be trimmed to floor length if necessary. The coat on a Yorkshire's head is long and may have to be tied back with a single, or double, bow. The hair on a Yorkshire's muzzle should be left long. The hair on the ears and feet should be trimmed short.

When bathing, it is important to use a conditioner or at least a moisturizing shampoo made for dogs. Bathe them around once a week, but it would depend on the environment in which they are kept. They do not shed.

Proper care should be taken of a Yorkshires teeth as they are prone to early tooth decay. Yorkshire Terriers are also prone to severe dental disease. Because they have a small jaw, their teeth can become crowded and may not fall out naturally. This can cause food and plaque to build up, and bacteria can eventually develop on the surface of the teeth, leading to periodontal disease. The bacteria can spread to other parts of the body and cause heart and kidney problems. The best prevention is regular brushing of the teeth with toothpaste formulated specifically for dogs.

Diet

Exotic treats or sudden diet changes are not recommended as the Yorkshire Terrier has a delicate digestive system. It is important to feed a Yorkshire Terrierdry foodspecifically formulated for dental health to help keep tarter from building up on their teeth.

Barking

The Yorkshire Terrier likes to bark. This habit may be broken be with proper training.

Health

The http://www.caninehealthinfo.org/breeds.html recommends the Yorkshire Terrier is tested for:

- Eye problems
- Patellar Luxation
- Legg Calve Perthes (Optional)
- Autoimmune thyroiditis (Optional)
- Hip Dysplasia (Optional)

The Yorkshire Terriers may be prone to the following health issues:

- Bronchitis
- Low tolerance of aesthetic
- Delicate digestive system
- Difficulty delivering pups
- Spinal problems
- Paralysis in the hindquarters caused by herniated disks

Because of their small size, Yorkshires have fragile bones and care should be taken to make sure they do not suffer any fall, knocks or large jumps to the floor. There is also a chance for abnormal skull formations.

It is important to keep them current on immunizations and teeth cleanings. Because of their size they can be susceptible to fragile bones. High falls or jumps can lead to problems with joints. The 'teacup' Yorkshires can be even more prone to health concerns and behavioral problems.

409 The Best Dogs for Apartment Living

Breed Clubs

America - http://www.ytca.org/

United Kingdom - http://www.the-yorkshire-terrier-club.co.uk/

Health Glossary

Addison's Disease

Addison's Disease (hypoadrenocorticism) is a hormonal disorder which most commonly affects young to middle-aged female dogs. The dog's immune system attacks the outer layers of the adrenal glands, which causes the dog's muscles, including heart muscle, to function improperly. The outermost layer of the adrenal gland helps muscle function by producing hormones that help maintain the balance of sodium, potassium and water in the body. Symptoms include vomiting, diarrhea, weakness and collapse. Treatment for this potentially fatal disease involves medication. Affected dogs will need regular checkups and monitoring.

Atopic Dermatitis

Atopic Dermatitis (atopy) is a common canine skin condition. This condition is characterized by itchy, red, flaky skin resulting from a reaction to allergens such as house dust mites, pollen, or mould spores. Some dogs may also have a genetic predisposition to this condition. Treatments include low dust mite bedding, regular shampooing, regular sampling by the veterinarian to check for bacterial or yeast infections, antibiotics or anti-fungal medication and food supplements containing special fats to help reduce itching. Veterinarians may also prescribe steroids, antihistamines and immunotherapy.

Autoimmune Thyroiditis (Hypothyroidism)

This genetic disease involves the dog's immune system attacking the dog's thyroid gland (which sits in the throat below the larynx). As the thyroid gland cells are attacked and destroyed, the remaining cells work harder to compensate. Finally, when the gland has been destroyed by 75%, the remaining cells are unable to produce enough thyroid hormone, and the dog begins to display symptoms such as sluggishness, obesity, skin disease, intolerance to cold, hair loss, weakness, poor coat quality and infertility. Treatment includes hormone tablets – dosing depends on each dog's individual needs. This medication is administered throughout the dog's whole life.

Black Skin Disease

Progressive loss of hair and darkening of the skin in adolescent and young dogs can be caused by obesity, hormonal imbalances and allergies. Affected dogs tend to have a genetic susceptibility to a hormonal imbalance, which affects the function of cells at the base of the hair follicle. Hormone injections, melatonin supplements, baths using a benzoyl peroxide shampoo, weight control measures and desexing can all help with managing this condition.

Brachycephalic Breed

Bred to have relatively short muzzles and noses, brachycephalic breeds have undersized or flattened throats and breathing passages. Examples of brachycephalic breeds include the English Bulldog, Pug, Pekingese and Boston Terrier. Considered to be an inherited condition, all brachycephalic breeds are prone to breathing difficulties. The shorter the nose, the more likely the dog will have respiratory difficulties due to one or all of the three problems:

1. Elongated soft palate - the soft palate protrudes into the airway and interferes with inhalation.

2. Stenotic nares – the malformed nostrils are narrow or

collapse inward during inhalation.

3. Everted laryngeal saccules – when the dog inhales, the tissue within the airway in front of the vocal cords, is pulled into the windpipe and partially obstructs air flow.

Obesity will aggravate the problems. Brachycephalic breeds often show symptoms such as gagging, coughing, snoring, intolerance to exercise and breathing difficulties. One possible treatment is surgery to remove excess soft palate tissue and widen the nostrils.

Cardiomyopathy

Cardiomyopathy is a disease of the heart muscle that is characterized by an enlarged heart that does not function properly. The upper and lower chambers of the heart become enlarged, reducing the heart's ability to pump blood. An enlarged heart soon becomes overloaded, resulting in fluid gradually accumulating in the lungs or abdomen, and congestive heart failure. Common symptoms include coughing, swelling of the abdomen or other part of the body and loss of stamina. The cause of Cardiomyopathy in dogs is largely unknown. Nutritional deficiencies of taurine (an essential aide for cardiovascular function and development and function of skeletal muscle, retina and the central nervous system) or carnitine (used by cells to process fats and produce energy) have been found to contribute to the incidence of this condition in certain breeds such as Cocker Spaniels. Some breeds may have a genetic predisposition to this disease. In most breeds, male dogs are more susceptible to the disease than female dogs. Treatment is aimed at controlling symptoms and delaying the onset of heart failure. There is no cure for this disease and it will lead to heart failure. Symptoms of late stage Cardiomyopathy include heavy breathing and drooling even when the dog is at rest, a blue tongue, loss of consciousness, collapse and death.

Cataracts

Cataracts are the clouding of the lens inside the dog's eye, causing the dog to have blurry vision. If the cataract is small, it won't likely disturb the dog's vision too much, but cataracts must be monitored because the thicker and denser they become, the more likely it is they will lead to blindness. Cataracts can develop as a result of disease, old age and trauma to the eye, but inherited conditions are the most common cause. Cataracts may be present at birth or develop when a dog is very young (between one and three years of age). Cataracts are also often attributed to diabetes. Treatment for cataracts includes periodic checkups and anti-inflammatory eye drops prescribed by a veterinarian. If the cataracts are progressing rapidly, surgery is sometimes recommended to restore vision.

Cherry Eye

Cherry Eye is when part of a dog's eye, the third eyelid, flips over and a bright red mass (a tear gland) bulges out from the lower inside corner of the eye, resembling a cherry. This often happens suddenly and the causes are not well understood. It is more common in English Bulldogs and Cocker Spaniels. Cherry eye is not dangerous, but surgical correction is important to make the dog comfortable and reduce the risk of more serious secondary problems such as infection.

Chiari-like Malformation

Chiari-like malformation is a painful condition in which the rearmost part of the brain, the cerebellum, descends out of the skull through the opening at its base, called the foramen magnum, crowding the spinal cord. The exact cause is not completely understood. It is most common in Cavalier King Charles Spaniels. The type of treatment depends on the severity of the condition and dog's age. Surgical decompression for young dogs is often recommended to minimize the progression of the disease as the dog ages. Older dogs with little or no clinical signs may be treated medically, rather than surgically.

Chondrodysplasia

Chondrodysplasia is a genetically based syndrome leading to abnormal bone and cartilage development. Chondrodysplasia itself is not treated, rather secondary problems such as intervertebral disk disease may be treated with surgery. Cartilage supplements such as glucosamine and chondroitin may assist in maintaining healthy cartilage.

Collapsing Trachea

Collapsing Trachea is a chronic, progressive disease involving the windpipe, where the tracheal rings begin to collapse, resulting in obstruction of the airways and a honking cough. Treatments include cough suppressants, medications to increase the airflow to the lungs, corticosteroids (to control inflammation) and antibiotics. Surgery may be required if medication does not alleviate symptoms. A common surgery is the application of prosthetic polypropylene rings to the outside of the trachea or a stent within the trachea. Weight loss measures may also help obese or overweight dogs with this disease.

Color Dilution Alopecia

Color dilution alopecia is a relatively uncommon hereditary skin disease seen in 'Blue' colored dogs such as the Chihuahua, Chow Chow, Dachshund, Miniature Pinscher and the blue-gray Yorkshire terrier. Symptoms include dry skin, hair loss and recurring bacterial infection (folliculitis). This syndrome is associated with a color-dilution gene. This is caused by a genetic defect, affecting the way pigment is distributed in the hairs of affected dogs. There is no cure, however treatment options are aimed at controlling secondary skin infections. The avoidance of harsh grooming products or abrasive brushes can help reduce hair breakage. Mild shampoos which contain sulfur and salicylic acid may be helpful in reducing follicular plugging. In some dogs, oral ingestion of melatonin or retinoids can help to stimulate partial hair growth.

Craniomandibular osteopathy

This disease affects the bones of growing dogs; areas that are particularly susceptible are the skull, lower jaw, bone surrounding the middle ear and temporal region. The result is irregular enlargements of the affected bones. The cause is unknown and there is no treatment that will alter the progression of the disease. Therapy is usually targeted at making the dog more comfortable through the use of pain relievers and anti-inflammatory drugs. Proper nutrition must be provided, and in severe cases, it may be necessary to place a gastrostomy (stomach) tube.

Cryptorchidism

This hereditary condition (also called retained or undescended testes) is the absence of one or both testicles from the scrotum of a male puppy by the time it reaches 6 months of age. Testes normally descend within 6 to 8 weeks, although this can take longer. However, they can remain in the abdomen or may never develop at all. Cryptorchid dogs can still be fertile, depending on the number and location of the retained testicles. Treatment is castration (surgical removal of the testicles).

Cushing's Syndrome

Cushing's syndrome (hyperadrenocorticism) is a common condition in older dogs in which the adrenal glands produce excessive hormones. Affected dogs may have a "pot belly," weight gain, hair loss, and susceptibility to skin and urinary infections. They also have increased thirst, increased urination, and may urinate in the house. Treatments include surgery and medications.

Cystinuria

Cystinuria is a genetic defect which causes crystals and stones to develop in the urinary tract. If stones form, they can block the urethra and obstruct urinary flow, especially in males. There is no treatment for this defect, but measures to reduce the likelihood of stones and crystals forming can be taken, such as feeding the affected dog a prescription low protein diet to raise the pH of the urine which helps keep stones from forming. If a stone has blocked the urinary tract a retrograde hydropulsion is performed to unblock the tract by pushing the stone back up into the bladder. If stones are found in the bladder, a cystotomy (bladder surgery) is performed to remove the stones. Many dogs with this defect do not form stones, however there is no real evidence to suggest why this is so. Symptoms of obstruction include: frequent, scanty, dribbling, difficult or bloody urination, frequent urinary tract infections, pain during urination and a reluctance to urinate.

Degenerative Myelopathy

Degenerative myelopathy is a slow yet progressive, non-inflammatory degeneration of the spinal cord. It is most common in Welsh Corgis, but is occasionally recognized in other breeds. The cause is unknown, although genetic factors are suspected. There are no treatments that have been clearly shown to stop or slow its progression, that is, there no cure. Initially, the dog will suffer from muscle weakness and lack of coordination of the back legs. As a result, the dog walks with a staggering gait. The dog may also drag one or both rear paws whilst walking (causing worn toenails). As the disease progresses, the dog may display symptoms such as incontinence, paralysis of the back legs and a failure to maintain balance. Eventually the dog's front limbs and respiratory system are affected; progression of systems can be slow or fast, however there is no known indicator of how fast this disease will progress for each dog.

Demodectic Mange

These tiny mites, Demodex Canis, are microscopic – yet normal - inhabitants of the dog's skin. When a dog's immune system becomes weakened, the mites can overgrow and cause disease and inflammation. These parasites live primarily in the hair follicles of the dog and they may also may be found in the sebaceous (oil producing) glands of the skin adjacent to hair follicles. This condition causes hair loss (patchy or all over the body). Treatment for dogs with this condition includes improving the dog's overall health so that her immune system is restored. The underlying disease should be determined and the dog's overall health should be improved before attempting to treat demodicosis. Oral antibiotics are often needed for 1-2 months to treat secondary bacterial infection. Localized demodicosis will usually heal within 6-8 weeks with minimal or no medical treatment. Generalized demodicosis often requires a very intense and lengthy treatment plan.

Diabetes

Diabetes in dogs is a complex disease caused by either a lack of the hormone insulin or an inadequate response to insulin. Autoimmune disease, genetics, obesity, chronic pancreatitis, certain medications and abnormal protein deposits in the pancreas can cause the disease. Symptoms include excessive thirst, excessive urination, increased appetite, and weight loss. Diabetes treatment is dependent on the severity of the symptoms and whether there are any other health issues that could complicate therapy. For most dogs, insulin injections are necessary for adequate regulation of blood glucose.

Distichia

A distichia is an eyelash that grows from an abnormal location on the eyelid or grows in an abnormal direction, usually along the margin of the eyelid through the duct or opening of the meibomian gland. The reason why the follicles develop in different locations is not known, but the condition is recognized as hereditary in certain dog breeds. If the condition seems to irritate the dog, surgical correction is an option. The goal of surgery is to remove the offending eyelashes and kill the corresponding hair follicles to prevent recurrence.

Elbow Dysplasia

Elbow dysplasia is a progressive disease and is characterized by varying degrees of elbow incongruity, bony fragments (chips) and, ultimately, severe arthritis. Although hereditary, the severity of this disease can also be influenced by the dog's genetic makeup, growth rate, diet and exercise. Treatment is often a combination of medical and surgical management. Therapy helps to relieve pain and maintain limb function. Surgical removal of the fragments is recommended before the development of severe arthritis occurs.

Ectropion

Ectropion is a condition where one or both of a dog's lower eyelids roll outward. A primary cause of ectropion is genetics; dogs with loose facial skin are predisposed to this disorder. It can also be caused by trauma, foreign bodies, infection, corneal ulceration, marked weight loss or loss of facial muscle tone around the eyes due to old age. Treatments include a veterinary prescription of topical eye drops or ointments to help maintain moisture in the affected eyes. If a bacterial infection accompanies this condition, then topical treatments containing antibiotics will be prescribed to clear the infection.

Encephalitis

Encephalitis is an inflammation of the brain. Causes include immune-mediated disorders, post-vaccinal complications, viral and bacterial infections, fungal infections, parasitic infections and foreign bodies, although some causes are still not known. Symptoms include fever, depression, behavior changes (such as increased aggression), uncoordinated movement, seizures, neck pain, stupor and coma. Antibiotics can treat the infectious causes, whilst anticonvulsants like phenobarbital are prescribed if the dog is suffering seizures. Low doses of steroids may be used if there is significant inflammation in the spinal fluid or severe symptoms.

Endocardiosis

Endocardiosis or Mitral valve disease is a heart disease, believed to be hereditary and common in small-breed dogs. A low-grade heart murmur may be the only early warning sign. Later on, coughing, exercise intolerance, rapid breathing, or fainting may develop. Treatment generally involves medication to ease the burden on the heart and promote better function, as well as to help control blood pressure and reduce fluid retention. Other helpful measures include a low-sodium diet and exercise restriction.

Entropion

Entropion is the inversion, or rolling inward, of all or part of the edge of an eyelid, which causes the rim of lashes to come into contact with the eyeball. This creates friction, irritation and discomfort and can severely damage the dog's eye. Entropion is primarily caused by a hereditary abnormality. Treatments include the application of eye lubricants, or surgery.

Epilepsy

Epilepsy is a brain disorder that causes the dog to have sudden, uncontrolled, recurring seizures, with or without loss of consciousness. This may sometimes occur due to genetic abnormalities. Treatment is necessary if seizures occur more often than every once 1-4 months. Medication can be used to treat epilepsy, but anti-epileptic drugs are not totally effective. The aim of treatment is to therefore reduce severity and frequency of the seizures and increase the amount of time between seizures.

Eye Prolapse (Proptosis)

Eye Prolapse is when the eye falls out of place (protruding forward out of the eye socket) and occurs as a result of trauma, such as an injury to the head or face. It is more common in breeds with prominent eyes, such as Pugs and Shih-Tzus. In rare cases, eye tumors or other serious infections can cause the eye to move out of place. Surgery is the most common means of treating eye prolapse.

Food Allergies

Allergies to food ingredients can cause similar skin symptoms as atopic dermatitis, along with gastrointestinal symptoms of poor appetite, vomiting or diarrhea. Food allergies are treated with hypoallergenic diets.

Gastric Torsion

Bloat (gastric dilatation and volvulus) may occur 1–2 hours after eating. Canine bloat is the overstretching of the stomach by gases; the stomach can become twisted as a result. When the stomach twists around itself, its blood supply is cut off and the tissue begins to die. Bloat is more common in large-breed dogs but can occur in small dogs as well. The dog may also show signs of:

- Distress or pain (hunching over).

- Excess salivation.

- Gagging, retching, or trying to vomit but not bringing up any stomach contents.

- Restlessness, panting, whining, drooling.

- Dark red gums (early stage) or pale blue gums (late stage).

Bloat can be fatal so take your dog to the veterinarian immediately as emergency surgery is usually required.

Glaucoma

Glaucoma is a serious condition characterized by the abnormal build-up of fluid, called aqueous humor, inside the eye. Glaucoma can be genetic or be caused by eye damage or disease. Dogs develop increased intraocular pressure, pain, vision impairment from degeneration of the retina and optical nerve and, if untreated, eventually blindness. Cases of canine glaucoma are initially treated with some combination of topical and other systemic medications designed to decrease intraocular pressure and to dehydrate the fluid inside the eye. Often, surgery is required for long-term treatment.

Globoid Cell Leukodystrophy

Globoid Cell Leukodystrophy is a relatively rare group of disorders in which there is a deficiency of a particular molecule called myelin which is crucial to the normal conduction of nerve impulses. The progressive loss of myelin in the brain, spinal cord and/or peripheral nerves causes a variety of symptoms such as lack of coordination, tremors and weakness. There is no treatment for this condition.

Gonioscopy

Gonioscopy is the examination of the iridocorneal angle of the eye. The iridocorneal angle is where the base of the iris attaches to the cornea and sclera (the white, outer layer of the eyeball). It's the site where aqueous humor (the fluid within the eye) drains from the front chamber of the eye. A normal eye produces and drains watery fluid. This fluid nourishes the lens and cornea and maintains the proper ocular pressure. Poor drainage of this fluid can cause glaucoma. Pressure within the eye builds up if this fluid does not drain properly. This pressure can damage the optic nerve, leading to vision loss.

Granulomatous Meningoencephalitis (GME)

Granulomatous meningoencephalitis is a disease where the dog's central nervous system is inflamed. Closely related to GME is Pug Dog Encephalitis. Female dogs, as well as young and middle-aged dogs are more commonly affected. Granulomatous Meningoencephalitis behaves in a similar way to cancer and as it spreads throughout the dog's nervous system, symptoms such as depression, uncoordinated movement, head tilt, nystagmus (involuntary eye movement) and seizures may arise. Meningitis may also manifest, causing fever and neck pain. Most dogs with this disease eventually die, however, immunosuppressive medications and radiationtherapy may slow its progress.

Heart Murmurs

Heart Murmurs are extra heart vibrations caused by blood flow disturbances associated with outflow obstruction (abnormal forward flow through diseased valves or into a dilated great vessel), regurgitant (backward) flow due to an incompetent valve, patent ductus arteriosus, or a defect in the wall that separates the heart's left and right sides. The course of treatment will be determined based on the associated clinical signs.

Hemophilia

Hemophilia A is a severe inherited coagulation disorder. In dogs, the disease arises spontaneously. The bleeding tendency of Hemophilia A is caused by specific deficiency of a single clotting factor. The clotting factors are critical for normal blood clot formation. There is no cure for this disorder. With more severe hemophilia, the affected dog will require periodic transfusions when bleeding occurs, to replace the deficient coagulation factor.

Hip Dysplasia

Hip dysplasia is the failure of the hip joints to develop normally (malformation), gradually deteriorating and leading to loss of function of the hip joints, which is composed of a ball and socket structure. Treatments such as surgery will depend on the dog's size, age and the intended outcome. It will also depend on the severity of the condition, degree of osteoarthritis and the veterinarian's preferences for treatment. Weight control for overweight or obese dogs is an integral part of the recovery process as the pressure applied to the painful joint as the dog moves is decreased as the dog loses weight.

Hydrocephalus

Hydrocephalus is the abnormal expansion or dilation of the ventricular system (which is a set of structures containing cerebro-spinal fluid in the brain) due to an increased volume of spinal fluid. The abnormal dilation may affect only one side of the brain, or both sides. This may be caused by genetics, prenatal infection, parainfluenza virus, exposure to drugs that interfere with fetal development in utero, brain hemorrhage in the newborn after a difficult labor, Vitamin A deficiency and inflammatory diseases or masses in the cranium. The treatments could include medications and surgery.

Hypoglycemia

Hypoglycemia is when there are critically low levels of sugar in the blood, often linked to diabetes and an overdose of insulin. It is also seen in young small-breed puppies if they don't eat for a prolonged period. Symptoms include lethargy, weakness and seizures. If hypoglycemia it is not treated quickly, the brain may be damaged irreversibly, leading to death. There are two types of treatments for hypoglycemia, one of which is given when the episode is occurring, to raise blood sugar levels immediately, and the other is to treat the underlying condition, to prevent hypoglycemia from recurring. The treatments could include medications.

Hypothyroidism

Hypothyroidism is the most common hormone deficiency in dogs, and usually manifests between 4 - 6 years old. Most cases of hypothyroidism are caused by the dog's own immune system attacking its own thyroid gland tissue. Hypothyroidism is treated with oral administration of thyroid hormone. Medication may also be prescribed and may be regulated to smaller doses after thyroid control has been achieved.

Hyperadrenocorticism

Hyperadrenocorticism is a disease which results from a chronic surplus of cortisol. Cortisol is a glucocorticoid steroid which is secreted from the adrenal glands. There are two mechanisms which can cause. The most common mechanism is called pituitary dependent hyperadrenocorticism, which is a tumor in the pituitary gland in the brain. The second mechanism is functional adrenal tumors. In functional adrenal tumors there is a tumor on the adrenal gland which causes an excess of glucocorticoid steroids to be released. One type of treatment is to remove the tumors. Drugs can be used to reduce the amount of steroids being produced.

Ichthyosis

This is a rare genetic condition in which there is marked thickening of the outer layer of the skin and footpads. The affected dog's skin is rough and covered with thick greasy flakes or scales that stick to the skin and hair. Treatment includes frequent washing with mild anti-seborrheic shampoos and moisturizing rinses.

Immune Mediated Hemolytic Anemia

Is a condition where the immune system attacks the red blood cells, resulting anemia. Symptoms include weakness, pale or jaundiced (yellow) gums, and difficulty breathing. IMHA can also occur as a secondary response to a drug, toxin or disease. IMHA is the most common form of anemia in dogs. Treatment depends on the severity of the condition and can include a variety of medications and blood transfusions. Without immediate treatment, the dog can suffer severe anemia and die.

Intervertebral Disc Disease

Intervertebral disc disease is a condition where the cushion between the vertebrae of the spinal column either bulge or burst (herniate) into the spinal canal. These discs then press on the nerves running through the spinal cord causing pain, nerve damage and paralysis. A common type of this disease often affects small and toy breeds and results in damage and weakened discs in the dog's neck region. Any forceful impact such as jumping and landing can cause one or more of these weakened discs to burst and press on the spinal cord. Another type of this disease involves the discs becoming hardened and fibrous over a long period of time and eventually become herniated, which results in the compression of the spinal cord. Treatment can include medication such as steroids and anti-inflammatories to reduce both swelling of the spinal cord and pain. Emergency surgery may be required to treat paralysis and incontinence.

Keratitis

Keratitis is any inflammation of the cornea that does not retain fluorescein stain, a dye that is used to identify ulcers of the cornea. Symptoms include neovascularization (the process by which the transparency of the cornea is lost due to an ingrowth of blood vessels), pigmentation, haziness, pain, and squinting . Your dog will only need to be hospitalized if it does not respond adequately to medical therapy. There are medications that your veterinarian may prescribe as a part of the treatment regimen for the various forms of this condition, and to relieve discomfort.

Keratoconjunctivitis Sicca

Keratoconjunctivitis sicca is a disorder of the tear glands that results in insufficient tear production and a correspondingly dry cornea. With this disease, the tear film comprises a higher mucus content than normal. The most common cause of dry eye is an immune disorder, however other causes may be a reaction to drugs and a side effect of the removal of a gland of the third eye to treat cherry eye (this is rarely done because of the risk of dry eye). Topical medications, such as artificial-tear medication, medication to stimulate tear production, and possibly a lubricant can be prescribed and administered to compensate for the dog's lack of tears. The dog's eyes need to be kept clean and free of dried discharge.

Legg-Calves-Perthes Disease

Legg-Calves-Perthes Disease involves spontaneous degeneration of the head of the femur bone, located in the dog's hind leg. This results in disintegration of the hip joint as well as bone and joint inflammation. The exact cause of this disease is unknown, though some research suggests it might be related to blood supply issues to the head of the femur bone. Rest, pain relief medication and cold compresses may assist in treating the dog's lameness. Surgery and rehabilitation of the affected limb are also options.

Lip Fold Pyoderma

Lip fold pyoderma is a condition that can affect dogs that have pendulous lower lips. This is caused when the dog's lower lip may have an extra fold that traps saliva. This and other folds around the mouth, including the area where the upper canine teeth touch the lower lip, tend to remain moist and warm, providing bacteria with an ideal environment to grow. As a result, the area becomes inflamed, smelly and quite painful. Treatment includes a special or medicated shampoo to help keep the affected areas clean and to discourage bacteria. Antibiotics can be used to treat infections, with surgery being an option of last resort if infections recur frequently.

Liver Shunt

A canine liver shunt (portosystemic shunt) is when the blood stream bypasses the liver. Since the liver cleans the blood, a shunt needs to be corrected to remove toxins that may accumulate. Symptoms include abnormal behavior, lethargy, seizures, vomiting and diarrhea. The exact reasons for this congenital defect are unknown. The liver shunt appears to be an anomaly of prenatal development and may be caused by some insult to the puppies in utero. Treatment options include medications and surgery.

Luxating Patella

Luxating patella is a canine condition in which the kneecap (patella) is dislocated or moves out of its normal location. This condition is common in small and toy breeds and becomes evident between 4 to 6 months of age. The condition is often congenital and frequently presents on both sides. However, obesity and, rarely, blunt trauma can also cause this condition. This condition can be corrected with surgery.

Musladin-Lueke Syndrome

Musladin-Lueke Syndrome is a genetic disease of the Beagle that affects the development and structure of connective tissues of the bone, heart, skin and muscle. Affected dogs have tight skin and noticeably reduced 'scruff' as well as shorter toes (which makes the dog look as if she is standing on tiptoes), as well as a flat skull. The condition can worsen as the puppy grows, but tends to stabilize at about 1 year old. There is no treatment or cure for this disease.

Myotonia congenita

A painful, hereditary condition, Myotonia congenita is when the voluntary muscles continuously contract. Affected dogs have significant excessive muscle growth, a stiff gait, difficulty swallowing, excessive salivation and abnormal bark. Procainamide, a drug used to treat heart arrhythmias, has been found to reduce the symptoms in affected dogs. Also, exercise has shown to improve the dog's gait.

Open Fontanelle

The skull is made up of soft plates that normally come together during development in utero. However, in some puppies these plates do not fuse, leaving a soft gap at the top of the skull, which may be up to coin-sized. The gap is called an open fontanelle or a molera. The molera is quite soft and can vary in size and shape. Molera is most commonly seen in toy breeds, especially Chihuahuas. The molera in itself is not dangerous, however, care should be taken to ensure trauma in the soft spot is avoided. The affected dog can still live a long and active life. There is no treatment for this congenital condition.

Optic Nerve Hypoplasia

Optic nerve hypoplasia is a genetic, yet uncommon, defect in which the optic nerve fails to develop normally, leading to blindness. There is no treatment for this condition. With their acute senses of smell and hearing, dogs can manage well despite reduced vision.

Otitis Externa

Otitis Externa is an inflammation of the ear canal caused by bacteria, yeast or mites. The fold of the ear can prevent air from entering, and it also creates a warm, moist environment where organisms grow. Treatment for the more common causes often includes flushing the ears with an antibacterial solution. In some cases, anti-inflammatory medication is prescribed.

Patent ductus arteriosis

Patent ductus arteriosis is the most common congenital heart disease in dogs, occurring more frequently in females. Patent ductus arteriosis is an abnormal vessel which causes unnecessary recirculation of blood through the heart, greatly increasing the workload of the heart and potentially causing terminal heart failure. Treatment consists of surgery to close the blood vessel.

Periodontal Disease

Periodontal disease is an inflammation of some or all of a tooth's deep supporting structures. If food particles and bacteria are allowed to accumulate along the dog's gum line, it can form plaque, which, when combined with saliva and minerals turns into a hard, adhered substance called tartar or calculus. This can boost the growth of harmful bacteria, resulting in inflammation and tooth decay/loss. Toy breeds with crowded teeth are at higher risk of acquiring the disease. Poor nutrition is said to contribute to the speedier onset of this condition. In the early stages, treatment is focused on controlling plaque and maintaining the gum's integrity with daily brushing, professional cleaning and prescribed fluoride. If the condition is a little more advanced, treatment involves the cleansing of the space between the gums and teeth and the application of antibiotic gel to rejuvenate gum tissue and decrease the size of the space. In more advanced stages, tooth extraction, bone replacement procedures, periodontal splinting and guided tissue regeneration may become necessary.

Phosphofructokinase Deficiency

Destroys red blood cells and leads to anemia and muscle degeneration, muscle cramps and pain during movement. The only way to treat phosphofructokinase deficiency, however, is through bone marrow transplantation, an expensive procedure that requires a healthy donor. Treatments prior to surgery are fluid therapy or blood transfusions, especially if the dog is suffering severe anemia.

Primary Lens Luxation

Primary Lens Luxation is a painful, blinding genetic eye condition. In affected dogs, the lens falls into the wrong position within the eye. The onset of glaucoma and loss of vision is accelerated if the lens falls into the anterior (front) chamber of the eye. Treatments include operations to remove the lens, however, loss of vision may or may not be permanent. Medication, if given soon enough, will also reduce the pressure in the eye.

Progressive Retinal Atrophy

Progressive Retinal Atrophy is a genetic condition of the eye's retina, which either stops developing prematurely or degenerates early in life. Both eyes can be equally affected. There is currently no treatment for Progressive Retinal Atrophy.

Pulmonic Stenosis

Pulmonic stenosis is a congenital heart defect characterized by the narrowing and obstruction of blood through the heart's pulmonary valve. Depending on the severity of the obstruction, it can cause anything from a murmur to an arrhythmia to congestive heart failure. The course of treatment will ultimately depend on the severity of the valve obstruction. If the dog suffers congestive heart failure, emergency treatment will be required. Surgeries to relieve the obstruction include inserting a balloon catheter at the site of obstruction or incising the obstructed valve.

Retinal Degeneration

The cells of the eye's retina decline in health, leading to impaired vision and blindness. Causes include genetics, long-term glaucoma, scarring, inflammation or separation of the retina due to trauma, abnormal retinal structure, secondary cancer affecting the retina, Vitamin A or E deficiency and (secondary) infections of the retina. There is no cure for retinal degeneration. A healthy diet may mitigate some of the damage caused by this condition.

Rheumatism

Rheumatism in dogs is a form of canine arthritis where the immune system attacks the joint membranes. The most common cause of arthritis is old age as well as the accumulation of minor traumatic episodes to the joint. Treatment is aimed at reducing the dog's symptoms and restoring some quality of life. Medications that relieve pain and glucosamine supplements may be prescribed by your veterinarian to restore some of the dog's mobility and movement.

Schnauzer Comedone Syndrome

Dogs with this syndrome have multiple comedones on their backs. These plugs of keratin and sebum block the hair follicles, and are commonly called "blackheads." They cause crusts, pimples, hair loss and itching. This condition cannot be cured but it can be controlled. Regular cleaning with acne cleaning products or mild anti-seborrheic shampoos will be required. If a secondary bacterial infection develops, your dog will need to take antibiotics for 3 or 4 weeks.

Sebaceous Adenitis

Sebaceous adenitis is a rare type of inflammatory skin disease that affects the skin glands of young and middle age dogs. Symptoms include silvery dandruff, hair loss, thickening of the skin, a dull and brittle and smelly coat. As the condition worsens, lesions appear on the dog's back and ears. The exact cause is unknown and treatment depends on the stage of the disease. Treatments include brushing lightly to remove flaking, medication, antibacterial products and antibiotic-based shampoos, and massaging oil throughout the skin to encourage sloughing of flaking skin and scales.

Seborrhea

Seborrhea causes flaky skin and greasiness of the dog's skin and hair. This genetic skin condition is very common and can lead to a secondary infection of the skin. It usually afflicts the dog before they reach two years of age and progresses as they get older. Treatment focuses on controlling the condition's symptoms through a combination of shampoos and conditioners to keep the skin clean and to soothe itchiness. Secondary infections can be treated with antibiotics, anti-fungal medication, and sometimes, anti-histamines.

Slipped Stifle

Slipped stifle is genetic condition common in toy breeds. It occurs when your dog's 'knee joint' (just above the hock in the hind leg) slips, sometimes as a result of trauma. Sometimes the stifle corrects itself, whilst more stubborn cases are treated by the veterinarian maneuvering the joint into place or surgery. Treatments include anti-inflammatory medications, glucosamine, and surgery, the latter reduces the risk of arthritis and osteoarthritis.

Syringohydromyelia

Syringohydromyelia, which is often associated with Chiari-like malformation, is a condition where a sac filled with fluid develops inside the dog's spinal cord. This causes fluid to accumulate in the cervical spinal cord of the dog. This is a congenital disease and small dogs are much more at risk than medium sized and big dog breeds. Several types of treatment are available for dogs diagnosed with Syringohydromyelia. The four basic options are surgery, medical pain control, drugs that reduce the production of cerebro-spinal fluid formation and corticosteroids (drugs that closely resemble cortisol, a natural steroid hormone that increases blood sugar, suppresses the immune system and aids the metabolism of fat, protein and carbohydrates).

(Canine) Thrombopathia

Canine Thrombopathia is a blood disorder where the dog is more susceptible to bruising and hemorrhage. This condition cannot be cured but can be managed, depending on the severity. Mild bleeding may be controlled by applying prolonged pressure. Severe bleeding will require transfusion of blood or platelet-rich plasma. If your dog requires surgery, your veterinarian may recommend a transfusion pre-operatively as a precaution, depending on the severity of your dog's thrombopathia and the type of surgery.

Vitreous Degeneration

Vitreous degeneration is a common eye disorder which can cause retinal detachment. There is no specific treatment for the condition as it is usually a symptom of other diseases.

Von Willebrand's Disease

Von Willebrand's disease is a genetic blood disorder where a molecule that promotes blood clotting is absent from the dog's blood; this can lead to excessive bleeding following an injury. Although many dogs have this disease, only a small proportion of dogs actually develop severe symptoms. Symptoms include nosebleeds, blood in the dog's stool, bloody urine, bruising, bleeding from the gums, prolonged bleeding after injury or during heat (which may also cause the dog to become anemic). Many affected dogs can still lead normal lives, with bleeds being treated with appropriate first aid measures. Stress can worsen symptoms.

White Dog Shaker Syndrome

White dog shaker syndrome is thought to be an autoimmune-induced disorder where the dog suffers body tremors. This syndrome is found primarily in small white dog breeds. In most situations, the veterinarian initially gives the dog high doses of medication, and then gradually decreases the dose over the course of several weeks. Even if the dog seems completely recovered treatment should not be stopped until given the all-clear by the veterinarian; symptoms can resurface if treatment is ended prematurely. Dogs that receive early treatment will normally get better and recover completely within a week. Lifelong treatment can however be necessary to keep this syndrome under control.

First Aid & Emergencies

Two of the biggest concerns dog owners have about their pet's safety are:

1. Have I done everything I can to make sure my dog is protected?

2. How do I know when an incident requires an immediate visit to the veterinarian?

Knowing how to protect your dog against obvious or hidden dangers and knowing what to do in a variety of situations are your best defenses against hazards. This chapter will explain things you can do to protect your dog and be prepared for different kinds of emergencies.

It is recommended for pet owners to familiarize themselves with the contents of this chapter, so, they are always prepared with the equipment and knowledge to act responsibly during an emergency situation. A book cannot accurately diagnose and propose effective treatments for any condition, so, when in doubt, consult your veterinarian.

In this chapter, I'll explain:

- What to do if your dog stops breathing or is vomiting.
- What to do if your dog is bleeding, or has been run over by a vehicle or been in a fight.
- What to do if your dog is bitten by a snake.

- What to do if your dog is dry-retching or vomiting.

- How to bandage your dog's ear, tail or leg.

- What to do if your dog has eaten poison.

- What to do if your dog has eaten chocolate.

- What to pack in your dog's first aid and evacuation kits.

- How to handle your dog's heat stroke or heat exhaustion.

- How to give your dog a pill.

- The tell-tale signs of shock and how to manage a dog in shock.

Obvious Signs Your Dog Needs Veterinary Attention

If any of the following occur to your dog, you should contact your veterinarian *immediately*:

- The dog has been involved in a car accident or has been run over by a vehicle (car, motor bike or bicycle).

- The dog has been fighting with or bitten by a snake.

- The dog is suffering convulsions.

- The dog has ingested poison, such as anti-freeze, rat or mouse poison, or has eaten an animal that has been poisoned. Common poisons are listed later in this chapter.

- The dog is suffering from signs of shock (which may manifest in one or more of the following ways):
  - Panting
  - Shivering
  - Drooling
  - Vocalization (whimpering, yelping)
  - Hiding
  - Reluctance to move or walk
  - Very dark or very pale or bluish gums
  - Cold feet

- The dog is displaying an extreme and sudden mood swing such as uncharacteristic aggression, timidity or agitation.

- The dog is extremely listless or lethargic.

- The dog is experiencing difficulty breathing, or is gasping or choking.

- The dog has a tense, swollen stomach.

- The dog collapses, loses consciousness or fits.

- The dog vomits several times, and especially if vomiting persists for more than 12 hours.

- The dog suffers from diarrhea for 24 hours or longer.

- The dog's feces are bloodstained.

If in doubt about a particular incident, take your dog to the veterinarian. It's better to be slightly embarrassed about being overly cautious than to lose a pet for not being cautious enough.

Emergency Scenarios

What to do if your dog stops breathing

If your dog has stopped breathing you should give her artificial respiration. The three steps to artificial respiration are:

1. Wrap your hand around your pet's muzzle to seal her lips.

2. Blow into her nose with two quick breaths then give 15-20 breathes per minute. As you breathe, you should see her chest rise.

3. Continue until the dog starts to breathe on her own again or you reach medical help.

What to do if your dog is vomiting or dry-retching

If your dog is dry-retching

Dry-retching may be a sign of canine bloat. The dog may manage to puke some debris, but generally there will be no vomit.

Bloat may occur 1–2 hours after eating. Canine bloat is the overstretching of the stomach by gases; the stomach can become twisted as a result. The dog may also show signs of:

- Distress or pain (hunching over).
- Excess salivation.
- Restlessness, panting, whining, drooling.
- Dark red gums (early stage) or pale blue gums (late stage).

Bloat can be fatal so take your dog to the veterinarian immediately.

If your dog is vomiting

It's normal for dogs to vomit occasionally; they often will vomit after eating grass. Grass eating is normal and is a way to settle an upset stomach or aid digestion.

A dog can vomit as a result of a change of diet as some dog's stomachs are sensitive to changes.

Typically what causes an upset stomach is when there are dietary changes in the protein or carbohydrate in the dog's food or treat. This could be a change from beef to chicken, corn to potato, or simply a different makeup and distribution of ingredients. Most dogs do well with 12–24 hours of fasting after a sudden bout of nausea. This fasting should be followed by slowly reintroducing the normal diet in small amounts for a day or two. Keep in mind that this applies to otherwise healthy pets that aren't showing signs of discomfort, lethargy or dehydration.

If your dog vomits several times – especially if it persists for more than 12 hours – or is experiencing other serious symptoms (see the section above called 'Obvious Signs Your Dog Needs Veterinary Attention'), then take your dog to the veterinarian.

What to do if your dog suffers an allergic reaction

If your dog appears to be suffering an allergic reaction, use antihistamines, prescribed by your veterinarian. Talk to your veterinarian about correct dosage, as this will depend on your dog's weight and other factors. (Make sure the formula does not contain pseudoephedrine). Watch for a severe reaction such as difficulty breathing which will require an immediate visit to the veterinarian. Talk to your veterinarian about the possibility of mega-dosing of antihistamines and what amounts are recommended should mega-dosing be required.

What to do if your dog is bitten by a snake

Whilst the United States and Australia have a number of poisonous snakes, Britain's only poisonous snake is the Adder, which rarely attacks. Snakebites often occur on the dog's face, head or neck, because dogs use their nose to investigate other animals. However, bites to other areas can also occur.

If your dog:

- has been in a fight with a snake; or

- has been bitten by a venomous snake; or

- has been bitten by a non-venomous snake; or

- suffers sudden facial swelling during a walk or in a snake prone area then take the following action:

1. Check for difficulty breathing (as a result of shock or swelling in the nasal passage or wind pipe). Apply artificial respiration if your dog stops breathing (see above). Coral snake venom and some rattlesnake venom can paralyze a dog's respiratory system.

2. If available, use the vacuum pump that comes with commercial snakebite kits to remove up to 30% of the venom without an incision (when used within 3 minutes of the bite).

3. Keep your dog still and calm. Minimize the dog's movements whenever possible: if you're out on a walk, carry the dog; if she's too big, walk swiftly but don't run. Transport the dog to the veterinarian in a carrier, if you can.

4. Rinse the affected area. Do not cut or poke the area as this may assist the spreading of the venom or otherwise damage surrounding tissue.

5. Remove any paraphernalia such as a harness, collar or clothing so that the dog's breathing is not further restricted if swelling occurs.

6. Keep the dog cool by turning on the air-conditioning in the car – coolness slows circulation. You can also apply a cold pack or

other cold item (such as a pack of frozen vegetables) to the area. A pack should only be applied for 10-30 minutes. A cold pack's effect is three-fold: it reduces swelling, reduces pain and slows circulation.

7. Keep the bitten area below the heart's level. This reduces the circulation of the venom.

8. If medical help is more than 1 hour away, then tightly (the same as you would a person had they been bitten) bandage the bite area (if on a leg or the tail) to slow the spread of poison. Do not use a tourniquet.

Aftercare

Death from a venomous snakebite usually occurs within 1–2 hours after the bite. The prognosis for dogs who survive beyond that point is good, but the recovery period can last at least ten days.

Snakebites need antibiotics to fight possible infection from bacteria found in snakes' mouths. Your veterinarian may give tetanus and antibiotic injections, and may prescribe antibiotic, anti-inflammatory and painkiller medication. These will help stave off tissue damage and reduce pain.

Snakebite prevention

Treating snakebite can be a really expensive exercise and can cost anywhere in the vicinity of $USD500 to $USD3000. Faced with such an expense, many owners make the awful decision to euthanize their dog. Make sure any pet insurance you take covers snakebites so you never have to face that decision.

There are also three things you can do to help prevent the likelihood of snakebite:

1. Avoid areas where snakes reside, particularly in weedy areas. Snakes are most active at 77°F–90°F (25°C–32°C). As summer approaches, avoid night walks as snakes tend to loiter during these times. If walking at night, remain alert and use a flashlight.

2. Snakes are usually afraid of humans and large animals, so they tend to avoid contact. Thus, many snakebites occur because a dog has flushed an otherwise hidden snake. So, a good precaution is to keep your dog on a leash.

3. Consider 'Snake Avoidance' training. This type of training is offered by dog trainers and is increasing in popularity. The training usually involves using an electronic collar to administer 'shocks' to the dog as she approaches a snake, the objective being that the dog comes to avoid snakes. This is definitely not a type of training that you should try to do yourself as it takes some skill and experience to ensure the process is effective. Make sure any service you consider utilizes a trained and experienced instructor, as only a professional will be able to administer the shocks responsibly. Also ask questions to ensure the snake used in training is treated humanely and according to the prevailing animal protection laws.

What to do if your dog has been in a fight, injured or bleeding

Animal fights

Fights with cats or other dogs may not be as serious as snakebite, however your dog may suffer punctures that are hard to detect. After a fight, check every part of your dog for wounds, especially puncture wounds using both your hands and eyes. If you think your dog may have been bitten, contact your veterinarian. You may be able to ask for antibiotic prescription to stem possible infection. Prior to that, cleanse any wounds with antiseptic lotions.

If you don't see any wounds, it's best to monitor your dog for a few days after a fight anyway. If you see signs of lethargy or pain, then a visit to the veterinarian may be needed.

Profuse bleeding

If your dog is bleeding profusely, urgent veterinary attention is needed. In the meantime, you should take immediate steps to stem the bleeding. Apply a pressure to the wound with a sanitary napkin or large wad of cotton wool. Do not use a tourniquet.

Bandaging a paw or leg

Here are six steps to bandaging a paw or leg:

1. Clean the wound.

2. Place some padding between the dog's toes and over the wound.

3.   Wind   a   bandage over the wound, and above and below the wound, ensuring that the bandage is firm but not so tight as to restrict circulation.

4. Whether it is the leg or paw that is wounded, ensure the bandage includes the dog's paw.

5. Tie the bandage off well above the site of the wound.

6. Cover the bandage with adhesive dressing, firmly but not tightly, and secure it to the back of the dog's leg.

Bandaging an ear

Here are six steps to bandaging a bleeding ear:

1. Clean the wound.

2. Place some padding over the wound on the dog's ear.

3. Fold back the dog's ear and place another pad over (but not inside) the ear's opening.

4. Bandage the ear by starting at the base of the dog's neck and work forward. Enclose the wounded ear.

5. Ensure the unaffected ear is not included in the bandage.

6. Secure the bandage firmly but not so tightly that it places too much pressure on the dog's neck.

Bandaging a tail

Here are four steps to bandaging a tail:

1. Place a bandage along the length of the tail, making sure you also
cover the wound.

2. Lay bandage strips lengthways along the tail.

3. Bandage the tail by encircling it section by section.

4. The bandage should then be covered in adhesive dressing, which should extend beyond the bandage.

What to do if your dog has been run over by a vehicle

A dog that has been hit by a car or another vehicle will require urgent medical attention. Here are nine steps to handling this emergency:

1. Isolate the accident area so that the dog and the people surrounding her won't suffer further injury. A makeshift stretcher can be made out of clothing or blankets, place the dog gently onto this 'stretcher'. If on your own, lay the 'stretcher' along the dog's back and drag the dog onto it using your hands to support the dog's neck and hips.

2. Ensure the dog is contained by using a leash or makeshift noose. Place this over the dog's head without moving the dog.

3. Improvise a muzzle with a bandage, tie or scarf. A muzzle can be made by placing a bandage over the bridge of the dog's nose, then looping the ends under the dog's chin. Take the bandage behind the dog's ears and tie firmly on the back of the dog's head. The knot should be tight, but should not choke the dog. This should be done before you examine or move the dog, as a distressed dog may bite.

4. Bind any wounds that are bleeding heavily.

5. Have a bystander call the nearest veterinary surgery or pet hospital to advise them of the incoming emergency.

6. Try not to disturb or startle the dog. However, moving the dog may be necessary to obtain medical attention. If so, use the

makeshift stretcher to move her. If this cannot be achieved then carry the dog, allowing for any injured limbs to hang free.

7. Do not handle any injured limbs.

8. Do not try to resuscitate an unconscious dog.

9. Take the dog to the nearest veterinarian.

What to do if your dog is choking

Only remove an object from a dog's mouth if you can see it. Never try to remove an object you cannot see from a dog's throat, as this may cause more damage.

You can perform a Heimlich manoeuvre – an action which may help the dog eject the stuck object – on your dog in three easy steps:

1. Stand behind your dog and steady her.

2. Make a fist.

3. Thrust upwards on the belly below the ribcage.

What to do if your dog is suffering heat stroke or heat exhaustion

Heat stroke can be avoided by providing shade, fresh water and a cool retreat for the dog. Leaving a dog inside a car at any time of year (especially during summer) can have fatal consequences as the temperature inside a car can very quickly reach intolerable levels for a dog. Short-nosed breeds like Chow Chows and Bulldogs are particularly susceptible to over-heating.

Symptoms of heat stroke include distress, panting and/or a blue and swollen tongue. The dog's breathing will be shallow and may be accompanied by throaty noises.

In such cases, the dog needs to be cooled down immediately. Here are three things you can do to cool down your dog:

- Douse your dog, or sponge her, with cold water, paying particular attention to the dog's head.

- Immerse your dog in a cold bath.

- Place a wet towel over your dog's torso, changing it frequently.

After your dog starts to show signs of easier breathing, take her to the veterinarian.

What to do if your dog has been poisoned

Poisoning can occur due to a dog eating, inhaling or absorbing poison through the skin via contact. Since there are many types of poisons, there can be a wide variety of symptoms (most of which will manifest within 3 days). Symptoms of poisoning can include:

- Mouth or skin irritation
- Glassy eyes
- Listlessness
- Vomiting
- Diarrhea
- Loss of appetite
- Drooling or frothing at the mouth
- Staggering or a 'drunken walk'
- Over-reaction to sound or light
- Labored breathing
- Muscle tremor and rigidity
- Seizures
- Collapse

If you suspect your dog has consumed something poisonous then you need to seek veterinary help immediately! Talk to your veterinarian's office before trying to induce vomiting. There are cases where inducing vomiting will make things much worse, especially if your dog has ingested something caustic.

Do not induce vomiting if the poison has been ingested for around 30 minutes or more.

If your veterinarian recommends that you induce vomiting, choose one of three methods:

1. Give 1–2 teaspoons of 3% hydrogen peroxide every 15 minutes until the dog purges.

2. Give a single dose of 2–3 teaspoons of Syrup of Ipecac.

3. Place two washing soda crystals on the back of the dog's tongue, then make her swallow them by holding your dog's mouth shut and rubbing her throat.

The American Society for the Prevention of Cruelty to Animals (ASPCA) maintains a hotline (1-888-426-4435) which dog owners in the United States can call if they have any queries about suspected poisoning.

What to do if your dog has eaten chocolate

Although chocolate in small quantities is not harmful, as a precaution dogs should never be given any chocolate for they might eat more than what their system can tolerate.

Although you probably do not give your dog chocolate, accidents do occur. If your dog has eaten chocolate, the following information will help you decide what to do about it:

1. Determine if the amount of chocolate your dog has eaten is harmful. There are two main factors that will determine whether the dog will have a toxic reaction to chocolate: (a) the

concentration of theobromine in the chocolate compared to the dog's weight; and (b) her individual dog's age and health.

The concentration of theobromine compared to the dog's weight

Theobromine is a substance found in chocolate which is poisonous to dogs. Milk chocolate and white chocolate have a smaller concentration of theobromine and are therefore less toxic than dark or cooking chocolate. Here's a guide to each type of chocolate:

- White chocolate: it takes 250 pounds (113 kilograms) of white chocolate to poison a 20 pound (9 kilogram) dog.

- Milk or semi-sweet chocolate: approximately 1 pound (0.5 kg) of milk chocolate is poisonous to a 20 pound (9 kilogram) dog. As an example, it would take about 2 or 3 chocolate/candy bars to poison a 10 pound (5 kilogram) dog.

- Dark chocolate or cooking/baking chocolate: just 2 ounces (57 grams) of dark or cooking/baking chocolate is poisonous to a 20 pound (9 kilogram) dog.

The dog's age and health

The dog's tolerance to chocolate may be lowered, if she is elderly or not in optimal health.

2. See if your dog is exhibiting the following symptoms – if your dog has eaten a toxic amount of chocolate, she will show the following symptoms within the first two hours: vomiting, diarrhea or hyperactivity. The symptoms will then progress to increased heart rate, arrhythmia, restlessness, muscle twitching, increased urination or excessive panting. More dire symptoms include hyperthermia, muscle tremors, seizures, coma and, ultimately, death.

3. Treat Your Dog. There are three steps in the first aid treatment of chocolate poisoning:

Induce vomiting

In order to do this you can give 1–2 teaspoons of 3% hydrogen peroxide every 15 minutes until the dog purges. Or, give her a single dose of 2–3 teaspoons of Syrup of Ipecac.

Administer an absorption agent

Once vomiting has been induced, reduce the absorption of the theobromine by administering activated charcoal mixed with water. The ratio is 1 teaspoon for dogs less than 25 pounds (11.3 kilograms) and 2 teaspoons for dogs weighing more than 25 pounds (11.3 kilograms). Use a syringe to administer the dose.

Consult your veterinarian

Advise your veterinarian of the following details:

- How much chocolate the dog has eaten
- What type of chocolate
- How long ago the dog ate the chocolate
- The symptoms she is experiencing
- The age and general health of your dog
- Any first aid you have given her.

Health Hazards in Winter

Winter months especially in areas where snow and ice are common can be very hard on dogs, whether they live indoors or outdoors. Here are some tips for caring for your dog during winter:

Indoors

Most people think if their dog lives indoors that they are protected from the worst of winter but even indoor dogs have to go outside. Small dogs and toy dogs, especially, can suffer during winter months.

If you walk your dog on cold sidewalks you may want to consider getting your dog some dog booties. Booties not only keep your dog's paws warm but they will protect her paws from the de-icing chemicals used on sidewalks. These chemicals can be very harmful to a dog's paws, causing them to crack. When a dog licks these chemicals off her paws the chemicals can also be dangerous when ingested.

You can use petroleum jelly to help prevent your dog's paws from cracking.

Small dogs and toy dogs may also need a coat or sweater when they go outdoors during winter. They have less body mass to keep them warm. Dog clothing provides some insulation and heat.

If you have a long-haired dog who ventures outdoors during winter months, be sure to check her paws and long hair when she comes back inside. Ice and snow tends to accumulate on long hair, particularly between a dog's toe pads. Be sure to remove this ice so it won't hurt your dog.

Outdoors

If your dog lives outdoors during the winter you will need to provide your dog with a warm, and comfortable dog house. There are some good dog houses that have a heating element inside to keep your dog warm.

You may wish to provide your dog with a warm dog mat, too.

Be sure that you check your dog's water frequently since cold weather may cause it to freeze. There are waterers that incorporate heating elements to keep them thawed in even the coldest weather. Remember that snow is not a substitute for water.

During very cold temperatures consider bringing your dog into the house.

Remember that wind chill makes the temperature outdoors feel colder than what the thermometer indicates. Your dog will get colder than you think. Try to limit your dog's time outside. Dogs can get frostbite if they are left outdoors too long in freezing conditions.

Be careful if you take your dog near frozen ponds or lakes. These bodies of water sometimes aren't frozen as solid as they seem and it can be easy for a dog to fall through.

Do keep your dog groomed during winter months. Grooming helps keep your dog well-insulated which will keep her warmer.

Make sure you feed your dog some extra calories in the winter, especially if she lives outside. Your dog needs the extra calories to keep herself warm.

If your dog gets wet from rain or snow it's a good idea to use a blow dryer to dry her off. This will help her warm up faster.

Don't leave your dog alone in a car in the winter, even with the engine running. Carbon monoxide can kill your dog.

Each season has its hazards for dogs and winter is no exception. Watch out for these weather-related issues and you can keep your dog warm and safe during winter.

Your Dog's First-Aid Kit

You can store your dog's first-aid essentials with your family's first-aid kit, however it's best to ensure they are kept in a separate, labeled and water proof container so there's no possibility of mixing contents. Make sure it is out of reach of both children and pets. If you use the services of a pet sitter, remember to let this person know where the dog's first-aid kit is located.

Make a periodic inventory of the first-aid kit to ensure that the items in it have not expired or have gone missing.

When you are putting your kit together, ask your veterinarian for any suggestions in relation to your dog's breed and age, and your own lifestyle.

Here is a list of supplies which should be included in a dog's first-aid kit:

- A card detailing your veterinarian's name, location and contact number. The location of the nearest animal hospital, animal ambulance and poison hotline.

- Pet insurance details and contact numbers.

- An inventory of items and expiry dates.

- Bandages.

- Veterinarian wrap: a great adhesive which is not overly sticky to fur.

- Absorbent cotton wool.

- Gauze bandages (5cm/2in and 10cm/4in) and adhesive tape.

- Gauze swabs.

- Cotton buds.

- Sanitary napkins: good for wounds that are bleeding profusely.

- Bottle of hydrogen peroxide.

- Mineral oil (which works well as a laxative).

- Anti-bacterial ointment cream (helps prevent infections and seals wounds). You may also want to keep eye ointments handy, but do not use them if there is a foreign object in the eye.

- Antibiotic or antiseptic ointment (like Betadine).

- Eyewash or eye drops (helps to wash away debris or dirt that may worsen eye injuries).

- Cleansing ear drops.

- Rectal or ear thermometer.

- Plastic syringe (½ fl. oz; 15ml): good for administering liquid medications. They should not be used to squirt any liquid directly into the ear canal.

- Rescue cream: good for bruises, cuts, abrasions, flaky skin.

- Activated charcoal: estimated to reduce the absorption of poisonous substances by up to 60%. Syrup of Ipecac and 3% hydrogen peroxide are also good for reducing the absorption of poison. Washing soda is also effective in inducing vomiting.

- Bismuth: helps to settle upset stomachs and can be used for diarrhea, nausea and motion sickness.

- Scissors with a blunt end, used for cutting bandages, tape or matted hair. Scissors are also good for trimming hair around wounds.

- Cold compress.

- Tweezers and a tick removal tool. Tweezers or forceps are useful for removing splinters from paws and faces. Forceps, which should *not* be used as a probe in any injury as this may worsen it.

- Pain reliever. Contact your veterinarian for advice on the best type and doses of human medication. Remember that some human pain medication is potentially harmful for dogs (and cats). Aspirin (given with food) can be used for mild pain, but only in very small doses – check with your veterinarian about the right dose for your dog. A dog cannot digest enteric-coated aspirin. Ibuprofen can be toxic. Never give a medication prescribed for another person or pet to your dog.

- Antihistamines are good for allergies, insect bites and itching. Make sure the formula does not contain pseudoephedrine.

- A large blanket to keep your dog warm and help to stave off shock.

- A soft muzzle is a good idea, because even a good natured domay bite when in pain or shock.

- Electrolyte fluids can help rehydrate a dog if she is suffering from chronic vomiting or diarrhea.

- Herbal remedies and supplements may be useful, but check with your veterinarian to ensure they do not react badly with other medications.

- Commercial snakebite kit (if you live in a country with poisonous snakes), including a vacuum.

- A first aid book for dogs.

Dog Essentials for Your Evacuation Kit

Many families have an emergency or evacuation kit stocked with essentials like food, water and other items to help through relocation as a result of fire, flood or other natural disaster. When stocking your evacuation kit, remember to include a first-aid kit for your dog as well as the following items:

Water and food

Make sure there is enough dried and canned food for your dog for two weeks. You should check expiration dates on the food labels and replace water every couple of months. Make sure you have a can-opener and spoons in the kit too! Your kit should also have a small portable water bowl made of soft material (these can be purchased at camping stores) and food bowls. Include your dog's favorite treats too.

Essential equipment

Make sure you have also packed the following items for your dog in your evacuation kit:

- Muzzle (frightened dogs may bite) - you can buy either a soft or hard muzzle from most pet stores.

- Bitter Apple or other product that discourages licking (some dogs do this when nervous).

- Pet carrier.

- Spare lead and collar (with a tag that has your contact details).

- A blanket/thermal blanket and some toys.

- Poo bags/plastic bags and disinfectant.

- Grooming, dental cleaning supplies and soap.

Essential papers

Your kit should have two copies of the following papers:

- Updated vaccination certificate.

- Pet insurance details and policy number.

- Microchip/tattoo ID and documentation.

- Bring proof that you own the dog, like pictures or video. Attach a copy of your contact details and those of your friends that you can trust to take care of your dog in case she gets lost. Proof of ownership, such as registration, purchase or adoption papers.

You should also have a list of the contact details for the following places:

- Your veterinarian and any secondary vets.

- Nearest emergency animal hospitals, clinics or poison centers (which may be required if your dog becomes ill or injured).

- Animal shelters, pet friendly motels, boarding facilities, microchip/tattoo ID centers. These numbers are good to have if you are either looking to find accommodation for your pet or if you are in the unfortunate position of looking for your dog.

One copy of these papers and the list of contact details can be placed in the evacuation kit with your other personal papers (in a zip lock bag or container). The second set of papers can be placed in a zip lock bag and taped to the inside wall of the pet carrier. Make a note with indelible ink on the outside of the carrier that there is important information about the dog and owner within. This is an especially useful measure if you want to make it easier to reclaim your dog, should you become separated.

Medication

The evacuation kit should have a supply of any medication your dog takes regularly, including monthly doses of heartworm/intestinal worm/flea preventatives. Keep these medications dry in waterproof containers.

Should your dog be prone to anxiety as a result of changes in routine or bad weather (such as storms), ask your veterinarian about any remedies that may be worth storing in your evacuation kit.

References

I would like to acknowledge the following great resources for dogs owners:

Bailey, Gwen. *What is My Dog Doing That? Understanding Your Pet's Puzzling Behaviour.* Octopus Publishing Group, 2009.

Larkin, Dr. Peter. *How to Look After Your Dog: An Expert Practical Guide to Dog Care, Grooming, Feeding and First Aid.* Anness Publishing Ltd, 2008.

Lindsay, Steven R. *Handbook of Applied Dog Behavior and Training: Volume One - Adaption and Learning.* Blackwell Publishing, 2000.

Lindsay, Steven R. *Handbook of Applied Dog Behavior and Training: Volume Two – Etiology and Assessment of Behavior Problems.*Blackwell Publishing, 2001.

MacDonald, Carina. *Dog Care & Training: A Complete Illustrated Guide to Adopting, House-Breaking, and Raising a Healthy Dog.* Morris Book Publishing, 2009.

Messent, Peter.*Understanding Your Dog.* A.P. Publishing Pty Ltd, 1979.

Reid, Pamela J. *Excel-erated Learning: Explaining How Dogs Learn and Best to Teach Them in Plain English.* James & Kenneth Publishers, 1996.

Rogers, Tammie. *4-H Guide Dog Training & Dog Tricks.*Voyageur Press, 2009.

Volhard, Jack & Wendy.*Dog Training for Dummies.*Wiley Publishing, 2005.

Wilson, Sylvia. *The Bark Busters Guide to Dog Behaviour and Training.*Simon & Schuster, 2003.

Made in the USA
Monee, IL
20 December 2023

50002689R00252